Journey into China

Arts in China

Jin Yong

translation by Wang Pingxing & Zhao Xiufu

CHINA INTERCONTINENTAL PRESS

JOURNEY INTO CHINA

Counsellor: Cai Wu
General Director: Li Bing
Chief Editors: Guo Changjian & Li Xiangping
Deputy Chief Editor: Wu Wei

图书在版编目（CIP）数据

艺术之旅：英文/靳永著；王平兴，赵秀福译．
—北京：五洲传播出版社，2007.8（2008.5重印）
（中国之旅）
ISBN 978-7-5085-1105-4

I．艺…
II．①靳… ②王… ③赵…
III．艺术–概况–中国–英文
IV．J12

中国版本图书馆CIP数据核字（2007）第064526号

ARTS IN CHINA

Author: Jin Yong
Translator: Wang Pingxing & Zhao Xiufu
Planner: Feng Lingyu
Project Director: Deng Jinhui
Executive Editor: Xu Weiran
Art Director: Tian Lin
Photo Credit: China Foto Press, Quan Jing Photo, Mei Lanfang Museum, Xu Chao, Fotoe, Zhang Jinliang, *Shengping Shu Xiqu Renwu Huace* (Album of Chinese Opera Characters of the Qing Court)
Publisher: China Intercontinental Press (6 Beixiaomachang, Lianhuachi Donglu, Haidian District, Beijing 100038, China)
Printer: Beijing Picture in Picture Printing Co., Ltd.
Tel: 86-10-58891281
Website: www.cicc.org.cn
Edition: Aug. 2007, 1st edition, May. 2008, 2nd print run
Format: 787×1092mm 1/16
Signatures: 9.75
Words: 46,000
Print Run: 7001–14,000
Price: RMB 95.00 (yuan)

Contents

Foreword *5*

Calligraphy *7*

Calligraphy: The Core of Chinese Culture *8*

Evolution of Styles: The Growth of Calligraphy *12*

The Four Treasures of the Study: They Record Civilization *18*

Forms of Calligraphic Works *21*

Inner Mirroring: The Way to Enjoy Calligraphic Works *23*

Lanting Xu: The Zenith of Running-Script Calligraphic Works *25*

The Four Masters of Regular-Script Writing *28*

Crazy Zhang (Zhang Xu) and Drunken Su (Monk Huaisu), Masters of the Grass Script *31*

Personality Decides Calligraphic Quality *34*

Chinese Seal: Dancing Beijing *37*

Painting *41*

Chinese Painting: Unity of Poetry, Calligraphy, Painting and Seal-Cutting *42*

The Childhood of Chinese Painting *48*

Figure Painting: Vivid and Lifelike *52*

Genre Painting: Snapshots of Ancient Life *57*

Landscape Painting: Indoor Tour of Mountains and Waters *61*

Flower-and-Bird Painting *65*

Noble Symbols in Flower-and-Bird Painting *68*

Dunhuang Frescoes: Treasures of Chinese Art *71*

Paintings and Poems: Sister Arts *74*

Meticulous Style and Sketching-Thoughts Style *76*

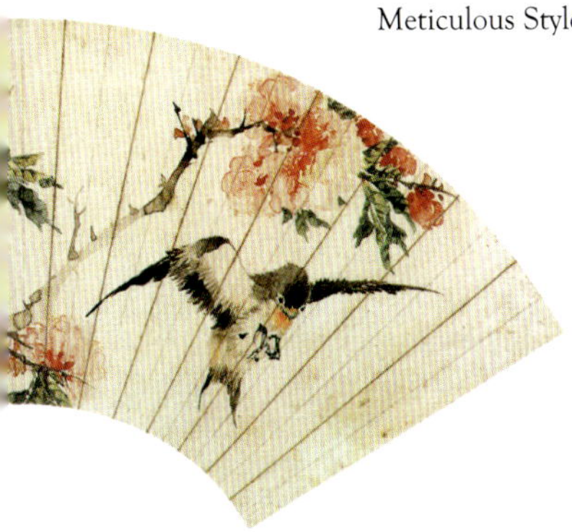

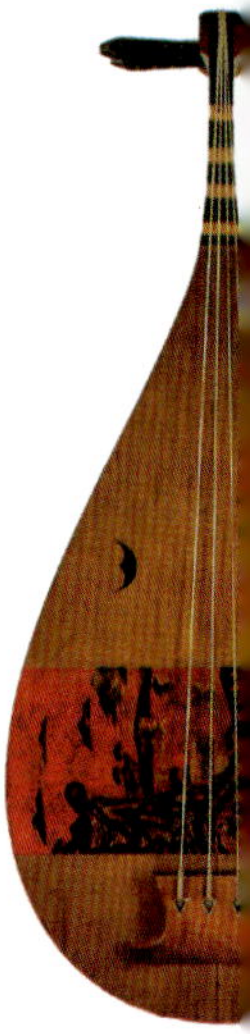

Music *81*

- Chinese Music: An Art of Harmony *82*
- Ritual, Music and Civilization *84*
- *Guqin*: The Oldest Plucked String Instrument of China *89*
- High Mountains and Flowing Streams: *Guqin* Music in Outer Space *91*
- *Pipa*: "Like Pouring Large and Small Pearls Onto a Plate of Jade" *93*
- *Zheng*: Another Chinese Zither *95*
- *Erhu* and Spring Water Reflects the Moon *97*
- The Butterfly Lovers: A Violin Concerto *99*
- What a Beautiful Jasmine Flower *101*
- *Shanqu* Folk Song *104*
- Muqam and Folk Long Song *106*

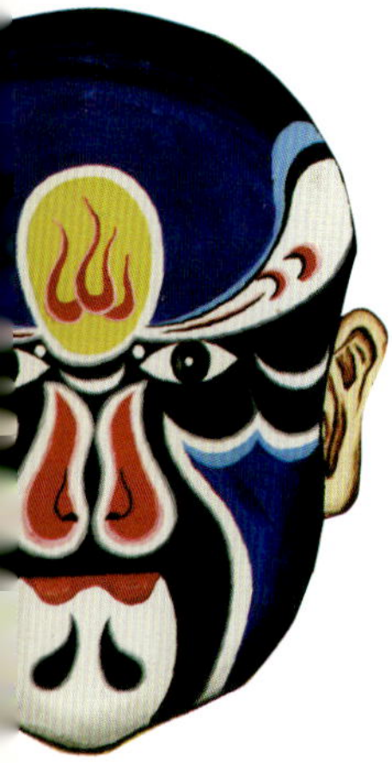

Opera *109*

- Four Basic Skills: The World as a Stage *110*
- The History: Over 2,000 Years *117*
- *Kunqu* Opera: Orchid in the Garden of Operas *122*
- Peking Opera: The National Drama *125*
- Mei Lanfang: Introducing Peking Opera to the World *128*
- Local Operas: The Significance of Gongs and Drums *131*

Dance *135*

- Chinese Dance: Close Ties with Music and Opera *136*
- Primitive Dance: The Dancing Shadows of the Primitive People *137*
- Ceremonial and Music Dance: Dancing for Ceremony and Propriety *138*
- Professional Female Dance: Carefree Soft Music and Graceful Dance *140*
- Religious Dance: Dancing upon the Encounter between Gods and Humans *142*
- Ethnic Dances: Flowing Customs *146*
- Modern Dance: Confluence of Oriental and Western Dance *149*

Epilogue *151*

Appendix: Chinese Dynasties *152*

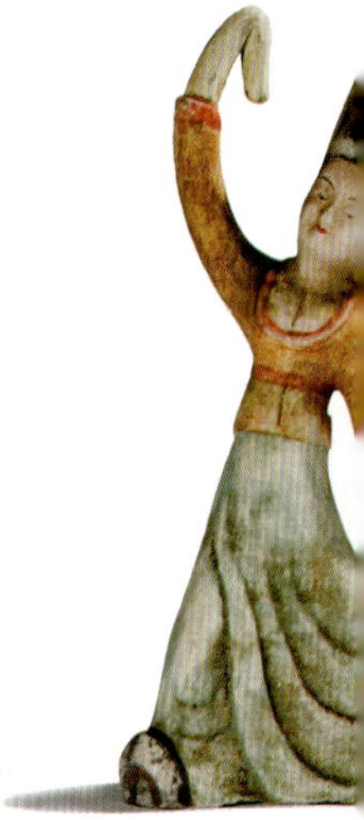

Foreword

With a lasting civilization of several thousand years, China offers the world a rich culture, which constitutes an important part of human civilization and wisdom. Chinese culture is both unique and inclusive, and consists of what is grown in this Oriental land as well as diverse elements from other cultures.

Chinese arts are the gems of Chinese culture. They carry the heritage of traditional Chinese culture, embody the personalities of artists and cultivate the national character. Chinese artists strive for an integration of beauty and goodness, communication between passion and reason and harmony between man and nature. For several thousand years, Chinese people have enjoyed their lives and creations through their artistic pursuits.

The culture and arts of a nation, with their captivating content, inform others about the way their people view the world, the way they think and the way they live.

In this booklet, we will take the readers on a journey of Chinese arts.

觀宇宙之大俯察品類之盛
所以遊目騁懷足以極視聽之
娛信可樂也夫人之相與俯仰
一世或取諸懷抱悟言一室之內
或因寄所託放浪形骸之外雖
趣舍萬殊靜躁不同當其欣

Calligraphy

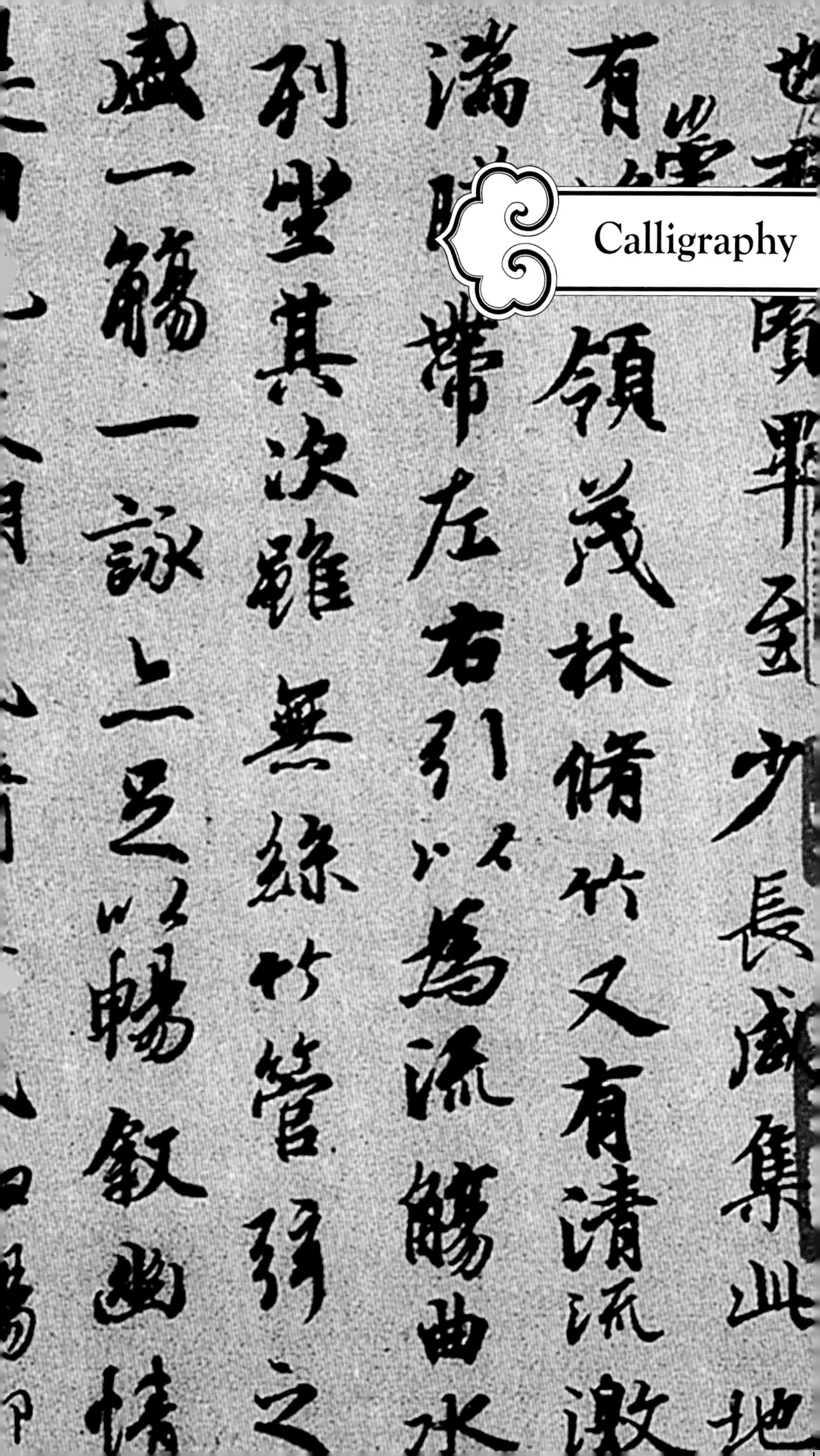

Calligraphy: The Core of Chinese Culture

Calligraphy, in which the characters of the Chinese language are written with brush on silk or paper, is one of the oldest art forms in China. This art has a history of several thousand years and remains full of vitality. Essential to the cultural activities of the Chinese, it is also the axis of their artistic lives. Chinese calligraphy is an abstract distillation of Chinese culture and reflects the spirit of the times.

This art of fine handwriting prospers in China, and is also popular in other Asian countries where Chinese characters are used, such as Japan, the Republic of Korea and Singapore. Calligraphy plays an important role in their cultural lives and serves as a channel for cultural exchanges between those countries and China. Wang Xizhi, the great Chinese calligrapher who lived in the 4th century, is also greatly admired in those countries.

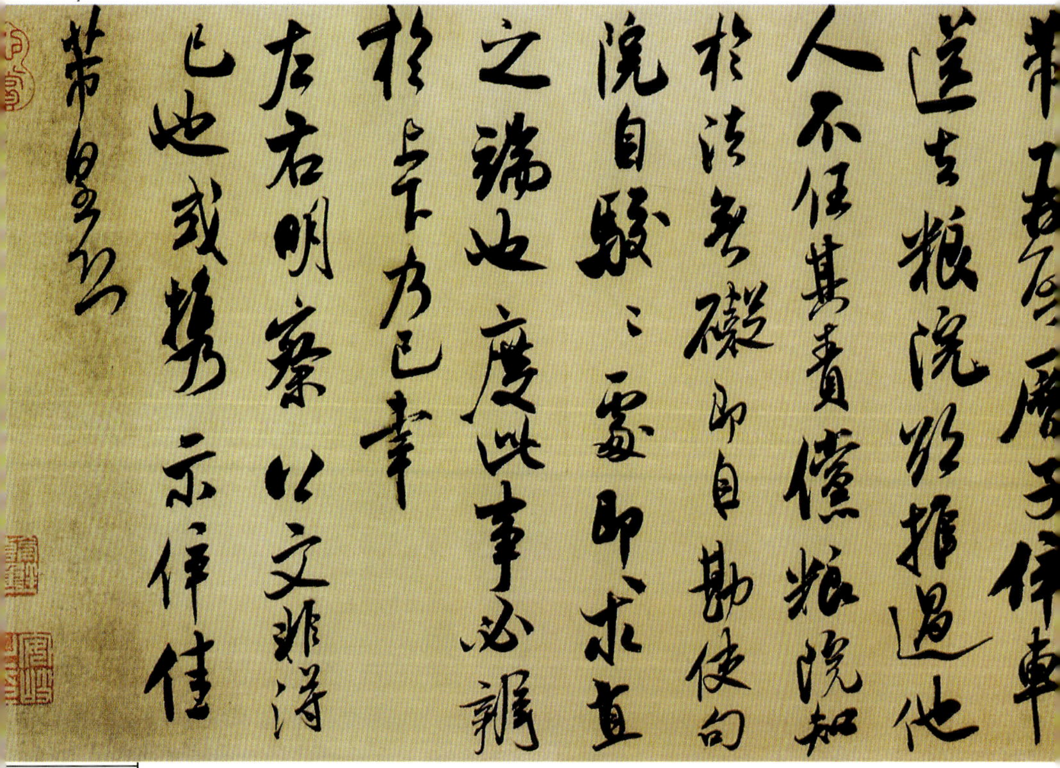

A scroll (partial) by Mi Fu, one of the four greatest calligraphers of the Song Dynasty.

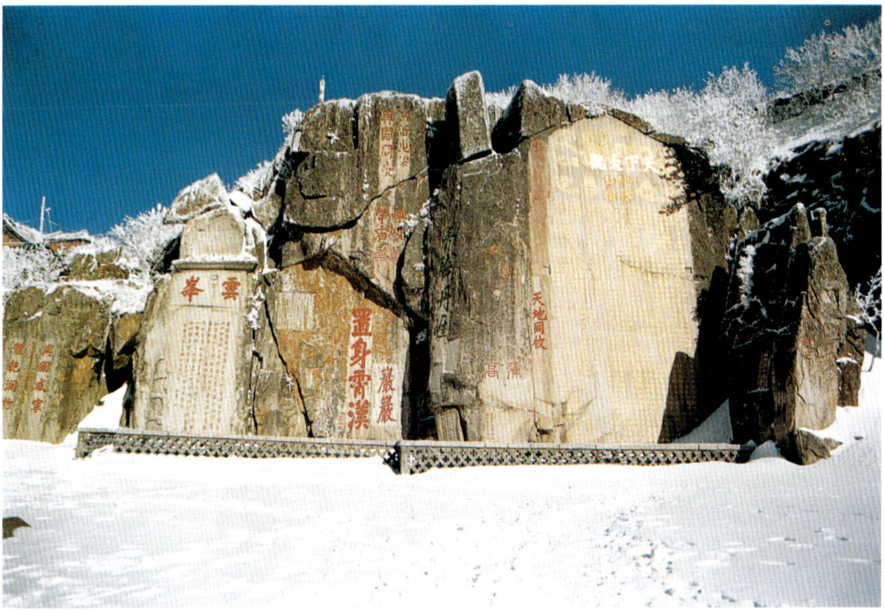

Calligraphic works on Mount Taishan in Shandong Province.

Many of the inscriptions were left by Chinese emperors during their pilgrimage tours of the mountain.

Calligraphy is an indispensable part of the cultivation of Chinese intellectuals. In the time of Confucius (551–479 BC), a great Chinese philosopher, calligraphy was considered to be one of the six basic skills of intellectuals. In later years, the art counted heavily in imperial examinations through which Chinese feudal rulers selected talented people to serve them. In ancient China, literary theory viewed calligraphy to be an exposition of a writer's personality, including his cultivation, mentality and interest; people could imagine the writer's character from his calligraphy. The four essential implements, writing brush, ink, paper and inkstone, accompanied an intellectual all his life. Many men of letters also set their wisdom into calligraphy, which served to carry their values, and won lasting great fame.

Calligraphy presently can be seen in daily life in China. A tourist can see signboards of all forms in Beijing, whether in commercial Wangfujing Street or cultural Liulichang Street. Most of the signs were written by noted calligraphers, and some of the oldest are regarded as relics of calligraphy. These unique signs embody the spirit of Chinese culture. Tourists to historic cities in China, such as

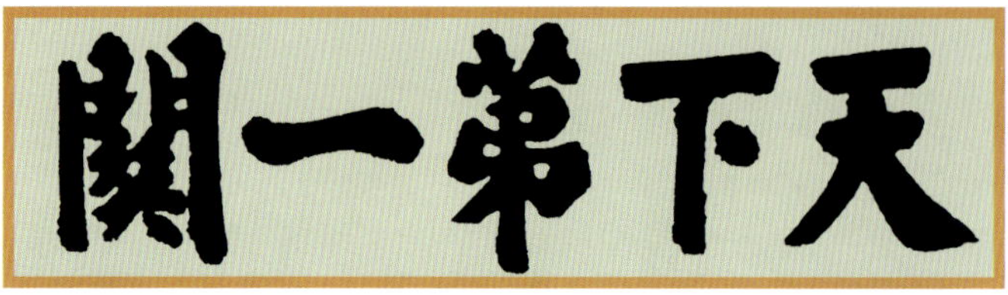

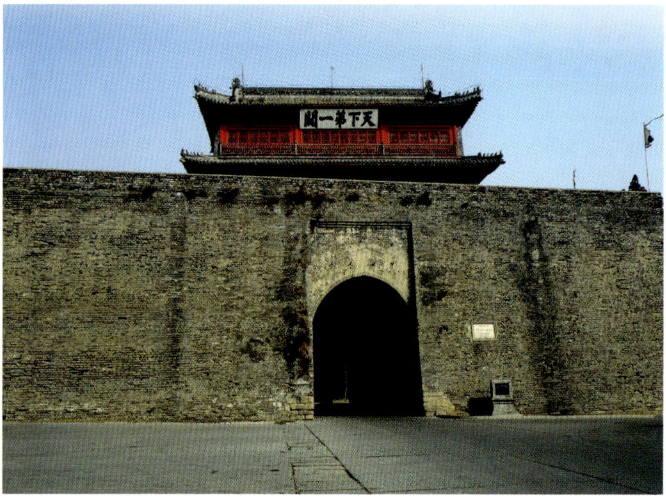

The giant tablet of Shanhai (mountain-sea) Pass, at the eastern end of the Great Wall.

The pass, built in 1381, is located in Qinhuangdao City, Hebei Province. The five characters "Tian Xia Di Yi Guan," meaning "the first pass under heaven," said to be written by calligrapher Xiao Xian in the Ming Dynasty, measure more than 1 meter by 1 meter each, in the standard script.

Xi'an, Nanjing, Qufu and Tai'an, are advised to visit their forests of steles, which carry not only historical records but treasures of calligraphic art. The delicate strokes on the steles might transport viewers back in history.

What is so fascinating about calligraphy? Even people who have devoted their whole lives to this art often ask themselves such a question. Calligraphy possesses in one form the beauty of music, architecture and dance, and is closely linked with other traditional Chinese arts. It gives an artistic turn to the characters and an understanding of traditional culture. Calligraphic works offer a description of traditional Chinese philosophy, a pursuit of aesthetic values, the rhythm and artistic conceptions of poetry, the melody and harmony of music, and the vividness of paintings. In calligraphy, the subtle hair of the writing brush lend great power to the Chinese characters, the single color of black ink produces numerous hues, and the simple strokes express the complexity of the art.

No wonder Nobel laureate physicist Chen Ning Yang

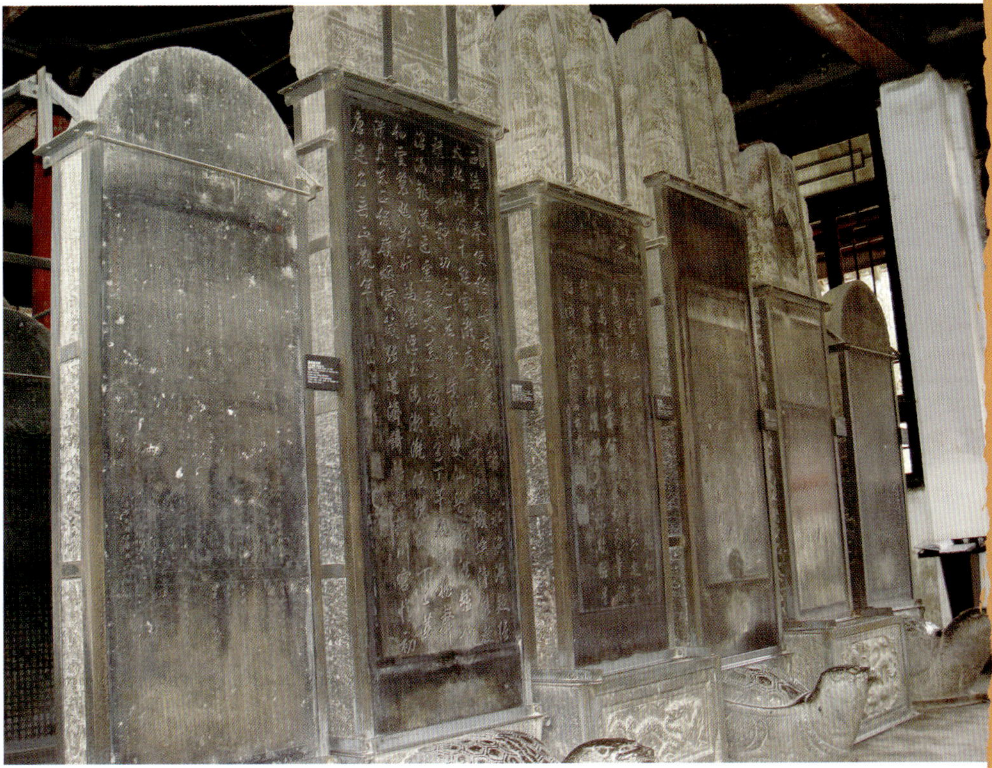

The Forest of Steles in Xi'an, capital of Shaanxi Province.

Construction of this forest of steles began in 1087. The steles and gravestones on display were built in different periods, from the Han to the Qing dynasties. It is the largest collection of calligraphic works of stone inscriptions in China.

once quoted a calligrapher as saying that calligraphy is at the core of philosophy-centered Chinese culture, and Yang approved his assertion. This is no exaggeration. The more that is known about Chinese culture, the more the beauty of calligraphy can be appreciated, and vice versa.

Evolution of Styles: The Growth of Calligraphy

Of the four original and major ancient civilizations—China, India, Egypt and Babylon—the Chinese civilization is the only one that has endured. Often, researchers attributed the continuation to the messenger of Chinese culture—the Chinese characters.

What is behind the wonder of the Chinese writing system that has sustained Chinese civilization for several thousand years? Let us trace the Chinese characters to their earliest forms—inscriptions on bones or tortoise shells, or the shell-and-bone script.

In 1899, a senior scholar who lived in Beijing fell ill. This scholar, Wang Yirong, examined the medicinal material his family got for him from a traditional Chinese medicine shop, and the *long gu* (literally "dragon bone" or "fossil fragments") among the ingredients caught his attention. Based on his study of ancient Chinese characters, he determined that the crossed strokes on the bones represented the writing system of the Shang Dynasty (16th–11th century BC; the latter part of this dynasty is also known as Yin, the name of its capital). As the oldest mature Chinese characters, they were inscribed on tortoise shells or animal bones and therefore are known as inscriptions on

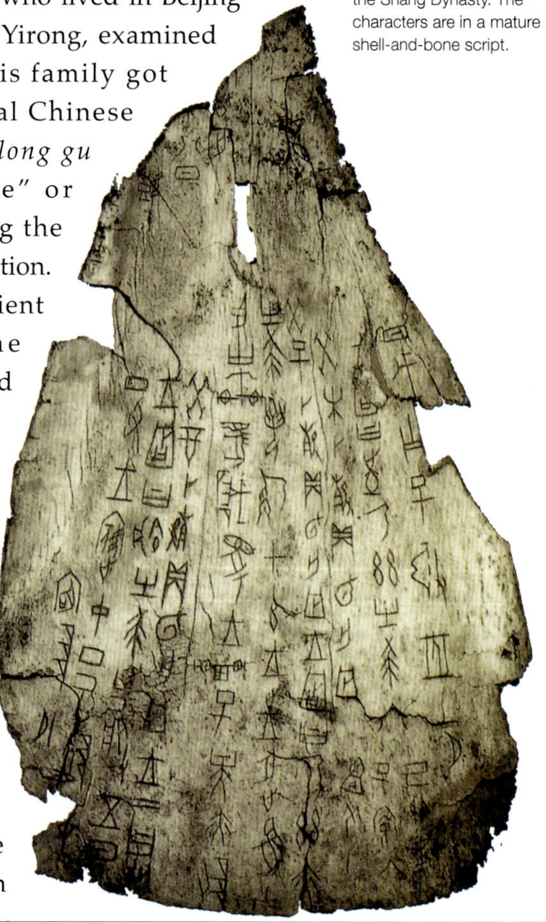

Shell-and-bone inscriptions.

The inscription on this piece of bone records sacrificial and hunting activities of a king of the Shang Dynasty. The characters are in a mature shell-and-bone script.

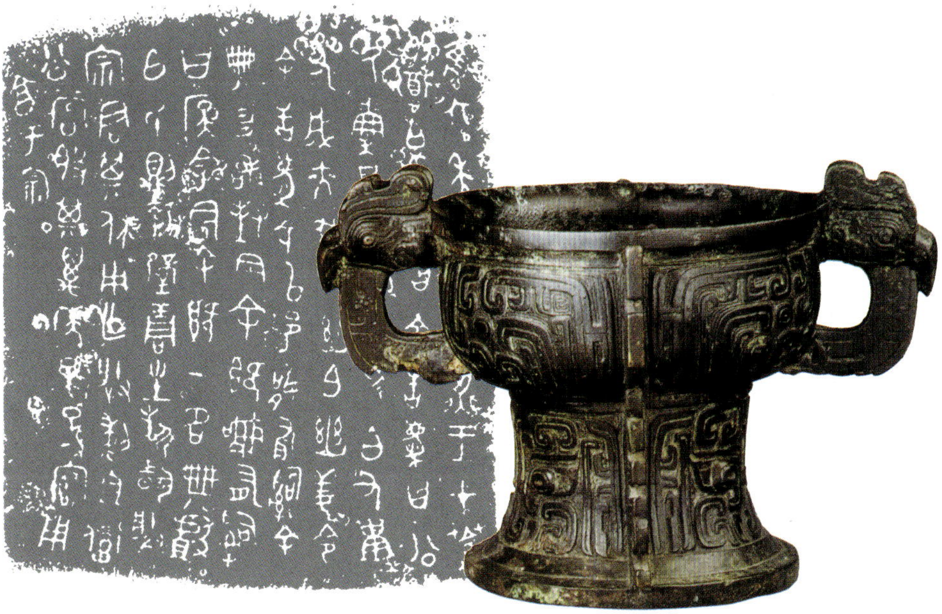

A bronze *gui* vessel from the Western Zhou Dynasty.

The owner of this bronze was a person named Diaosheng, and the inscription on the inner wall, with 104 characters, records a lawsuit over land ownership. The characters are in the typical bronze script of the Western Zhou Dynasty.

bones or tortoise shells. They had been buried for more than 3,000 years.

The characters of the shell-and-bone (the oracle bone) script are highly pictographic and many are easily recognizable. However, of the more than 3,000 characters found so far, only about 1,000 have been identified. The characters tell people many secrets of the Yin-Shang Dynasty, such as sacrificial rites, wars and farming. These characters also constitute the first source of calligraphic art, where more than a few calligraphers have received inspiration.

Inscriptions on bronze objects or the bronze script appeared almost in the same period as the inscriptions on bones or tortoise shells. In the Shang and Zhou dynasties, when a person rendered meritorious service to the state, the king would hand out largesse to him. Such a person would cast bronze objects with inscriptions to record the merits and show them to future generations. These inscriptions now have become treasures of Chinese calligraphy. As cultural relics, a large number of Chinese bronze objects are kept in the collections of

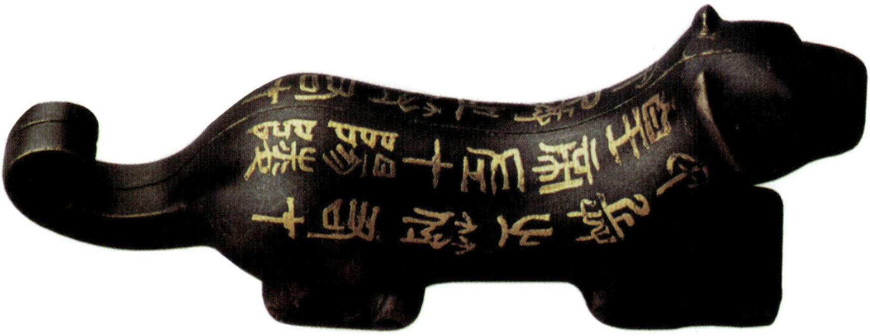

A tiger-shape military tally from the Qin Dynasty.

The military tally was an evidence of authority, but this tally is well known in Chinese history of calligraphy for the small-seal script inscription on it.

major museums in the world, such as the Freer Gallery of Art in the United States and the British Museum in the United Kingdom. We would like to remind visitors to the museums not to miss the beauty of the inscriptions on the bronze objects.

Qinshihuang, the first emperor of the Qin Dynasty, unified China and ordered that *xiao zhuan*, or the small-seal script, be adopted as the standard writing system. The small-seal script characters are highly artistic, with rounded end strokes and symmetrical structure. To parade his merits, the emperor toured various parts of the country and left a large number of steles and inscriptions recording his deeds. The actual steles are now used as source material for the study of the small-seal script.

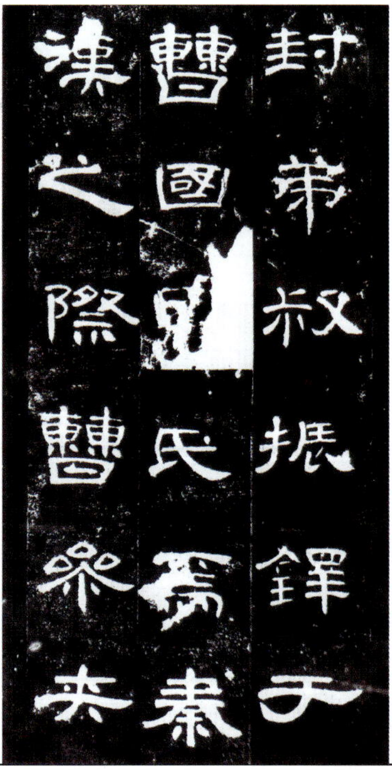

Part of a rubbing from a stele of the Han Dynasty.

This rubbing is an ideal example for learners of the clerical script.

As the small-seal script required focused effort to compose and, since in emergencies people would write hastily without much attention to style, a new style of writing—*li shu* or the clerical script—arose, created by clerks of a lower tier of society. As characters of this style are easy to write and read, they soon replaced the small-seal script and formed the writing system of the Han Dynasty. This transformation was extremely significant in the evolution of the Chinese writing system and marked a transition from

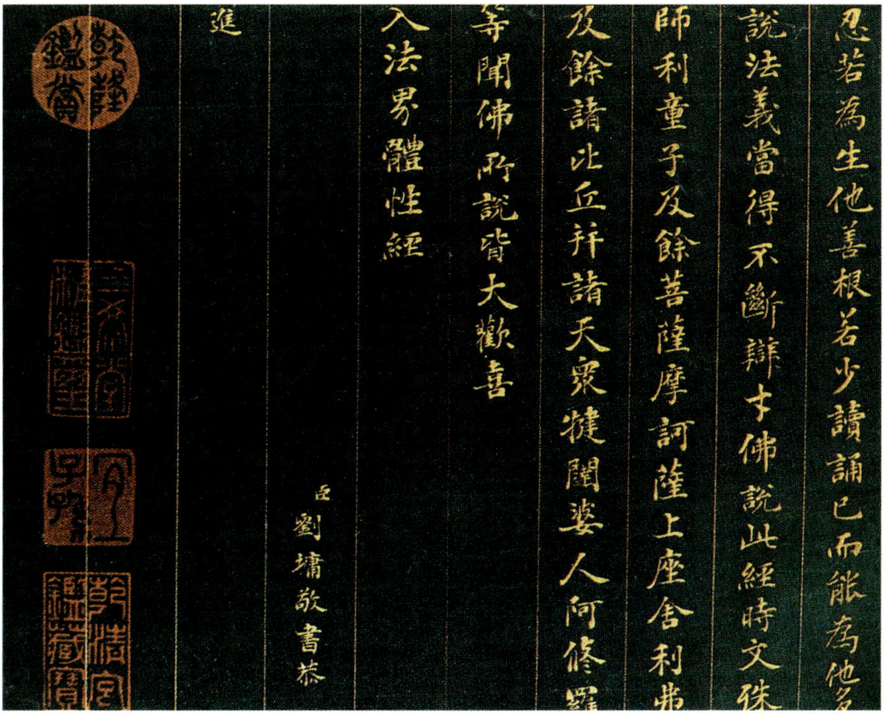

A calligraphic work (partial) of Liu Yong, one of the four most famous calligraphers of the Qing Dynasty. The Buddhist scripture was written in the standard script.

ancient to modern writing style.

The horizontal strokes of clerical script are curvy with a flared tail, and the characters have a dancing elegance. As making such strokes would slow down writing, people again improved the clerical script to create a new style that is easier to write—*kai shu* or regular script. As *kai* means standard in Chinese, this style is also known as the standard script. The regular script originated in the late Eastern Han Dynasty, and it still remains the most widely used writing style in present-day China.

What's apparent behind the evolution of styles was the pursuit of convenience and speed in writing. Roughly during the Wei and Jin dynasties, a new style, *xing shu*, the running script, emerged, which led to a writing speed much faster than the regular script. As *xing* means running, *xing shu* refers to a style in which characters run from the writing brush. This script is as popular as the regular script in scope and duration, and today most people use this style when they write by hand.

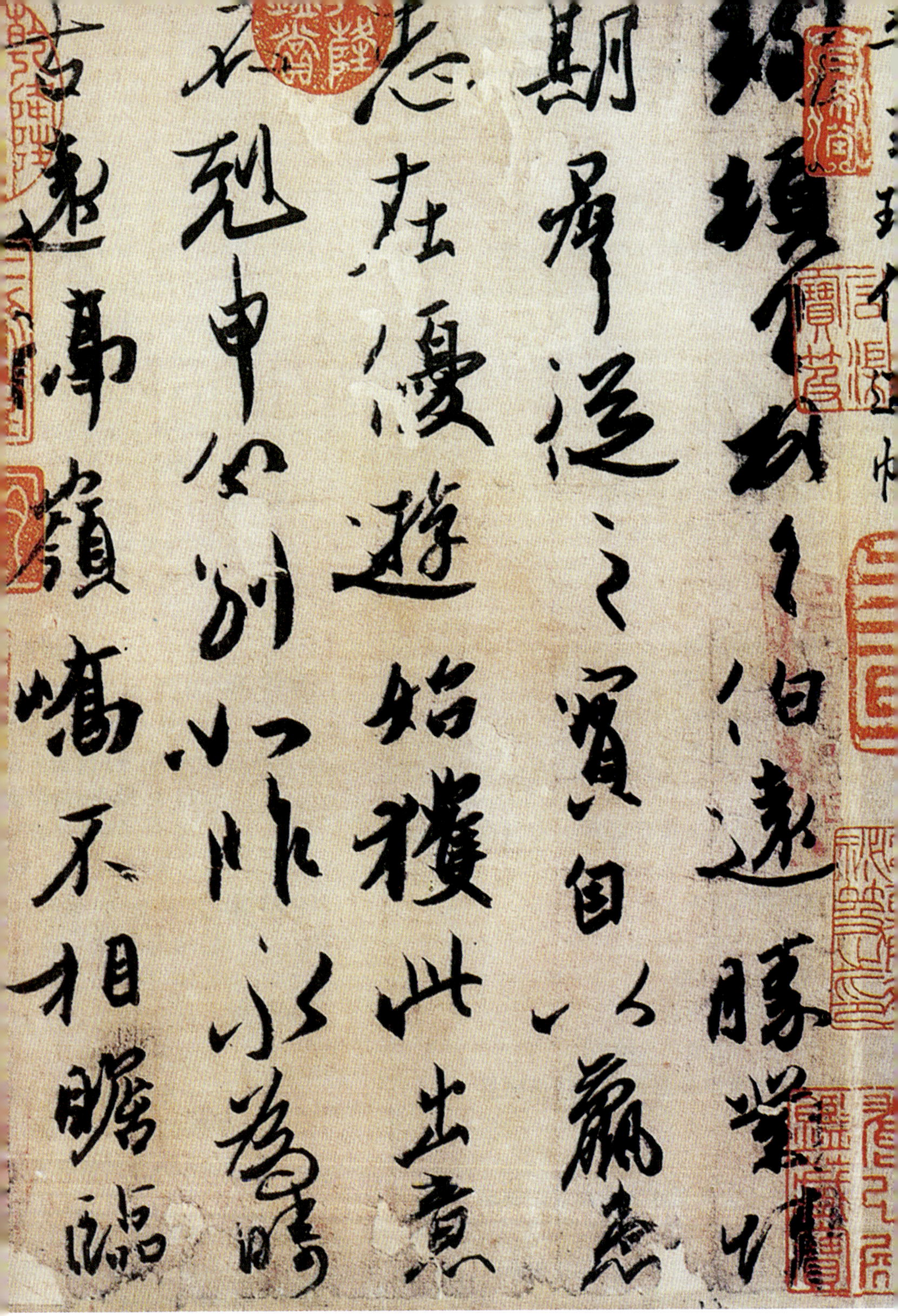

A running-script work by Wang Xun of the Eastern Jin Dynasty.

Now in the most treasured calligraphic collections of the Palace Museum in Beijing, this work used to be one of the favorites of Emperor Qianlong of the Qing Dynasty.

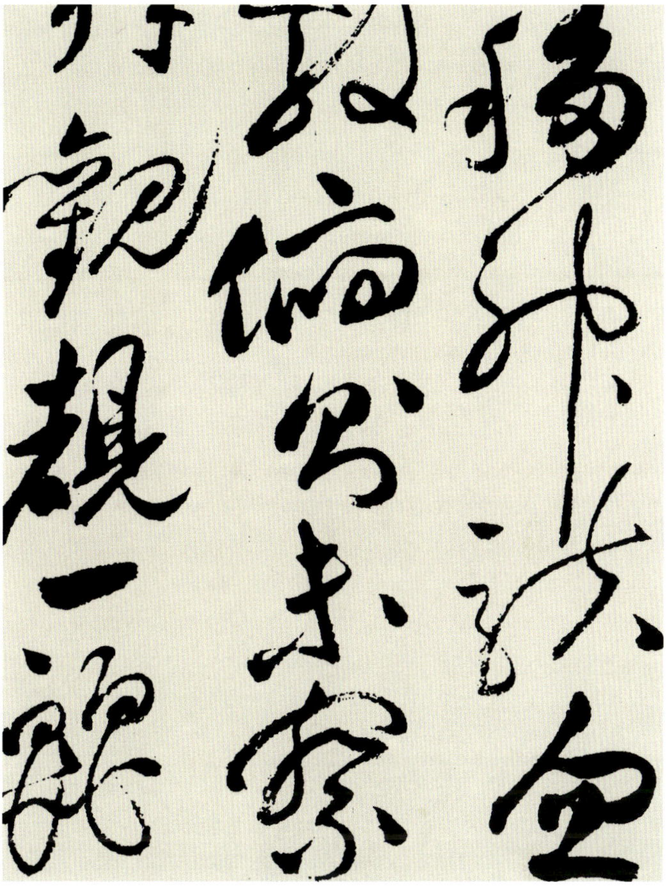

A grass-script work by Zhu Yunming of the Ming Dynasty.

The bold, unrestrained lines show the superb skills of the calligrapher.

Is there any style that can help the writer write even faster than the running script? Yes, the grass script (*cao shu*), especially the crazy grass script, offers an even faster writing speed. Some calligraphers would boastfully write in excitement that they could finish a calligraphic work of the crazy grass script before viewers could register their surprise. The grass script is highly abstract, and it requires special training to recognize the flying characters. But, for foreigners, the bold, unrestrained lines are most attractive.

The Four Treasures of the Study: They Record Civilization

Foreigners who have just encountered Chinese calligraphy find the instruments and materials used in this art to be quite novel. The writing brush, ink stick, paper and inkstone are called the "four treasures of the study," which shows their importance in the academic life of Chinese intellectuals.

The writing brush had been widely used at least as early as the Yin-Shang Dynasty. The character (聿) in the shell-and-bone script shows a hand holding a writing brush. But then writing brush was primitive. In the Qin Dynasty noted military general Meng Tian improved the making of the writing brush. Archaeological findings show the writing brushes from the Qin and Han dynasties were much the same as those now in use. Usually the bristles of a writing brush are made either of wool or

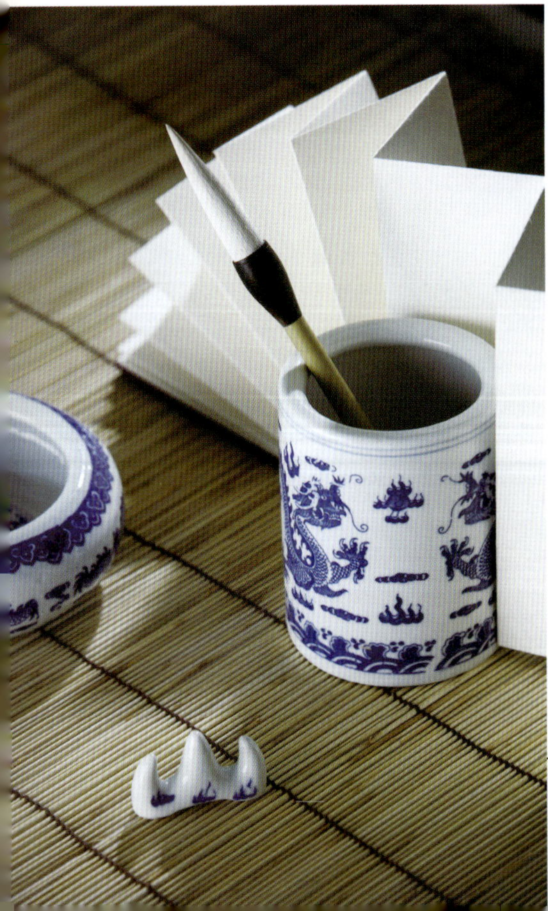

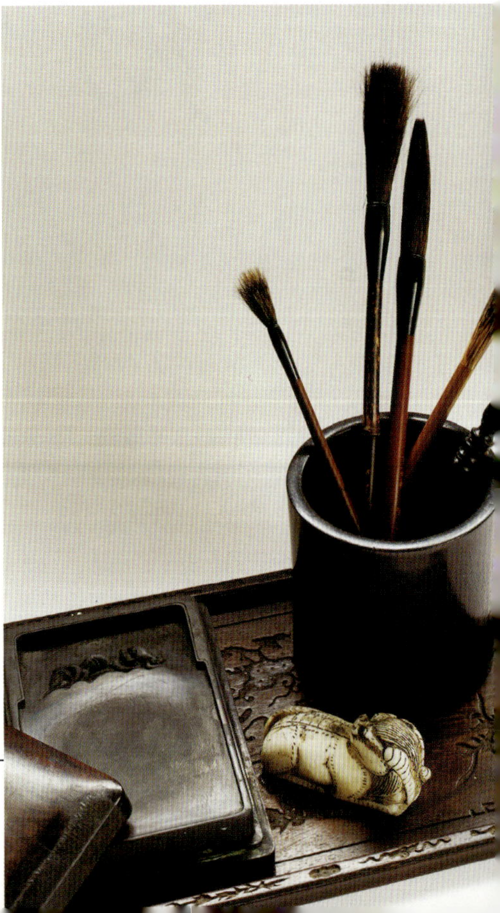

These instruments for calligraphy and painting used to be necessities in the study of a Chinese intellectual.

weasel hair. Many writing brushes can now be found in the collections of the Palace Museum in Beijing, which were tributes to the emperors of the Ming and Qing dynasties. These fine writing brushes represent the best workmanship of the times. For a calligrapher, a writing brush is as important as a weapon is for a warrior.

Before paper made of plant fiber was invented, Chinese characters were written on silk, which was so expensive that it could be afforded by only a few nobles. Archaeologists have unearthed writings on silk from the Warring States Period, which show a high achievement in calligraphy. But most people wrote on bamboo or wooden slips—bamboo slips were common in the south and wooden slips, in the north. Among the cultural relics that were found are a large number of writings on bamboo and wooden slips from the Warring States Period, which provide inspiration to today's calligraphers. In 105 inventor Cai Lun of the Eastern Han Dynasty improved the technology of paper-making by using various plant fibers to make inexpensive paper. The invention of paper has greatly advanced the progress of human civilization, and paper is listed as one of the four major inventions in human history. The Chinese further improved the technology by turning out Xuan paper, which is most suitable for calligraphy and painting. This paper is highly absor-

Ink stick

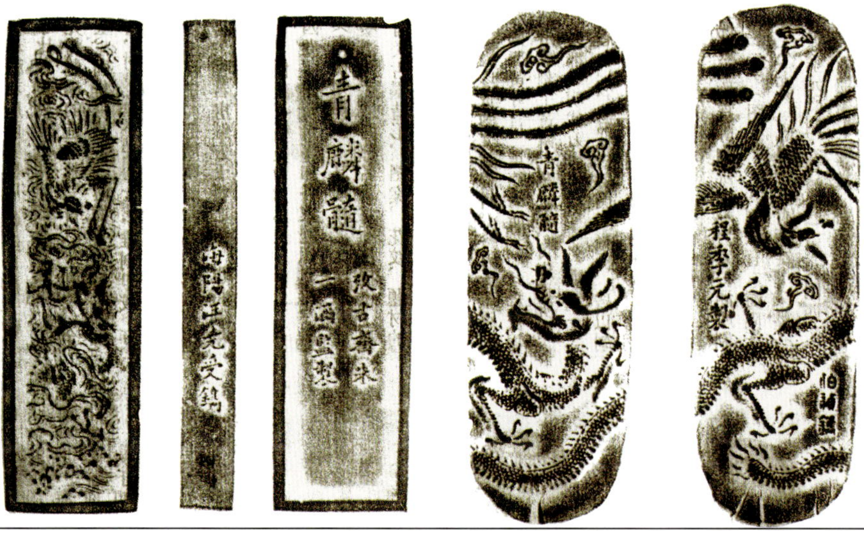

bent, which shows off the different hues and shades of ink, making it ideal for Chinese calligraphy and painting. As the paper was first produced in Xuanzhou of Anhui Province, it is called Xuan paper.

Top-rated Chinese calligraphers and painters are particular about the quality of the ink stick. The ancient Chinese collected soot from burning pine branches and mixed it with the powder of spices to make ink sticks. They rubbed the ink stick with water on an inkstone to prepare black ink for writing and painting. Depending on the amount of water added, the ink is thick or thin, and a successful artist can create different hues and shades from the ink. Once, a collector of ink sticks, although not skilled at calligraphy, would often prepare a pool of ink on an inkstone and sipped it to taste it. This story underscores how important the ink stick is for Chinese intellectuals.

The inkstone is also a prerequisite in traditional study in China. Inkstones from Shexian County of Anhui Province in east China and Duanzhou of Guangdong province in south China are highly valued by Chinese *literati*. When they get an excellent inkstone, men of letters would ask a skilled craftsman to process it and have the owner's name or favorite motto inscribed on the sides or bottom. Abundant collections of inkstones can be found in major museums in China. Touching an inkstone used by a historical icon is like conversing with a historical figure.

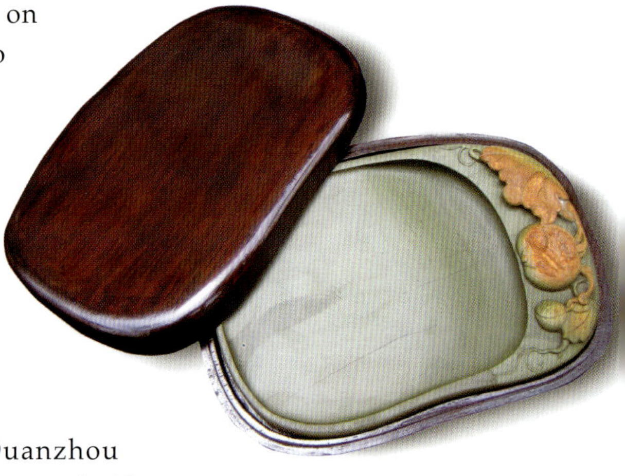

Inkstone

Perhaps no other people in the world attach such importance to writing instruments as the Chinese. These treasures of the study are not simply stationery, but have become part of a particular culture, the traditional Chinese culture, which is poetic in nature.

Forms of Calligraphic Works

A calligraphic work becomes an artwork when it is mounted in a special way. The forms of calligraphic works include the vertically hung or wall scroll, wide vertical scroll, horizontal scroll, hand scroll, fan covering and couplet. A basic knowledge of these forms will lead to better appreciation of the art.

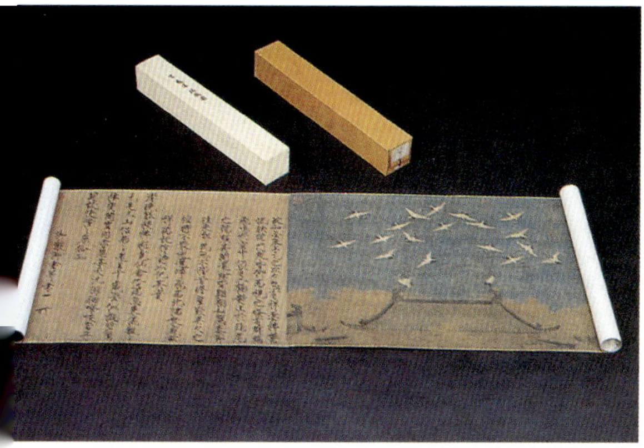

An unfolded hand scroll.

The scrolls, written on a narrow strip of Xuan paper, may be hung on the wall, either vertically or horizontally. If not hung, a scroll becomes a hand scroll, to be put on a table for viewers to appreciate.

In some movies ancient Chinese men of letters with a folding fan in hand can be seen; on one side of the fan is a painting and on the other, a calligraphic work. Such a fan was a necessary ornament of their lives, and also reflected their sentiments and tastes. Women carried a round or oval fan, also decorated with calligraphy and painting. When ladies went out and met strangers, they covered their faces with a fan out of courtesy. Emperor Huizong of the Song Dynasty wrote inscriptions on many round fans, and one is still in existence. A thousand years has passed, and yet this work still carries its charm.

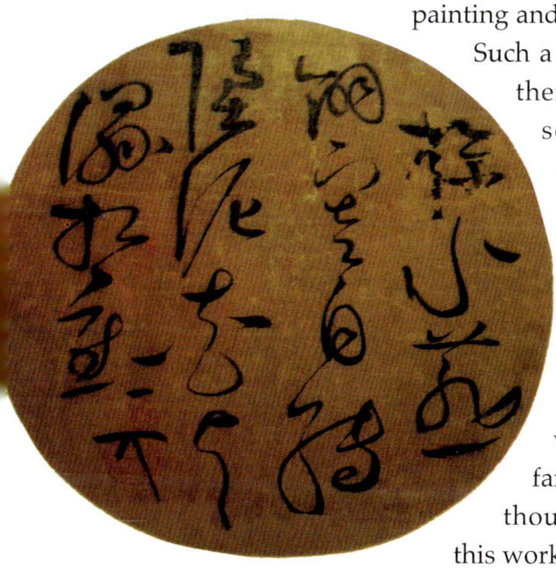

A round fan carrying a grass-script work by Emperor Huizong of the Song Dynasty.

The couplet is a unit of verse consisting of two successive lines to be hung on each side of a door or gate, and the words usually express the ideals and interests of their authors. During Spring Festival, Chinese households place Spring Festival couplets on their front doors. In China, even a remote, undeveloped village has a calligrapher who writes couplets. A calligrapher who can write Spring Festival couplets enjoys special respect, for even average Chinese regard calligraphy as a cultural symbol. This demonstrates the popularity of calligraphy in China.

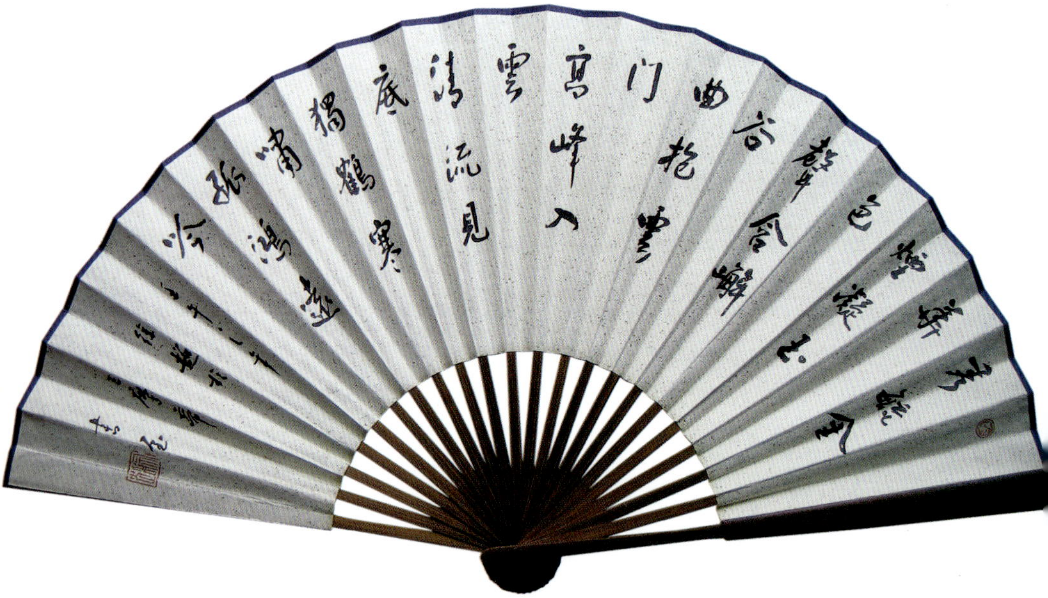

A fan covering with a running-script work by calligrapher Xu Chao. Quite a few Chinese still carry a fan in summer, not just to create a breeze but enjoy the artistic work on it as well.

Inner Mirroring: The Way to Enjoy Calligraphic Works

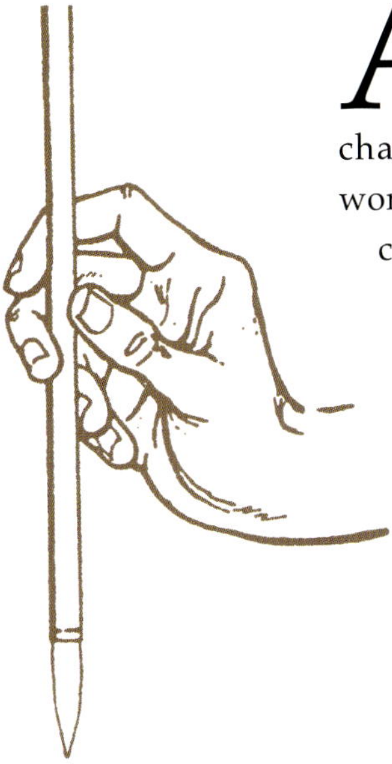

How the writing brush is held and moved.

A calligraphic instructor asks novices to pay attention to three things: the way the writing brush is held and moved, the structure of characters and the overall pattern of a calligraphic work. These factors are also important in appreciating calligraphic works.

Many people believe that the way the writing brush is held and moved is decisive in calligraphy, but such a belief is exaggerated. In fact, the writing brush is just like using chopsticks; the best way to hold and move it is up to the user, that is, when doing so feels convenient and comfortable. In the past several thousand years, the Chinese have summed up numerous ways of holding and moving the writing brush. Now the most popular is the way shown in the illustration. Anyone who is interested in learning calligraphy may follow this instruction. One can get different lines by moving the brush in different manners: fast, slow, randomly or abruptly pausing. Lines are the basic element of calligraphy.

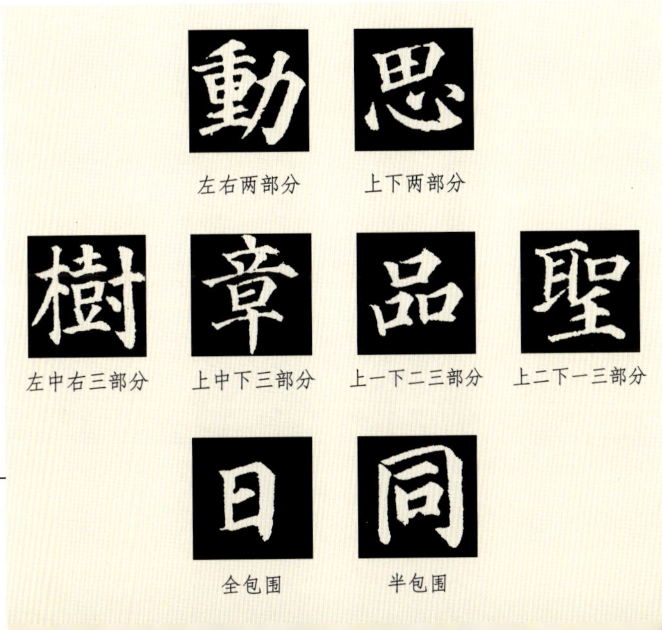

Dots and strokes form characters in various combinations.

A calligraphic work consists of Chinese characters, and a character, of dots and strokes. The composition of dots and strokes forms the structure of the characters, and the coordination of characters and rows of them decides the pattern of a calligraphic work. Both the structure of characters and pattern of calligraphic works call for harmony. A calligrapher must achieve order while avoiding rigidity by arranging the characters the way a general dispatches his soldiers.

The appreciation of a calligraphic work is just like an imaginary tracing of its creation. The viewer has to consider how the calligrapher created every stroke and every character by moving his brush. In literary psychology, this is called interior mirroring. In front of a celebrated calligraphic work, people are often seen meditating and moving their hands involuntarily—these people surely must be insiders of calligraphy, tracing and mirroring the artist-writer.

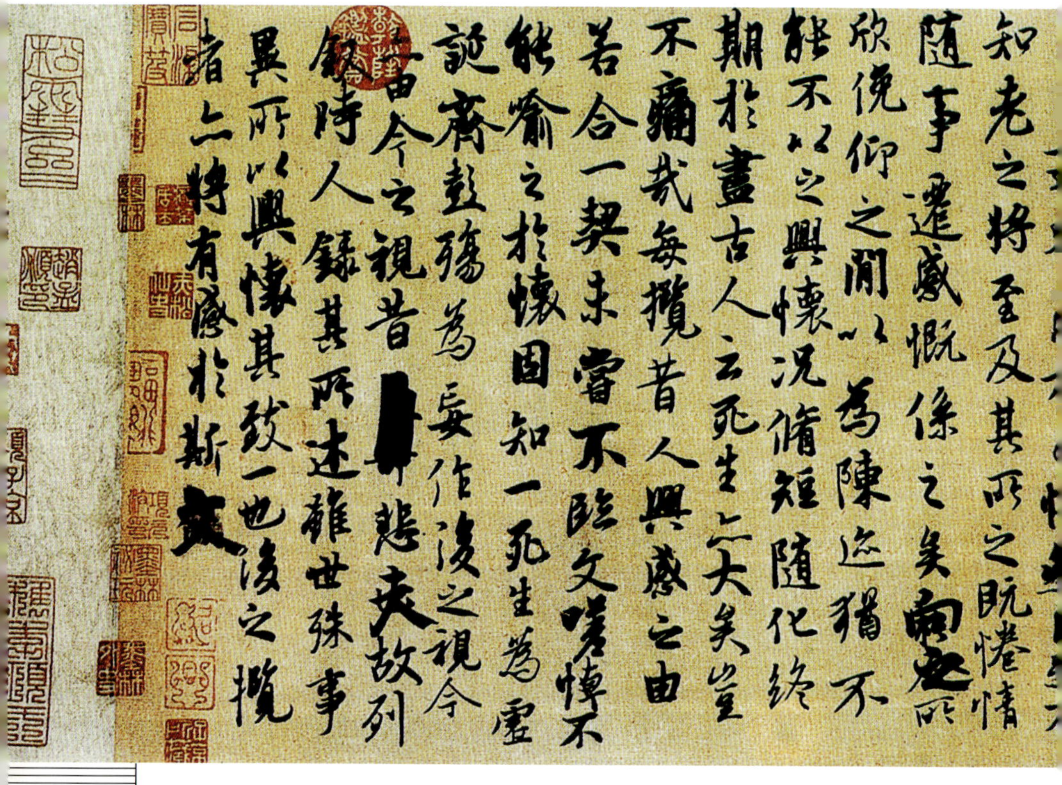

Lanting Xu: The Zenith of Running-Script Calligraphic Works

The Chinese worship heroes of various fields: the most celebrated are called the sages of their fields, such as poet Du Fu and painter Wu Daozi of the Tang Dynasty. Wang Xizhi of the Jin Dynasty is called the sage of calligraphy, and his *Lanting Xu* (Preface to the Poems Composed at the Orchid Pavilion), which he wrote during a gathering of intellectuals, is praised as the "zenith of running-script calligraphic works."

In Wang Xizhi's time Chinese intellectuals usually believed in Taoism, and they were both unconventional and talented artistically. On a warm, sunny day in 353, a group of top-ranking intellectuals gathered at the Orchid Pavilion and composed poems while enjoying wine. Slightly drunk, Wang Xizhi wrote in running

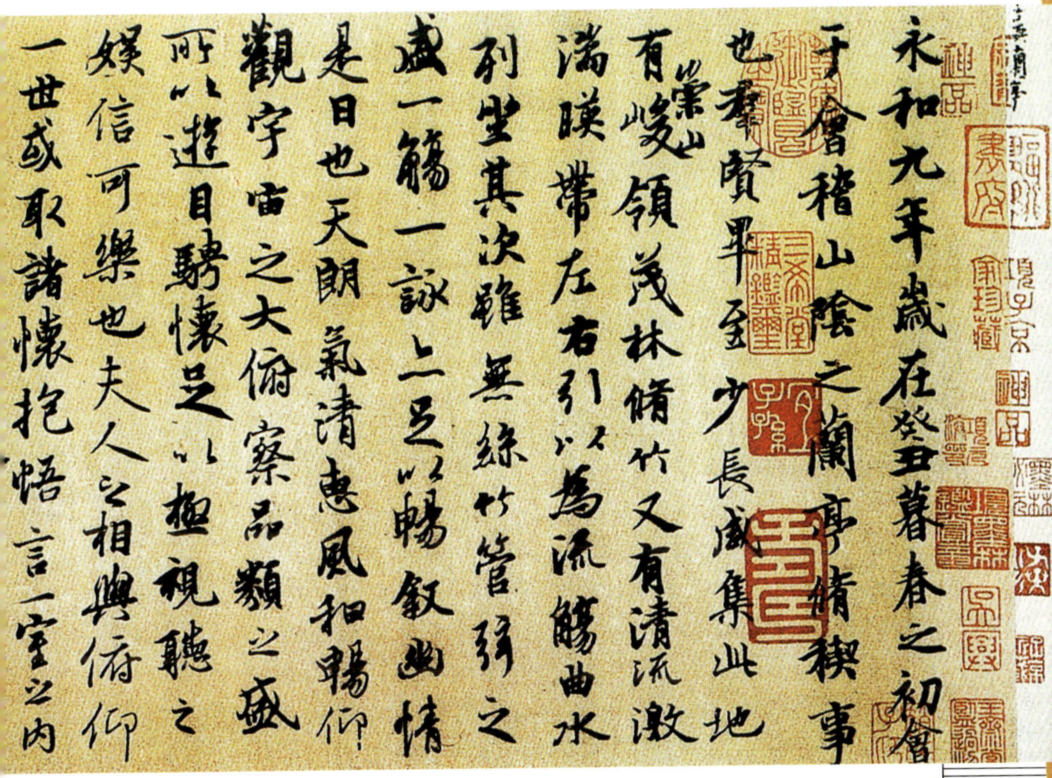

Lanting Xu (Preface to the Poems Composed at the Orchid Pavilion).

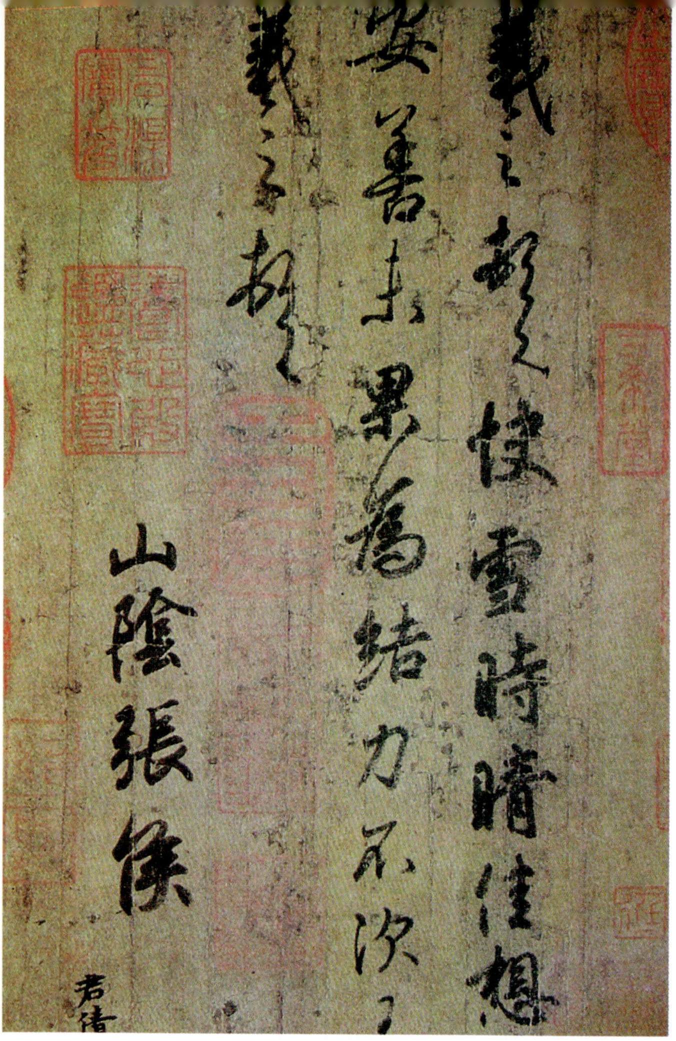

A note written by Wang Xizhi of the Jin Dynasty.

Wang Xizhi, known as the sage of calligraphy, wrote this note to one of his friends after a heavy snow. This note in the running style is among the few extant calligraphic works by him.

style the preface to the poems in a state of inebriation. Unintentionally written, the work later became the most celebrated in the history of Chinese calligraphy. Su Shi, an eminent writer of the Song Dynasty who was also good at calligraphy, wrote in one of his poems that a calligraphic work should combine strength with grace—which is exactly what *Lanting Xu* had achieved. Critics say this artistic work contains all the elements of the beauty of calligraphy, and all calligraphers after Wang can draw inspiration from this work.

Li Shimin, Emperor Taizong of the Tang Dynasty, was one of the best-known rulers in Chinese history. A successful statesman and artist, Li had a great love for the works of Wang Xizhi, and he even wrote a biography for Wang. The emperor sent a resourceful official to meet Wang's offspring and received the calligraphic work of *Lanting Xu* from them. In his will, he requested that the

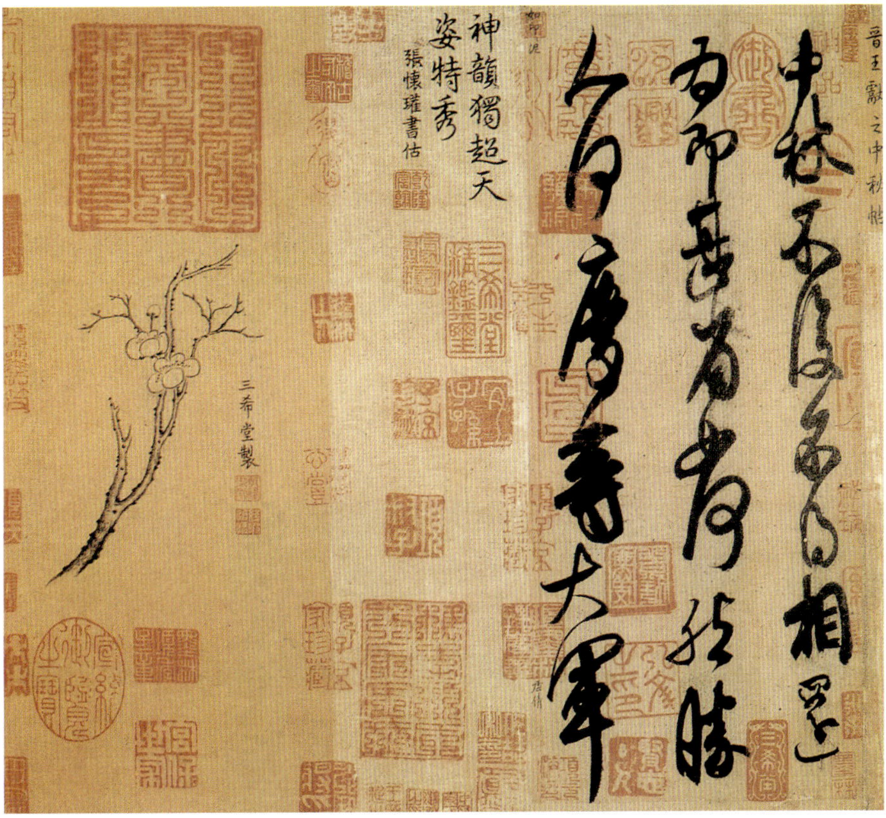

A grass-script work by Wang Xianzhi (son of Wang Xizhi) of the Jin Dynasty.

Wang Xianzhi was the first calligrapher that wrote in a crazy grass style with the characters linked to each other.

work be buried with him. The *Lanting Xu* seen today is in fact a reproduction of the work made in the Tang Dynasty, yet people who study calligraphy still revere it with devotion.

In Beijing, in the Hall of Mental Cultivation in the Palace Museum, a stele of San Xi Tang (The Hall of Three Rare Treasures) can be seen with Emperor Qianlong's inscription in the West Chamber. This dissolute, scholarly emperor kept three calligraphic works that he valued most in the hall: one by Wang Xizhi, another by his son Wang Xianzhi, and the other, by his distant nephew Wang Xun.

The Four Masters of Regular-Script Writing

In the history of Chinese calligraphy, the most adored regular-script works are those of four calligraphers: Ouyang Xun, Yan Zhenqing and Liu Gongquan of the Tang Dynasty, and Zhao Mengfu of the Yuan Dynasty. Their highly individual works are known as Ou-style, Yan-style, Liu-style and Zhao-style writings. Today, Chinese pupils are required to copy their penmanship when they learn calligraphy. This is called *miao hong*—tracing the red, printed characters with a writing brush

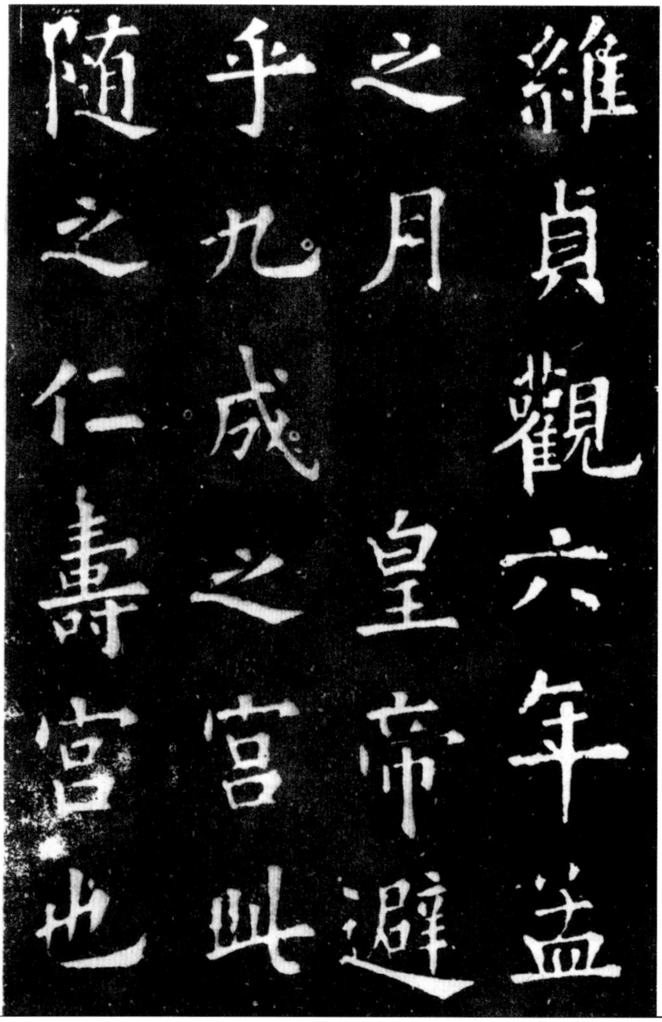

Part of a work by Ouyang Xun, regular-script master of the Tang Dynasty.

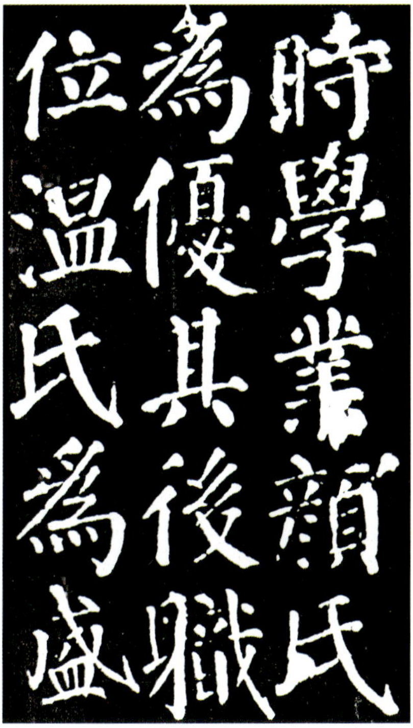

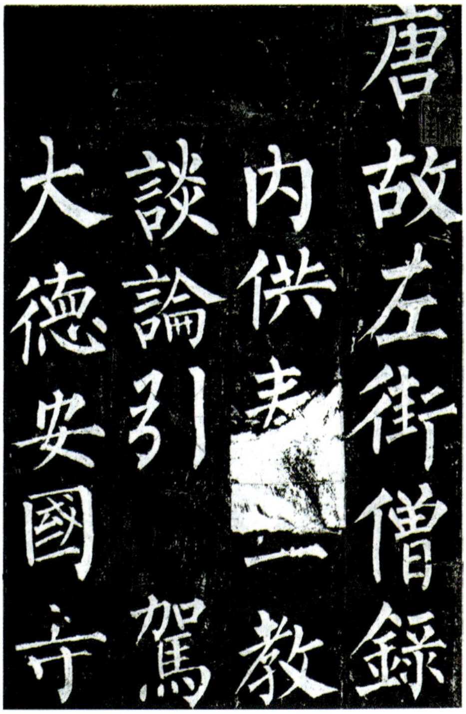

Part of a work by Yan Zhenqing, regular-script master of the Tang Dynasty.

Part of a work by Liu Gongquan, regular-script master of the Tang Dynasty.

in black, a must for calligraphic novices.

Emperor Taizong greatly admired Wang Xizhi, and, under his influence, the dynasty witnessed the ascension of Chinese calligraphy, with the Tang regular script being its peak. Ouyang Xun laid the foundation for the development of the regular script, and, after the technique of block printing was invented, most of the books adopted the Ou-style characters. Today, the Song typeface used in print and computers still bears some features of the Ou-style characters.

Yan Zhenqing was a role model of integrity for Chinese intellectuals. He died a hero's death at around 80 years old in the struggle against local rebel forces to safeguard the stability and unity of the empire. And Liu Gongquan, while explaining calligraphic principles to the emperor, told the ruler about the principles of integrity. In Liu's view, only calligraphic works of an upright person can have the scent of justice and strength. These people believed that calligraphy served not only to entertain but

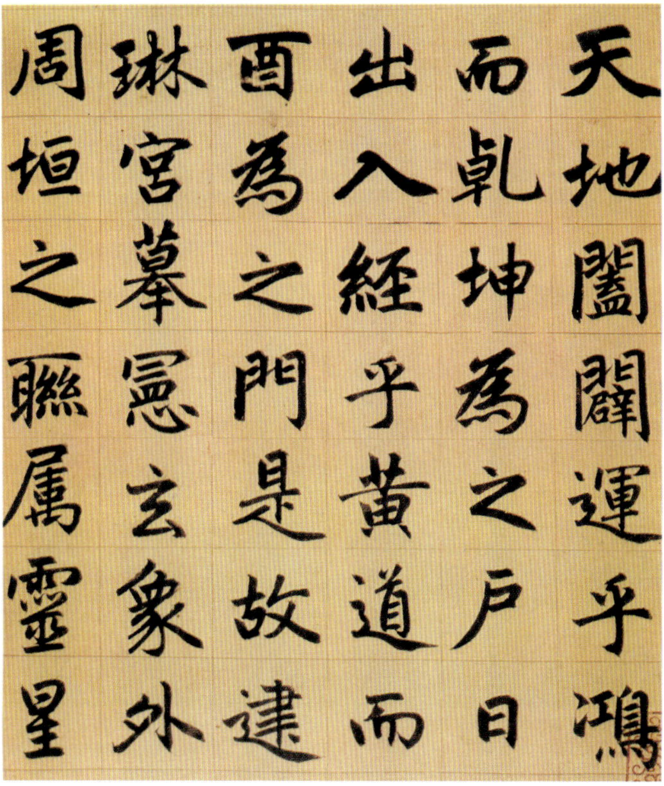

Part of a work by Zhao Mengfu, regular-script master of the Yuan Dynasty.

to cultivate noble values.

Zhao Mengfu was a descendant of the royalty of the Song Dynasty. His graceful style contrasts sharply with those of the three Tang calligraphers. Zhao is also well-known for his achievements in painting.

Crazy Zhang (Zhang Xu) and Drunken Su (Monk Huaisu), Masters of the Grass Script

Of all the styles of writing, the grass script is most suitable for artists to express their emotions and skills. Zhang Xu and Monk Huaisu of the Tang Dynasty were famous for their grass-script works, and poets of all eras have praised them unreservedly.

When artists in pursuing their creative endeavors enter a condition free from restriction or control, they become highly excitable and seem insane. Their nicknames Crazy Zhang and Drunken Su meant that the two artists were quite often in a feverish state. In such a crazy mindset, an artist can easily break away from convention, and, in drinking heartily, an artist can free

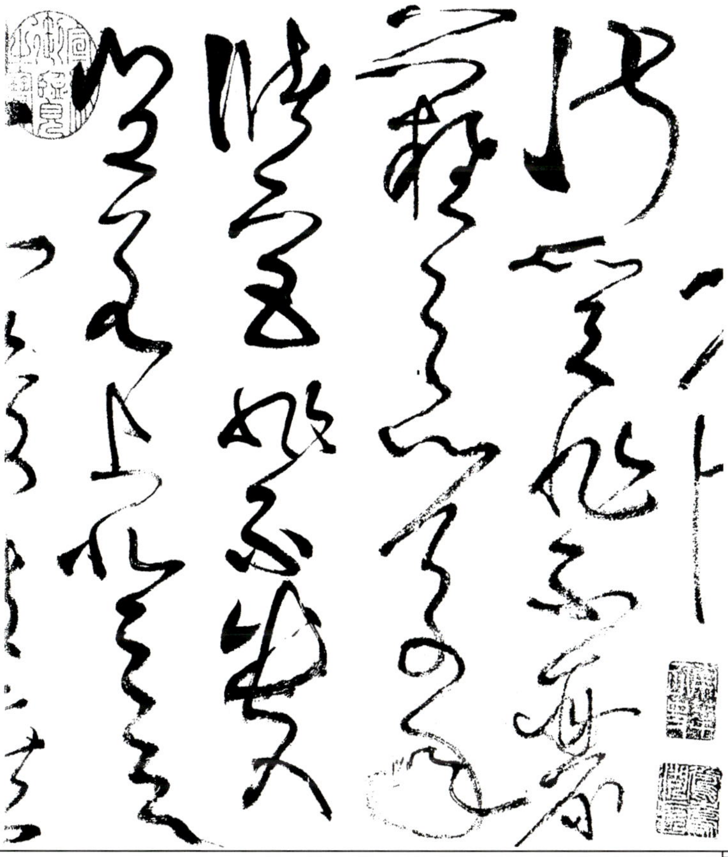

Part of a scroll by grass-script master Zhang Xu of the Tang Dynasty.

himself from inhibitions. Crazy Zhang and Drunken Su were emotional, sensitive and impulsive, and they poured all their feelings into their works. They were highly skilled in their writing, and their works flowed from the tips of the writing brushes like violent eruptions. Often, viewers of their works would vicariously share the writers' joy and agony.

Extant works of the two artists include a letter written by Zhang Xu to one of his friends when Zhang had a stomachache and an autobiography written by Monk Huaisu. Both are regarded as immortal in the history of calligraphy. A poet once wrote that the writings by Crazy Zhang and Drunken Su could never be placed by the water, lest the characters turned into dragons and flew away. When we view the works of Zhang Xu and Monk Huaisu, we often think of the Chinese idiom, "*long fei feng wu*," literally meaning dragons flying and phoenixes dancing—lively and vigorous flourishes in calligraphy.

Here the readers must be reminded that the grass script is not written recklessly but by following strict rules. Zhang Xu and monk Huaisu had gone through strict calligraphic training before they broke from convention. Their exposition of craziness and drunkenness is in fact like "dancing in chains." This is similar to the way traditional Chinese intellectuals themselves behave in society: those seemingly arrogant scholars who defied rituals and regulations were actually clinging to them. The core of Confucian philosophy is

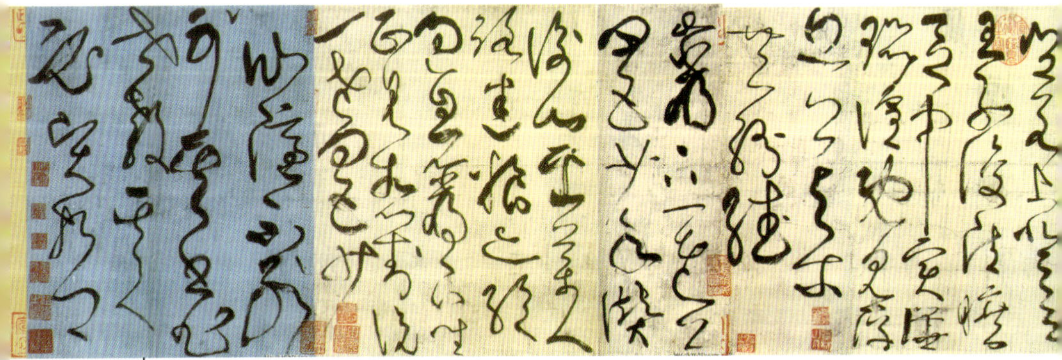

This scroll is the most well-known work by Zhang Xu, who wrote four ancient poems on five pieces of colored paper in the crazy grass script.

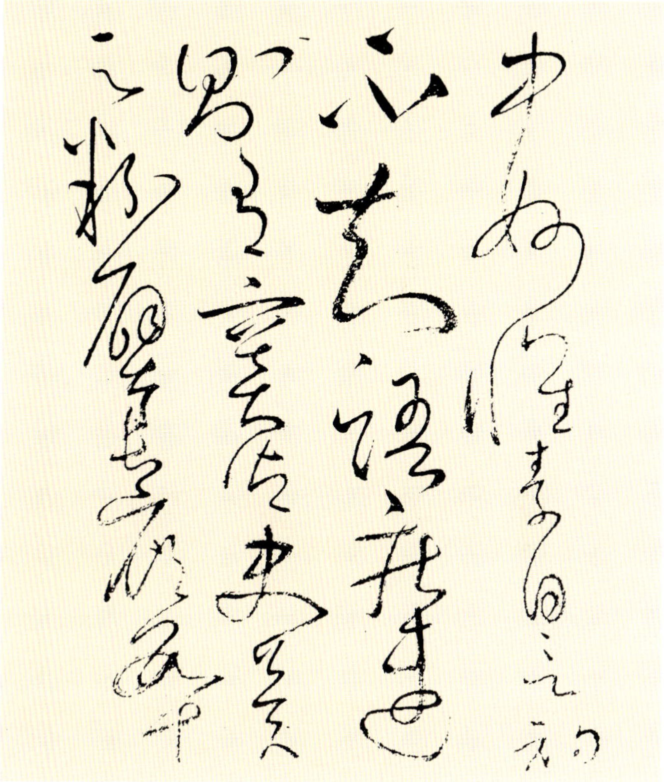

Part of a work by Monk Huaisu, grass-script master of the Tang Dynasty.

The work was an autobiography of the monk, in which he wrote about how he learnt calligraphy.

the doctrine of the mean, of observing discipline and regulation in the artistic field. Artists who approach the boundaries as closely as possible but do not overstep them will win the highest respect.

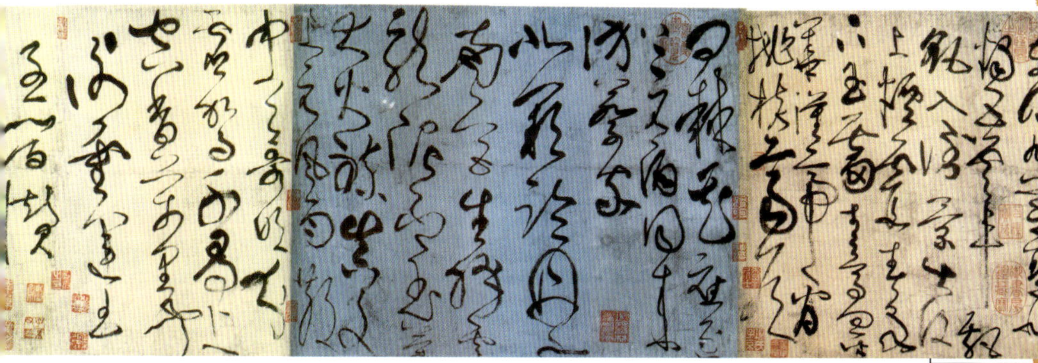

Personality Decides Calligraphic Quality

The Chinese believe that calligraphy reflects the writer's cultivation, including temperament, academic achievement, tastes and character. In short, calligraphy reveals personality. Artistic factors are not the only criteria for the judgment of calligraphic works; the political stance and personal character of the calligrapher are also considered in deciding the quality. For instance, General Yue Fei of the Southern Song Dynasty, who led Song troops in resisting nomadic invaders, has been honored as a national hero and the few words written by him have been highly valued, although he, rising from the ranks to become a general, was not skilled at calligraphy. In contrast, Qin Hui, a prime minister who lived during the same period, has

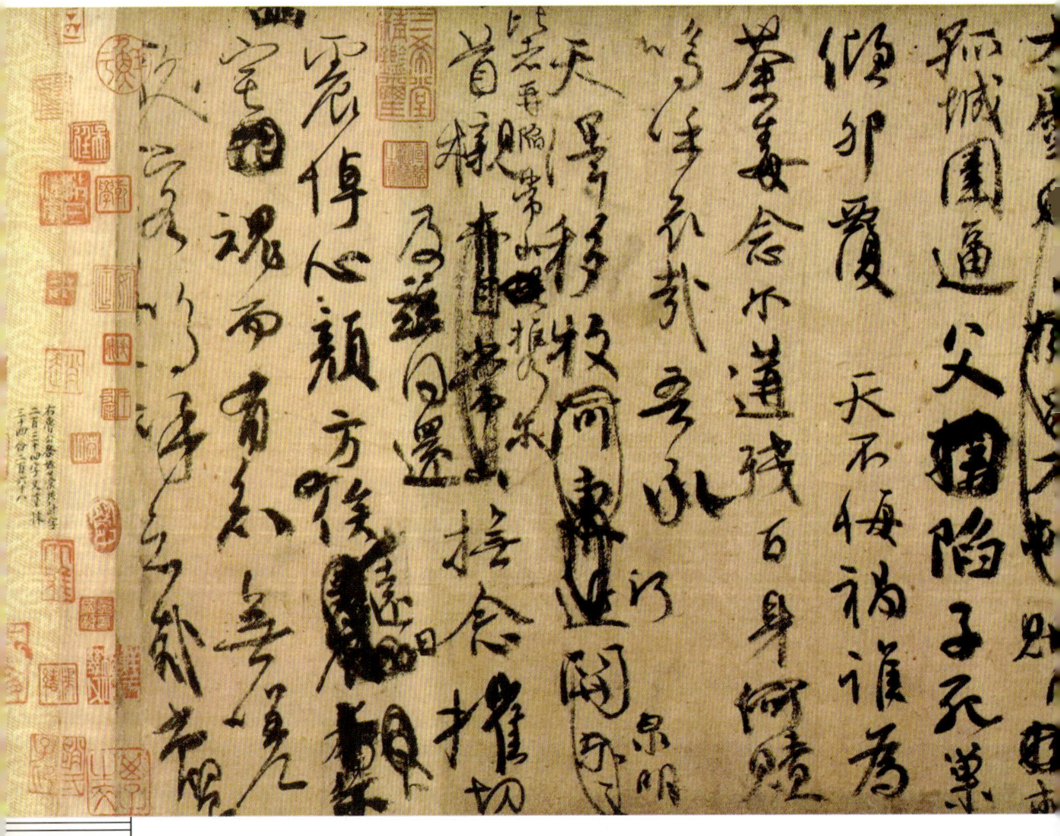

A manuscript by Yan Zhenqing of the Tang Dynasty.

This manuscript in the running script was the draft of an article Yan wrote in memory of his nephew who was killed in a war against rebels.

long been condemned as a traitor for betraying national interests. Despite the fact that Qin once won first place in the imperial examination and was an established calligrapher, he has simply disappeared from the history of Chinese calligraphy.

In evaluating calligraphic works, people often talk about the scent. Although intangible, the Chinese believe excellent literary and artistic works must have their scent. A well-known Chinese collection of short stories, *Strange Tales from the Liaozhai Studio*, includes a tale of an immortal who disguised himself as a blind monk in the temporal world to judge the quality of scholars' articles; he would burn the articles and smell the scent to discern the quality. The scent of a calligraphic work is like the temperament of a person. Chinese critics believe that the literary style of calligraphy is linked with the character and academic achievement of the writer, which determine

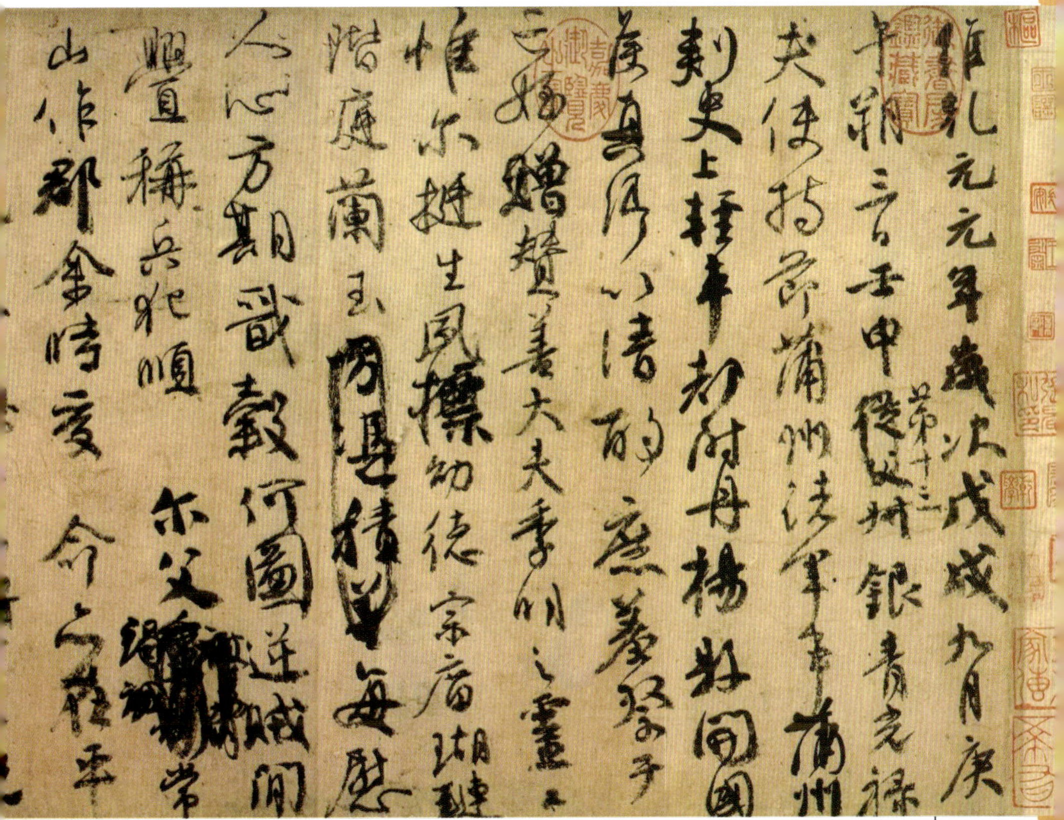

the quality of his works. And in turn people wish to imbue their writings with their tastes and learning. As a Chinese proverb goes, "The writing reveals the writer." Two people can learn much about each other from the calligraphic features of letters that they exchange, though they may live a thousand miles apart and have never met. Therefore, nearly all Chinese devote some time in improving their handwriting.

In Chinese literary criticism, it is a general rule to link the personality of the artist with his works. This is true for painting and other literary works as well as calligraphy. In the literary field, the top criterion is morality, and this criterion is exclusively decisive.

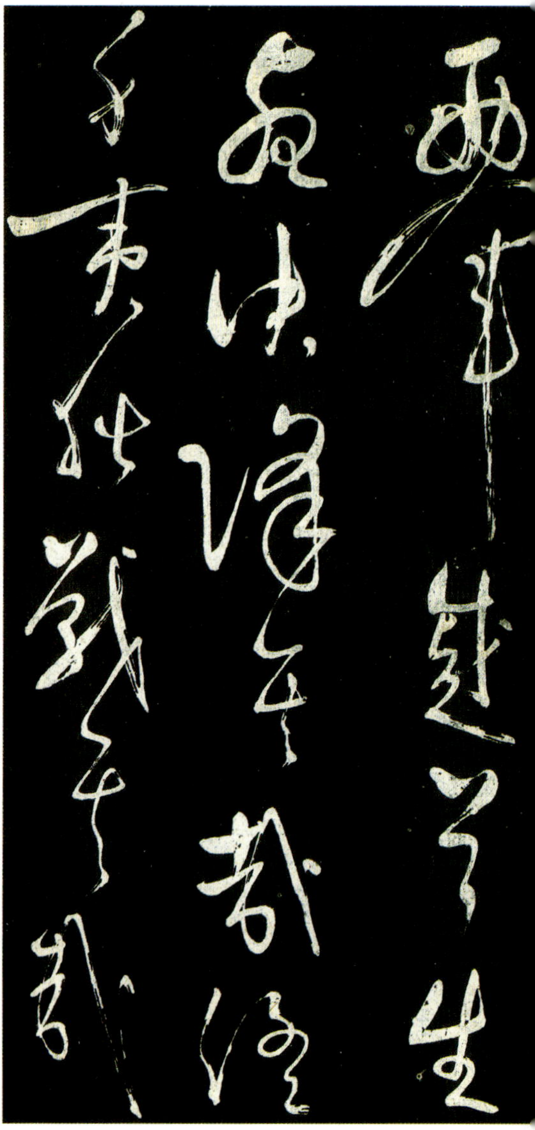

A calligraphic work said to be written by Yue Fei, a patriotic general of the Song Dynasty.

Chinese Seal: Dancing Beijing

In 2008, the Chinese people will host the 28th Olympic Games in Beijing, a great event for the nation and the world. When the emblem of the Beijing Olympic Games was published, the world witnessed an excellent combination of traditional Chinese art and the modern Olympic spirit.

The emblem, "Chinese Seal: Dancing Beijing," presents a running figure by integrating traditional Chinese arts such as seal-cutting and calligraphy, which have a history of more than 5,000 years, with sports images. The design crystallizes traditional Chinese culture in a seal: red is the color of celebration in Chinese culture; the logo carries multiple images—the Chinese character 京(capital), which implies the site for the event, a runner making the final sprint in the Olympic spirit and a dancer symbolizing the

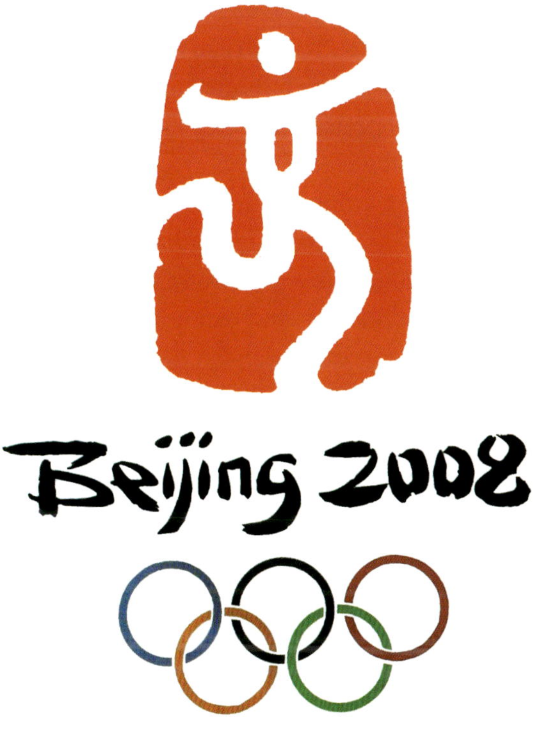

Chinese Seal: Dancing Beijing

This emblem of the 2008 Olympic Games is a combination of traditional Chinese art and the modern Olympic spirit.

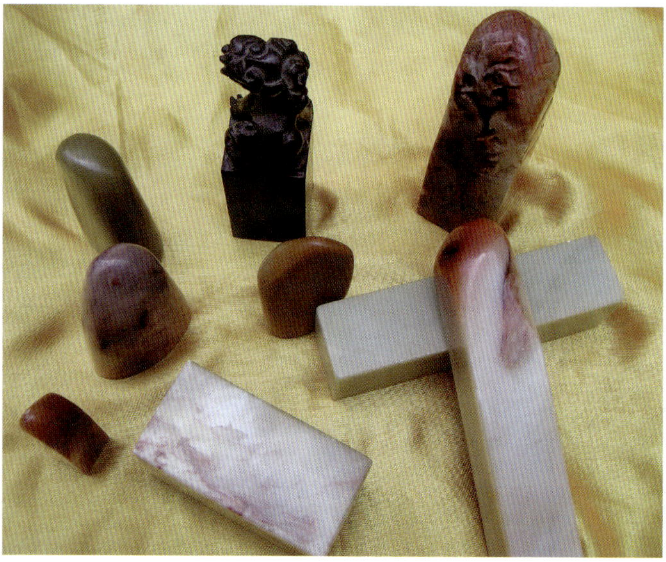

Stones for seal-cutting.

1.3 billion Chinese people's aspiration for the Olympics and their welcome to guests from all parts of the world.

Seal-cutting is a Chinese art that is derived from calligraphy, in which skillful artists inscribe elegant words and graceful writing on stone or metal. It is really a wonder that so much artistic content can be concentrated on a small piece of fine stone. Through the Olympic emblem, the ancient Chinese art of seal-cutting is once again renewed and enters the world arena.

In ancient China, emperors and officials had their own seals as symbols of authority, and regular people also used seals cut by craftsmen as a proof of credit in correspondence. Probably the Song and Yuan dynasties is when artists began to stamp their seals on their works, and collectors also began to put their seals on items in their collections to show ownership and love. A red seal print and black lines on white paper—these colors add to the charm of a calligraphic work or painting. An artist who excels in poetry, calligraphy, painting and seal-cutting is praised as "fourfold excelling" —the highest honor for artists.

Chinese readers like to stamp seals on their own books, just as Western readers use *ex libris*. Foreign friends who wish to taste the charm of Chinese art may ask for a seal to be cut so that they may stamp their names on the title pages of their books. And fans of Chinese arts or collectors simply cannot do without a seal with Chinese characters.

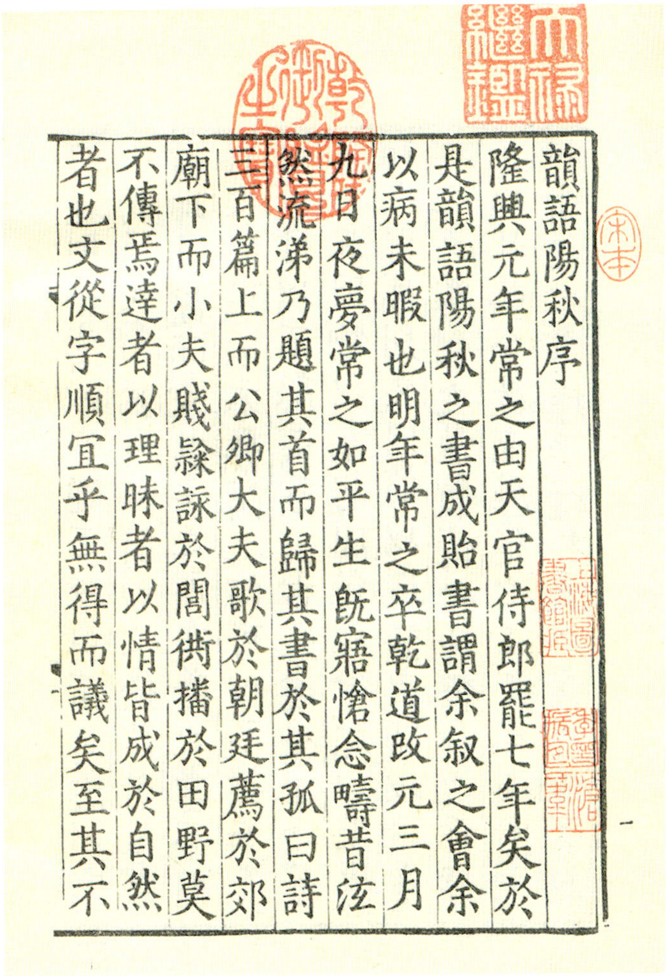
韻語陽秋序
隆興元年常之由天官侍郎罷七年矣於是韻語陽秋之書成貽書謂余敘之會余以病未暇也明年常之卒乾道改元三月九日夜夢常之如平生既寤愴念疇昔泫然流涕乃題其首而歸其書於其孤曰詩三百篇上而公卿大夫歌於朝廷薦於郊廟下而小夫賤隸詠於閭衖播於田野莫不傳焉達者以理昧者以情皆成於自然者也文從字順宜乎無得而議矣至其不

Stamps of seals used as ex libris on a page of a book from the Song Dynasty.

The stamps record the circulation of the book. The number of stamps may indicate the history and values of the book.

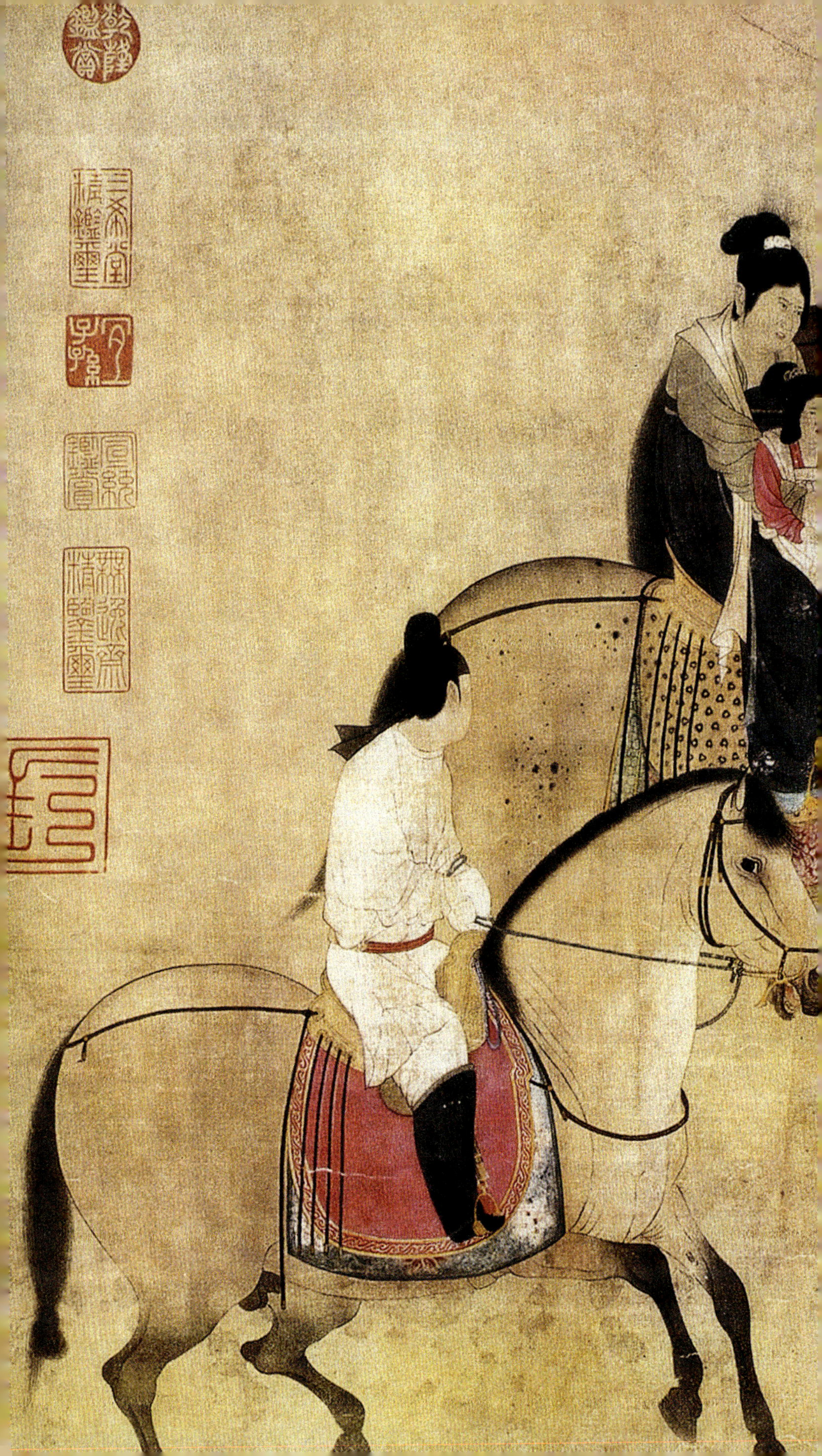

Painting

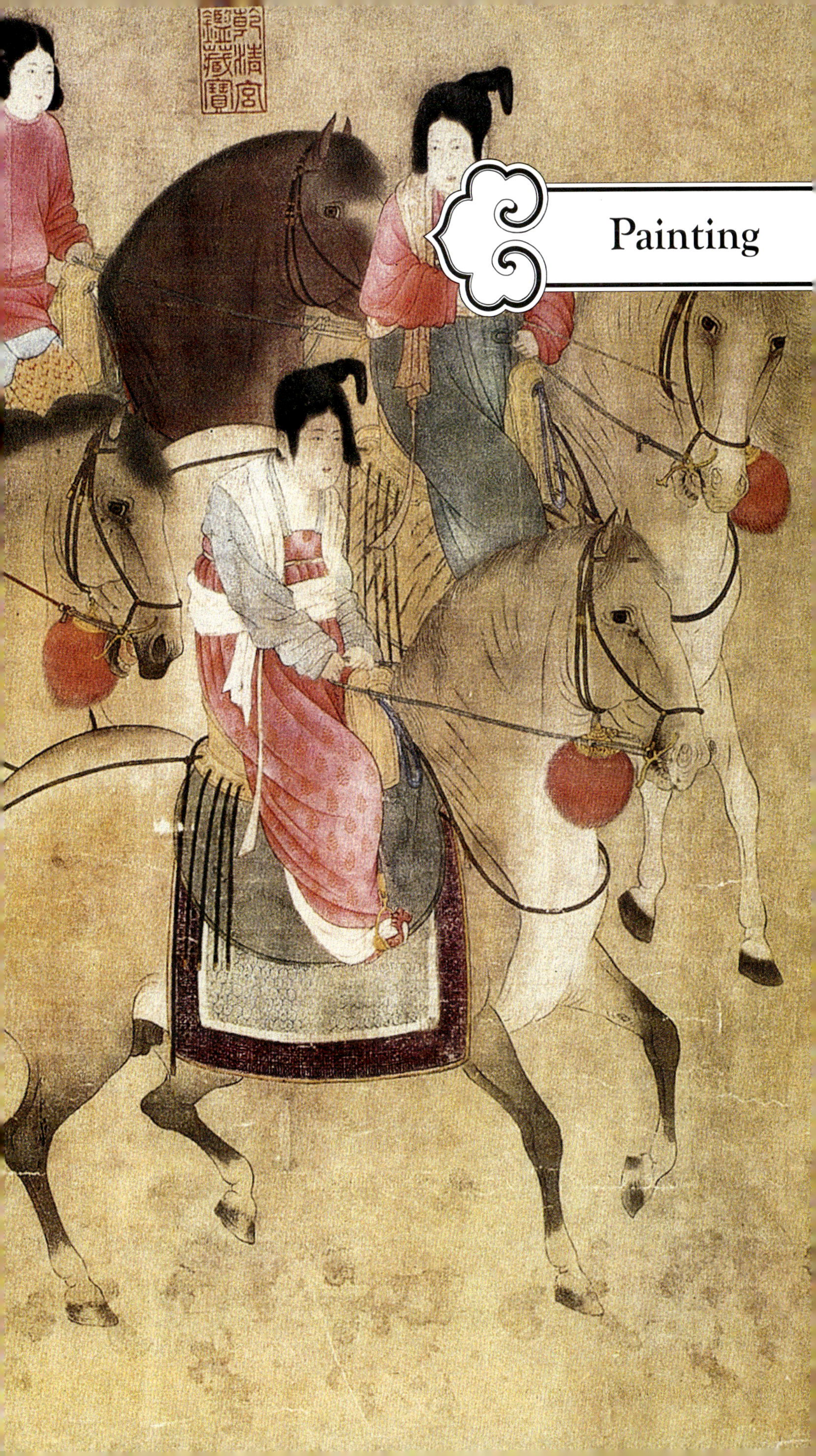

Chinese Painting: Unity of Poetry, Calligraphy, Painting and Seal-Cutting

Painting is an important branch of traditional Chinese arts. This branch has a history of several thousand years since the earliest drawings on painted pottery from the Neolithic Period. In this branch, traditional Chinese painting, or paintings created with long-haired brushes, ink and watercolor on paper or silk, is most fruitful and has the greatest influence on Chinese culture and art. Traditional Chinese paintings can be divided into figures, landscapes, and flowers and birds according to their themes, or *gongbi* (meticulous) and *xieyi* (sketching-thoughts) according to the techniques. Before the maturity of traditional Chinese paintings, there were rock paintings, silk paintings and mural paintings.

Chinese painting combines poetry, calligraphy, painting and seal-cutting to compose a stylized form of art. With all these elements, a traditional Chinese painting can fully display the artistic character of the painter, and provide much more aesthetic value.

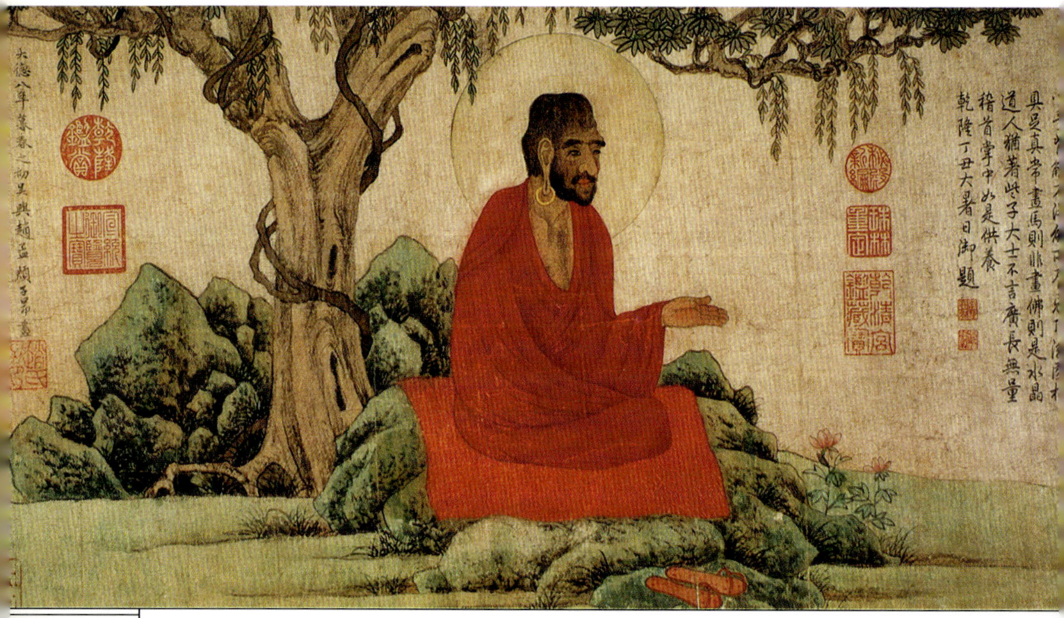

A Buddhist Arhat in Red by Zhao Mengfu of the Yuan Dynasty.

This work is an ideal combination of poetry, calligraphy, painting and seal-cutting.

Before the Song Dynasty, Chinese painters rarely made any inscriptions on their works except for signing their names in a corner in some cases. In the Song Period some painters, who were also poets and calligraphers, wrote an inscription or a poem on their works to explain the theme or express their emotions. And in the Yuan Dynasty, seals were stamped on paintings. By that time, all the four artistic elements had been combined in one form.

The inscriptions on Chinese paintings may include the name of the painter, the sender and recipient of the work,

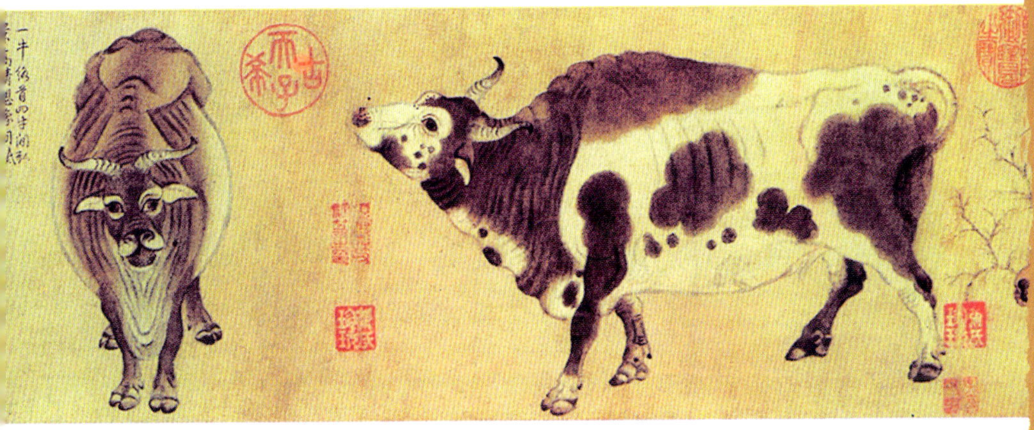

Part of the Five Oxen by Han Huang of the Tang Dynasty

a title, a few words from the painter, a poem or prose. An inscription should reflect the literary cultivation of the painter, its content should have an inherent link with the image so that it may help a viewer to develop a feeling from the painting, and should also act as a guide to understand the philosophies of history or life. Aside from its content, an inscription should also have a high calligraphic value. The style and script of the inscription must be in harmony with the pictorial work so that it adds to the beauty. Therefore, a painter must also be a calligrapher.

In the Tang and Song dynasties, many men of letters took up painting brushes and liked to write poems on their painting works. A pictorial work is direct and concrete but confined to a certain time and space. In contrast, unlimited by such constraints, a poem can describe things in different times and places and their developments to contain much greater content than the pictorial work. By combining a poem with a painting, the static painting becomes dynamic and more inclusive, and the poem also becomes more vivid—they are mutually complementary.

In Chinese painting, the blank space is important, and most images are in ink monochrome. As such is the case, the red impression of a seal can effectively add more color to a painting and make it livelier. Often more than one seal print can be seen in a Chinese painting, and the red seal prints of different characters and styles are arranged in different places, all out of careful consideration. This demonstrates that comprehensive cultivation is required in traditional Chinese culture and arts in forming an excellent painter.

In Chinese painting the painter strives for an artistic conception by infusing the image he creates with his views, feelings and ideals, turning the objective material image into a subjective artistic image. Take Mount Huangshan, for instance. Some people simply record the landscape of the mountain mechanically. Others observe the mountain and feel its life and temperament. In their aesthetic eyes, Huangshan is full of life, just like a human being—imposing peaks, floating clouds and flowing water, looming, surging and trickling. By selecting, processing and transforming the objective images and

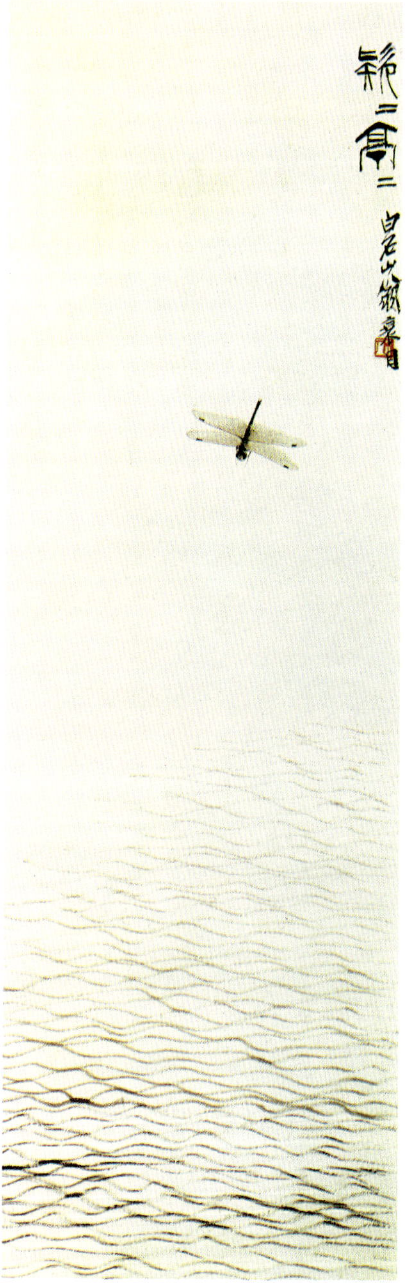

Dragonfly Flying above Water by Qi Baishi (1864–1957)

The blank in the painting invokes viewers' imagination of lake water and clouds.

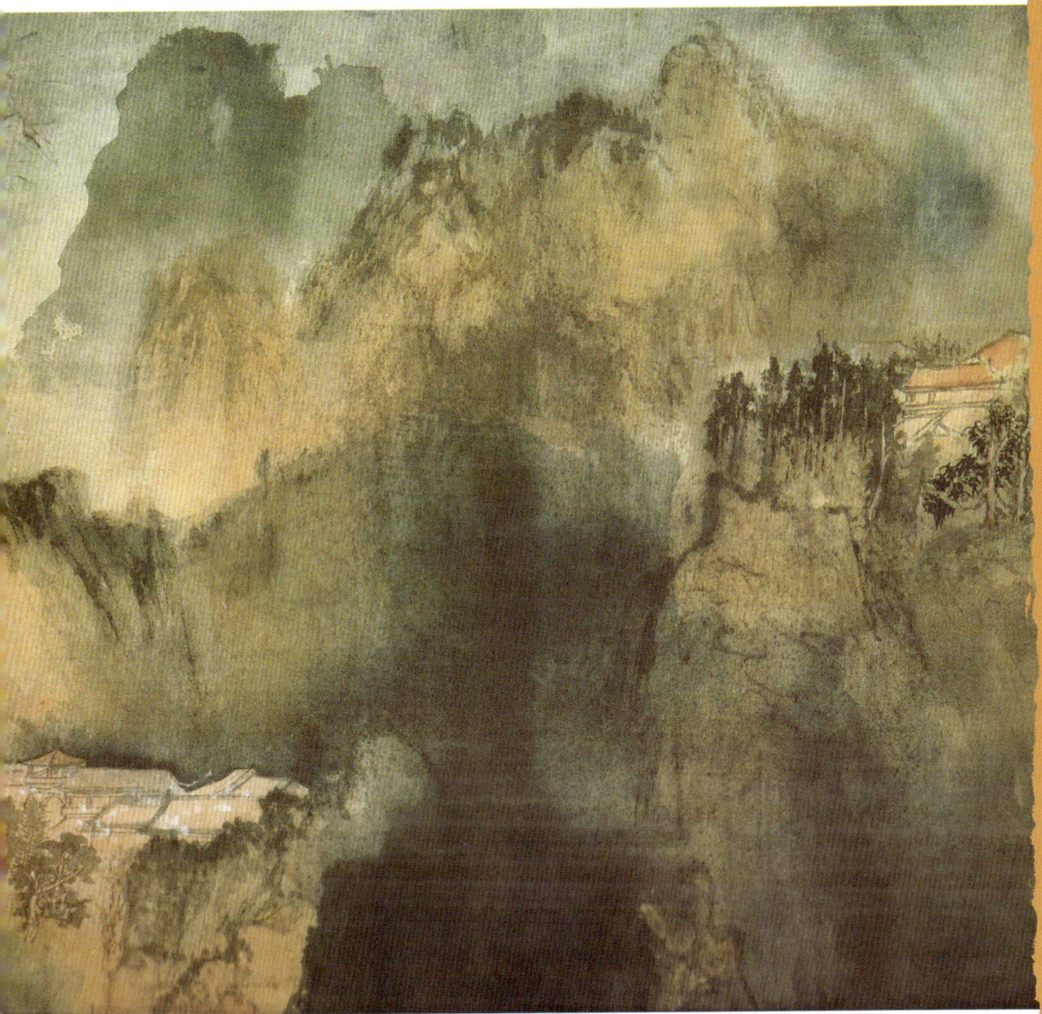

Part of the Mount Lushan by Zhang Daqian (1899–1983)

The painter turns the objective image of the well-known tourist attraction Mount Lushan in Anhui Province into a subjective artistic image.

imbuing them with his own aesthetic values, the painter creates an artistic conception in highly generalized artistic images. Artistic conception is an important criterion for judging Chinese paintings. If the image of a painting —a hill, a river, grass or trees—fails to invoke viewers' imaginations, it is considered a failure on the part of the painter.

The language of Chinese painting is quite different from that of Western painting, where oil colors, watercolors and brushes create colorful images. As the main medium is color, the painter must have a keen eye

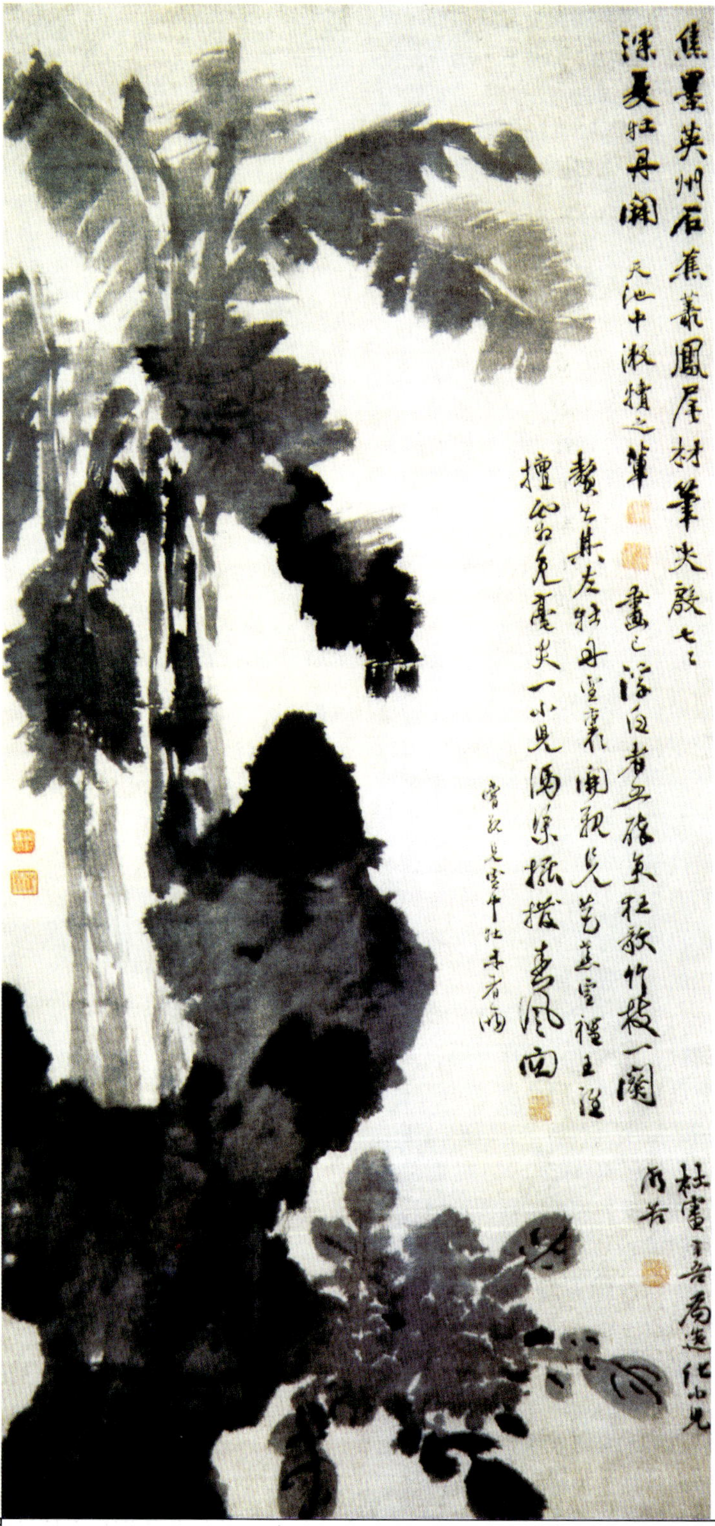

Peony and Rock by Xu Wei of the Ming Dynasty.

The painter was highly skillful in using the brush and ink.

for hues. Chinese painting is mainly a linear art, and the painter uses Chinese brushes, ink, paper and special watercolors. A Chinese painter must be poetic and skillful in applying the brush and ink to create not only images but artistic conception.

The Childhood of Chinese Painting

In Chinese culture, people believe calligraphy and painting spring from the same source. As Chinese writing is ideographic, Chinese ancestors were in fact drawing graphs when they wrote the highly ideographic characters. But before the Chinese writing system was developed, ancient Chinese had begun painting in primitive society.

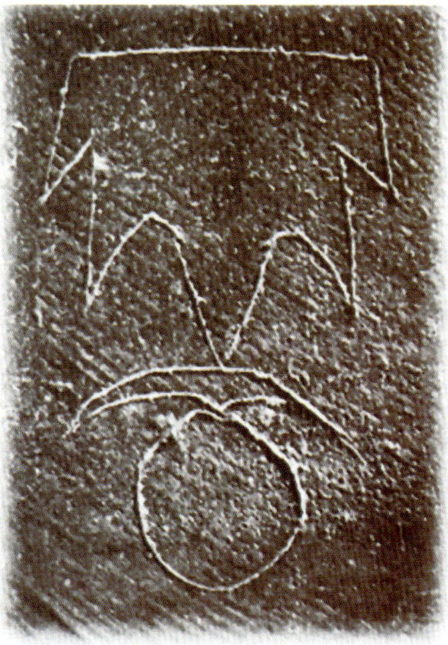

A pictograph from the Neolithic period.

This is a proof of the belief that calligraphy and painting spring from the same source.

Painted pottery was an important symbol of human civilization of the Neolithic Period, and a large number of painted pottery vessels were unearthed at the Banpo site in Xi'an city, Shaanxi Province in northwest China. The decorations painted on the vessels include geometric graphs as well as animals and plants. On the pot shown here are patterns of a human face and fish. On the top of the human face is a triangular hat, and there are two fish on both sides of the face and in the mouth. The parts above the eyebrow and below the mouth are painted a decorative color. In front of the human face is a big fish. Probably the human face represented a figure of a primitive clan at a religious ceremony, and the fish in the mouth displayed the people's wish for abundant food in the fishing and hunting season. This imaginative artwork shows the lives of Chinese

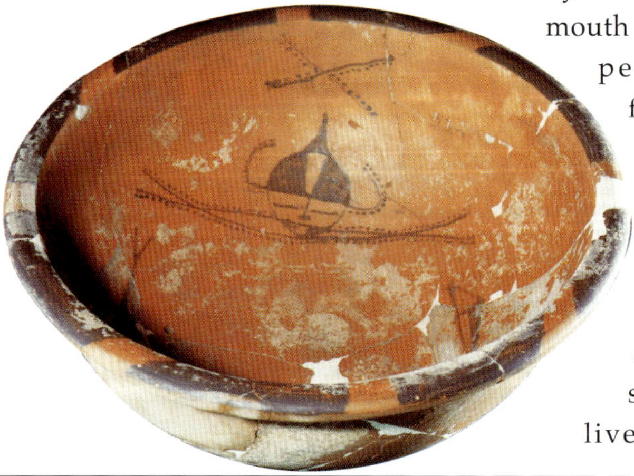

Human-Face-and-Fish pottery pot.

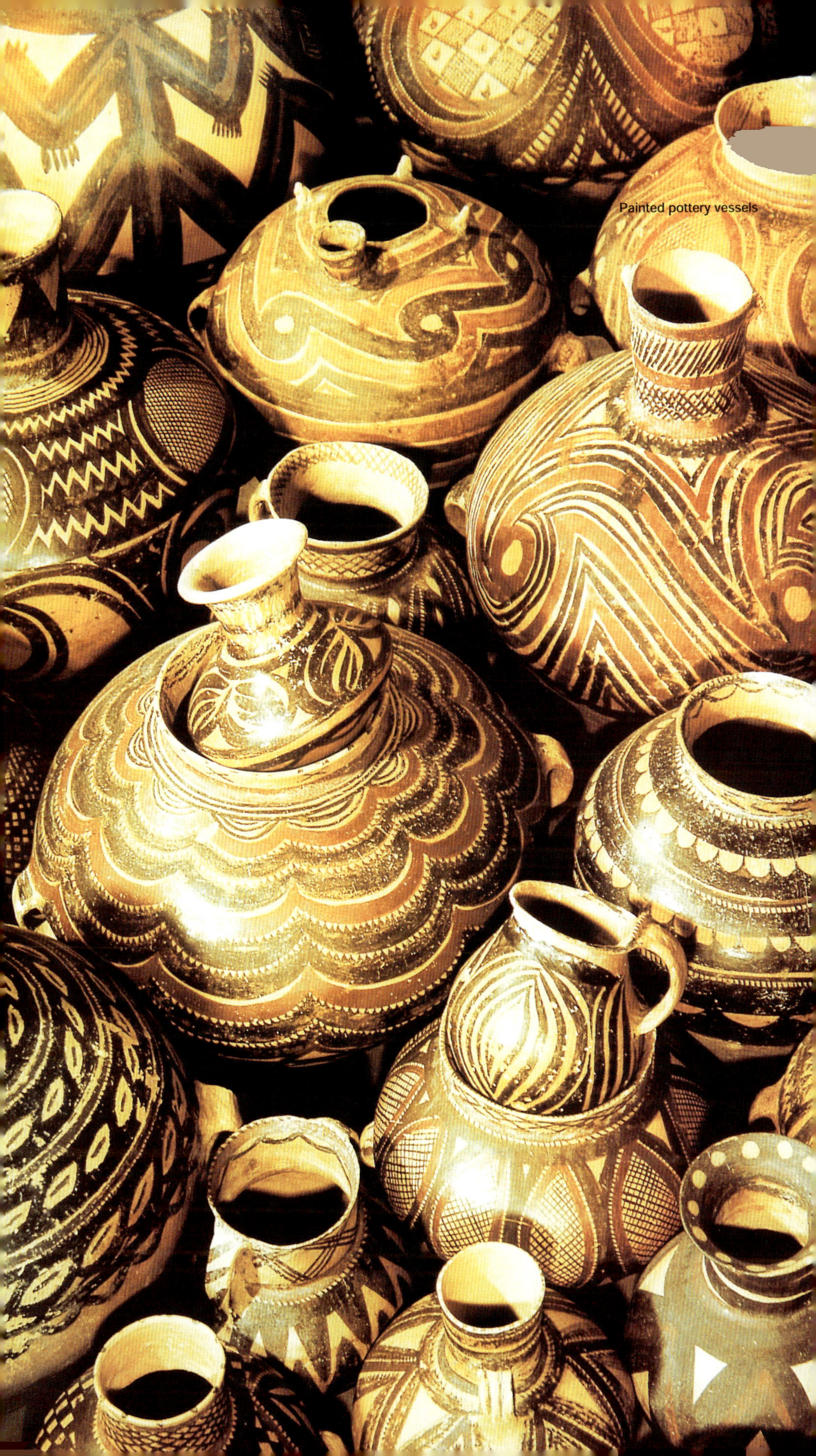

Painted pottery vessels

ancestors in the Neolithic Period. In another pottery pot unearthed at the Shangsunjiazhai site in Qinghai Province, also in northwest China, painted on the inside are dancing primitive people. The ancestors, five in one group, move rhythmically. The figures are clear and vivid; they are not copies of objects but artistic abstractions created from imagination. The Chinese ancestors also left a large number of paintings on rocks, which depict fishing, hunting, war and nomadic life.

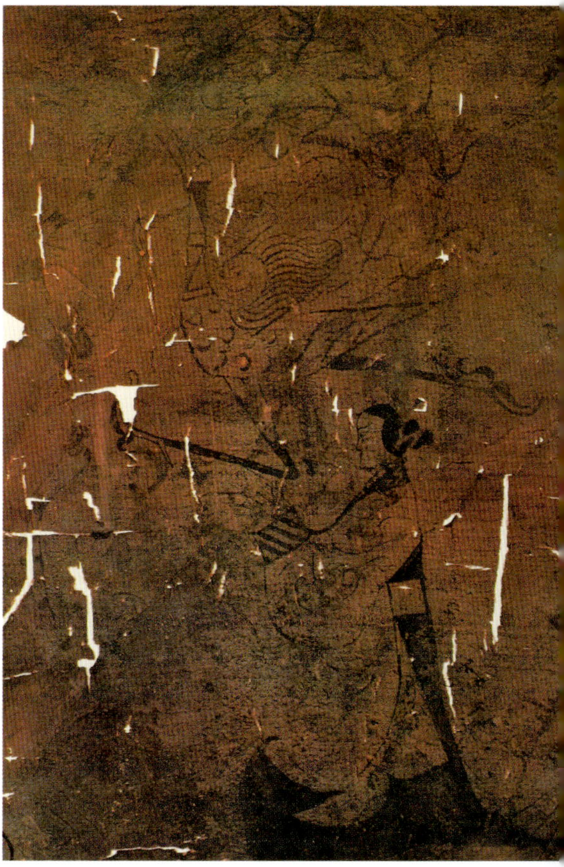

Dragon, Phoenix and Witch, a silk painting from the Warring States period.

By the Spring and Autumn and Warring States periods, people began painting on silk, which is a more suitable texture for the painting brush than pottery or rock. This silk painting of Dragon, Phoenix and Witch (*Long Feng Renwu Bo Hua*) is one of the earliest extant paintings in China, unearthed in 1949 from a tomb of the ancient Chu state in Changsha, Hunan Province in central China. The witch has a slim body and slender waist and her lips and sleeves are vermilion. The dragon and phoenix fly in the sky, guiding the soul of the dead character to heaven. The whole painting was sketched in smooth, black lines with striking images. The ancient Chinese had a great concern for the other world, and many paintings were devoted to the theme of souls ascending to heaven. Another silk painting, unearthed from a tomb of the Western Han Dynasty at Mawangdui in Changsha, depicts the reality of this world, and the imaginary life underground and in heaven. The main character had enjoyed a luxurious

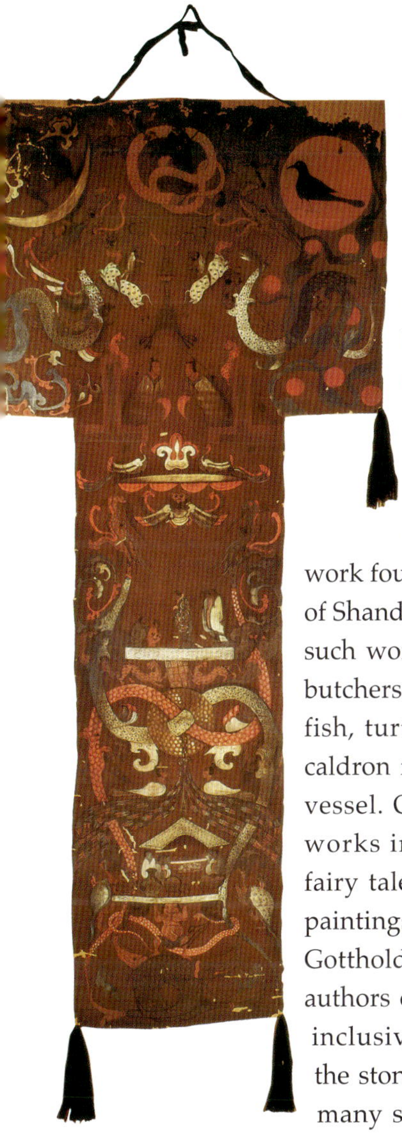

life in this world; after his death, as prayed for by his family, two dragons led his soul to heaven to enjoy a life for immortals. The painter used precise, expressive lines to depict both grand scenes and details. The mineral dyes between the lines are still bright, even after being buried in the tomb for more than 2,000 years.

Stone relief and brick relief were a major part of the pictorial works of the Han Dynasty, depicting the material and spiritual lives of the time. The stone relief work found in Wu's Ancestral Hall in Jiaxiang County of Shandong Province, east China, is one of the best of such works. The relief depicts scenes from daily life: butchers kill chickens and sheep, and cooks prepare fish, turtles and ducks in the kitchen. Outside, the caldron fire rages, and steam rises from the cooking vessel. Other themes for the stone and brick relief works include historical events and figures, and fairy tales. These works are similar to the narrative paintings of Western countries. German aesthetician Gotthold Ephraim Lessing wrote in his *Laocoon* that authors of narrative paintings should select the most inclusive scenes and moments for their works. In the stone and brick relief works of the Han Dynasty many such wonderful scenes and moments can be found, and they have had a far-reaching influence on figure painting and genre painting in China.

A silk painting from the Western Han Dynasty.

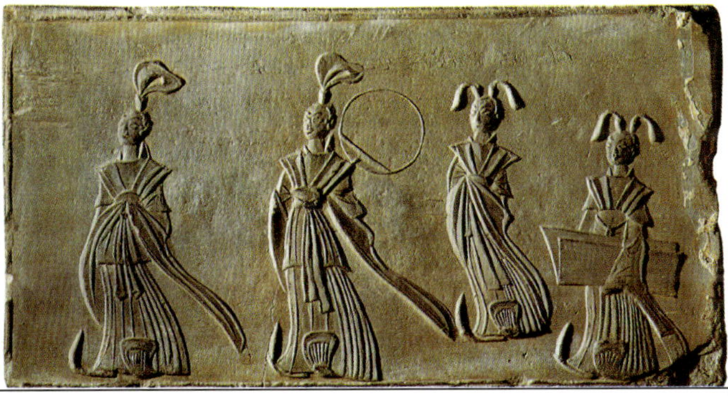

A brick relief of noble women on a tour.

Figure Painting: Vivid and Lifelike

Chinese paintings can be divided into figure painting, landscape painting and flower-and-bird painting, according to their themes. Figure painting, which focuses on the activities of human beings, was the first to reach maturity.

In figure painting, Chinese painters aspire to reveal the inner being of the person rather than simply present the external qualities. The following story may help explain this: Gu Kaizhi, a great painter of the Eastern Jin Dynasty, left his works of figure painting half-finished for several years before he painted the pupils of the eyes of the figures. When people asked why, he explained that for figure painting the most important part was the eyes, which revealed the inner being of the figures, and he would spend years to catch the right expression in the eyes. According to another widely circulated story, painter Zhang Yao once painted several dragons on the walls of a temple. When he finally painted the pupils of the eyes of the dragons, thunder boomed in the sky and the dragons flew away. This story gave birth to a Chinese proverb, "*hua long dian jing*" —make a picture of a dragon come to life by putting in the pupils of its eyes, meaning: add the touch that brings a work of art to life.

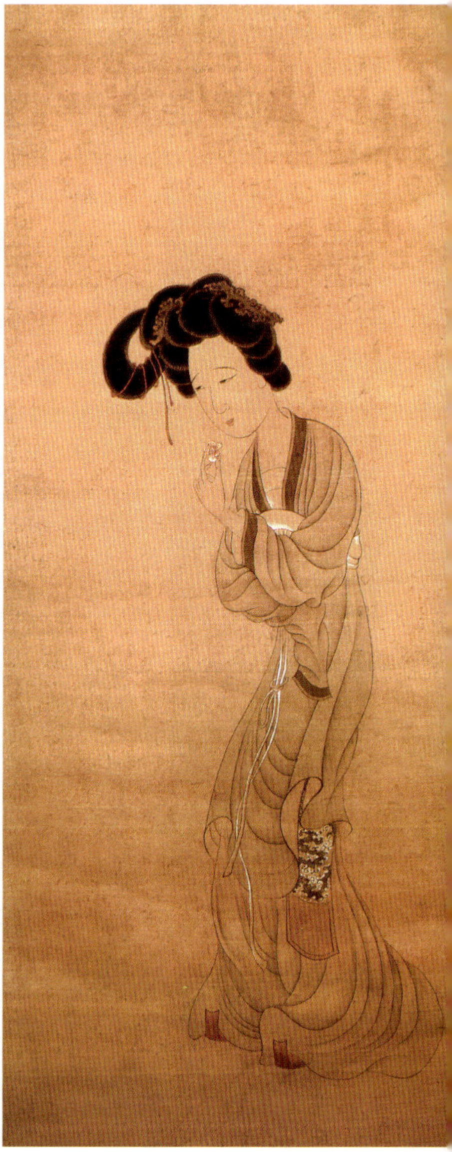

Beauties by Chen Hongshou of the Ming Dynasty.

Chen represented the artistic distortional trend in painting of his time.

In its several thousand years of development, Chinese figure painting has achieved highly mature techniques of applying the brush and ink, which may be divided into two groups: *gongbi* (meticulous) and *xieyi* (sketching thoughts). For centuries, meticulous lines and heavy color were in vogue, and such a style came to its peak during the Tang and Song dynasties. In the Yuan Dynasty the *xieyi* style emerged. Shown here is The Feast of Han Xizai (*Han Xizai Ye Yan Tu*), a heavy-color painting by Gu Hongzhong of the Five-Dynasties Period.

Han Xizai was a statesman of the Southern Tang Dynasty. As the emperor suspected that Han was attempting to usurp the throne, he sent Gu Hongzhong, a royal painter, to spy on Han. Gu made close observations in Han's mansions and later included them on a scroll painting. Gu's skills were so superb that the emperor recognized those who had dined and wined with Han, one by one. This painting later became a celebrated work in Chinese figure painting, with its meticulous lines and bright colors in presenting the figures. In the fourth section of the scroll, Gu presented five female musical instrument players in great detail, even down to the embroidered patterns on their costumes. Their garments were mainly light, yet red and green were also used to form a contrast in harmony. The meticulous brushstrokes

The fourth section of The Feast of Han Xizai (*Han Xizai Ye Yan Tu*).

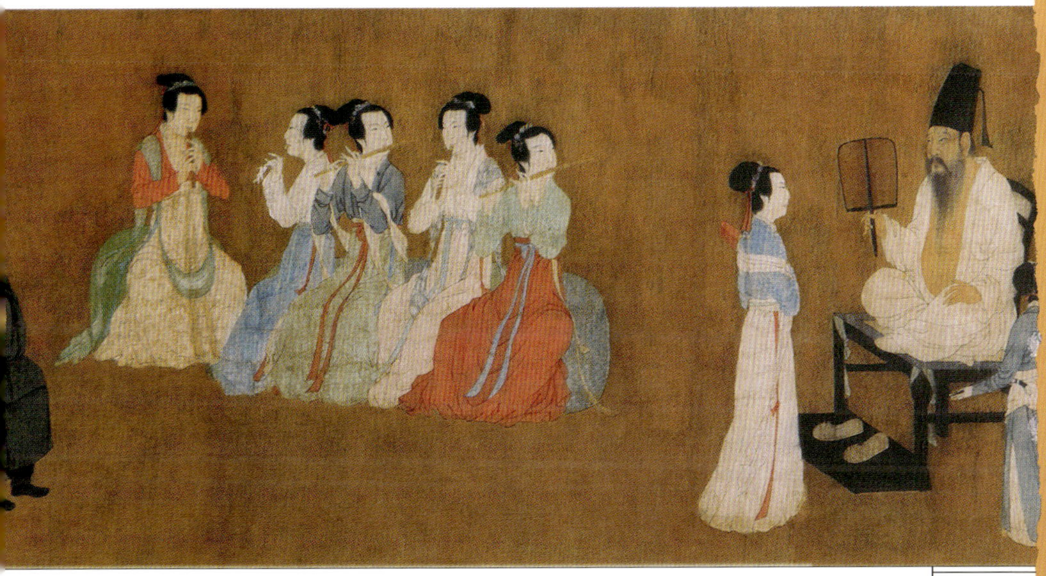

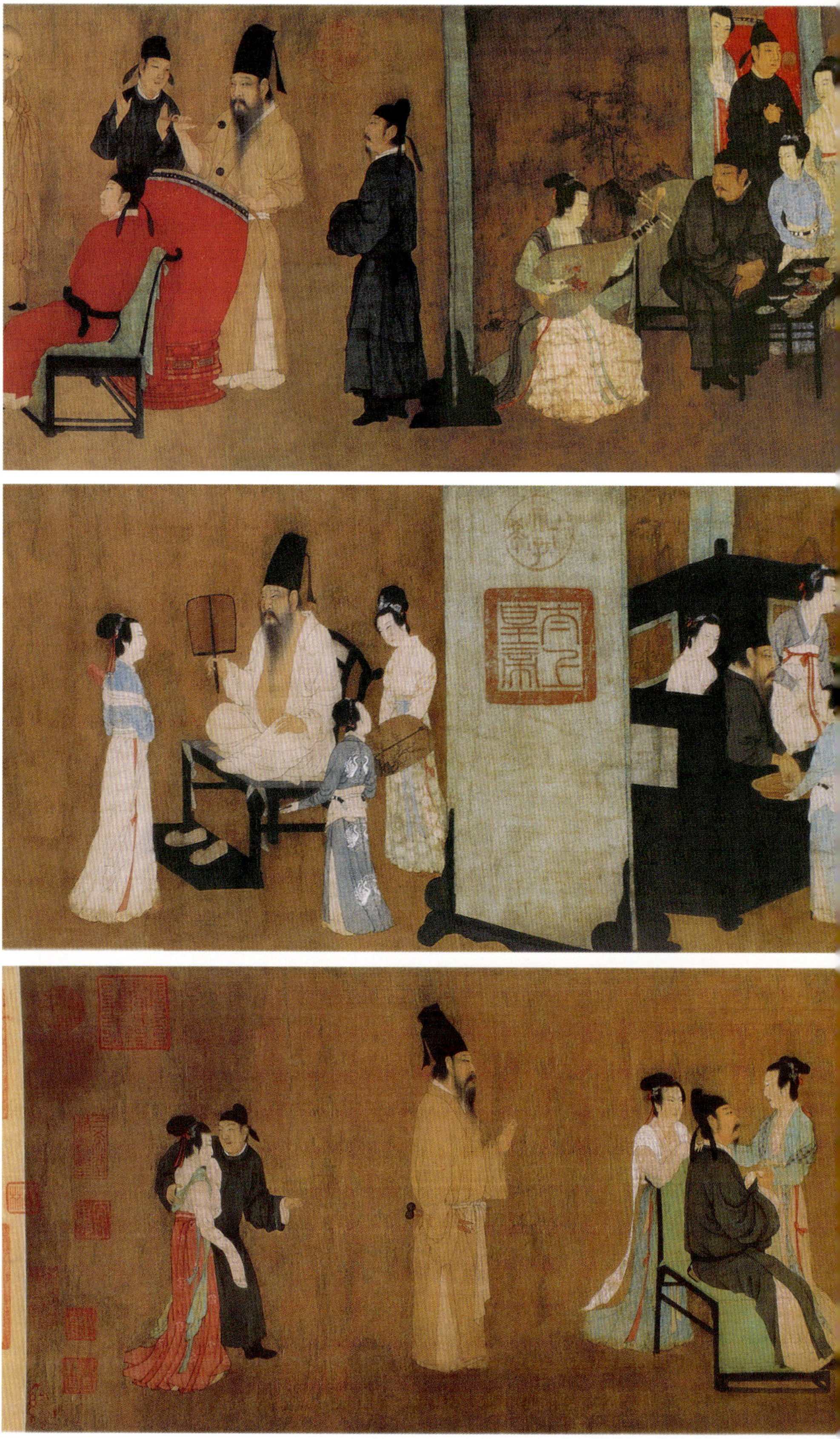

The Feast of Han Xizai (*Han Xizai Ye Yan Tu*), a heavy-color painting by Gu Hongzhong of the Five-Dynasties Period.

This is one of the best works in Chinese figure painting.

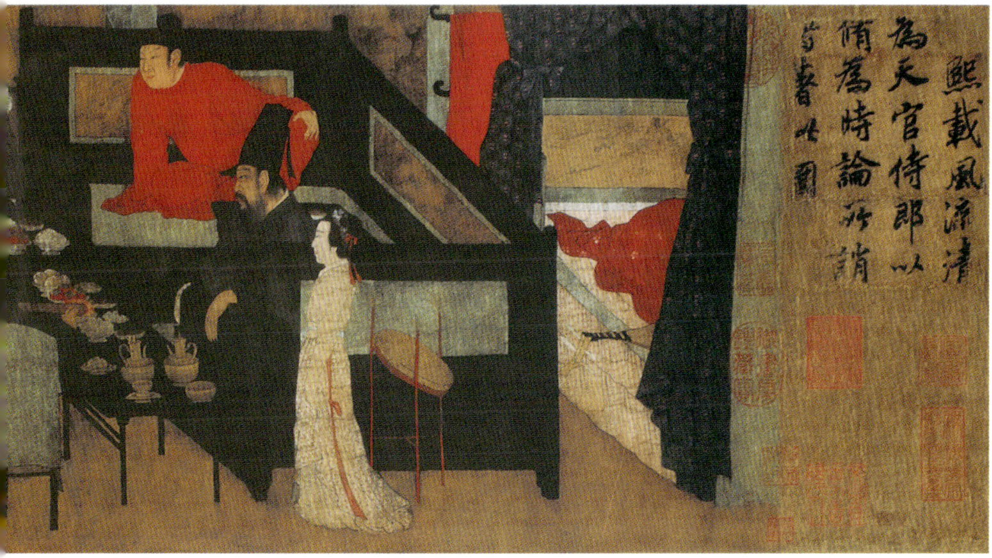

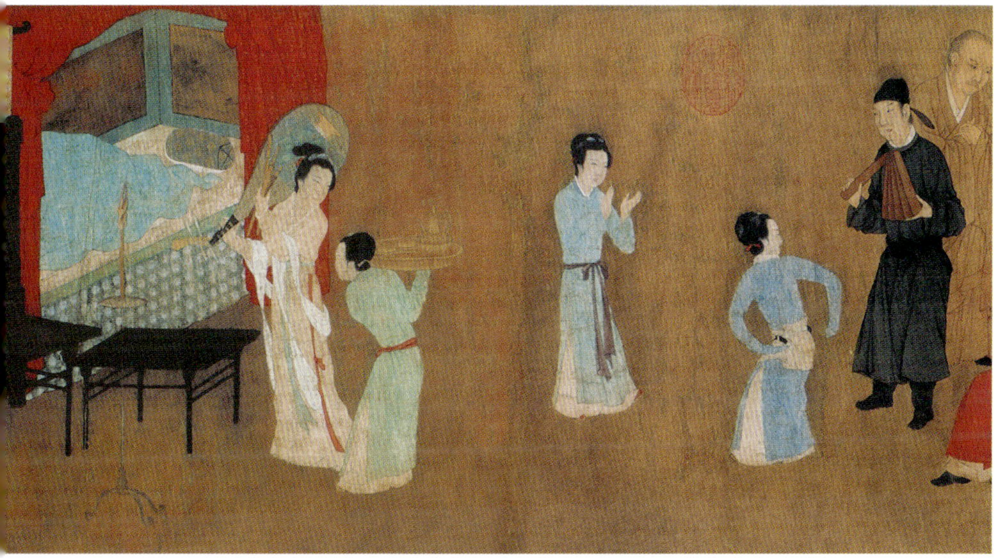

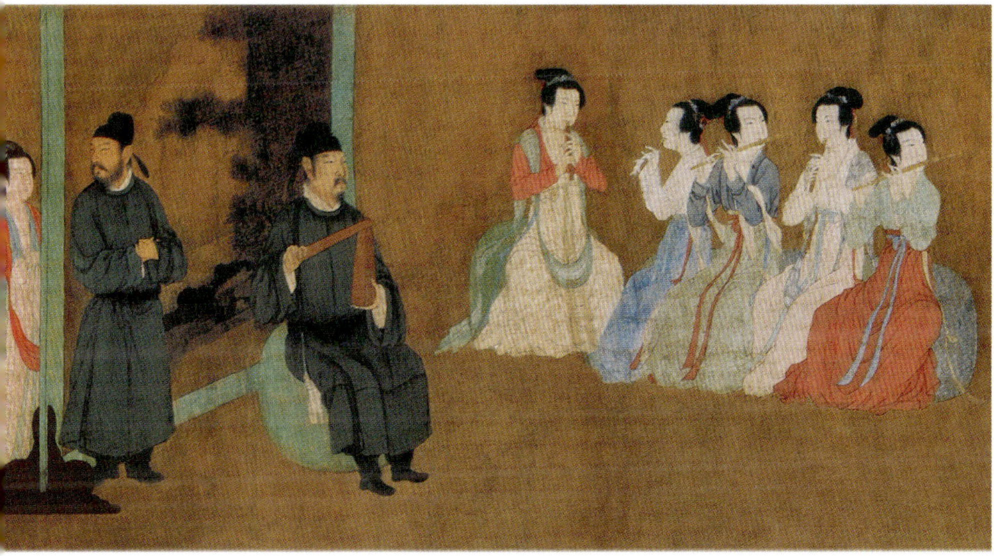

made Han's thick beard most vivid, as if grown rather than painted.

In sharp contrast with the meticulous style is the sketching-thoughts style. Typical of this style is Poet Li Bai (*Li Bai Xing Yin Tu*) by Liang Kai of the Southern Song Dynasty. Li Bai, known as the Poet Immortal, was a poet of the Tang Dynasty. In just a few lines Liang presented a lifelike Li Bai, a literary talent, proud and aloof. Quite a few artists from other countries are surprised to see that Chinese figure painting had reached such heights in the early 13th century.

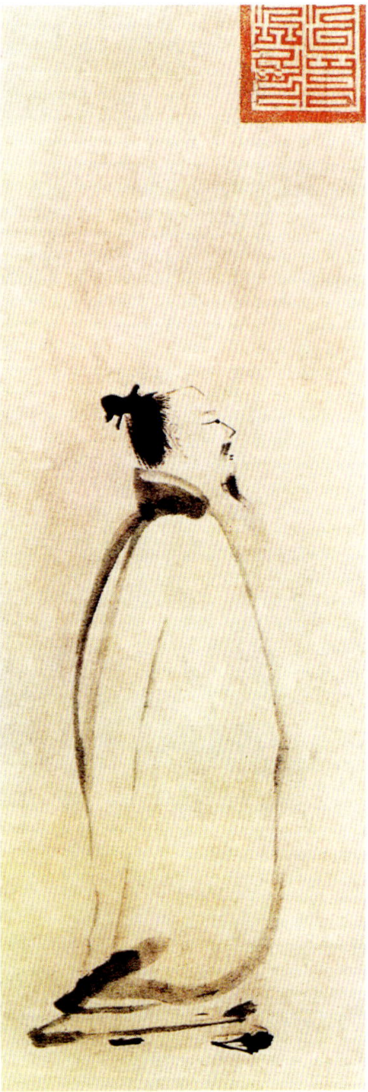

Poet Li Bai (*Li Bai Xing Yin Tu*) by Liang Kai of the Southern Song Dynasty.

The painter created a vivid image of the poet in a just few lines.

Genre Painting: Snapshots of Ancient Life

When people in China read classical works, they often regret that they can only imagine how their ancestors lived from the descriptions. "If only we have more realistic-style paintings like *Qingming Shang He Tu*!" Genre paintings from ancient times offer scenes of the past, just like snapshots of the lives of ancestors. Such a painting can take viewers hundreds or even thousands of years to the past.

Along the River During Qingming Festival (*Qingming Shang He Tu*) is a genre painting by Zhang Zeduan of the Song Dynasty. The painting, a hand-scroll measuring more than five meters in length, depicts life on the Bianhe River in the capital of the dynasty (now Kaifeng City of Henan Province), which was then one of the most prosperous cities in the world, during Qingming Festival in spring. The scenes begin from the rural outskirts of the city and move with the boats on the river, revealing the

Along the River During Qingming Festival (*Qingming Shang He Tu*) (partial) by Zhang Zeduan of the Northern Song Dynasty

This genre painting, showing more than 550 persons, is an encyclopedic work about urban life during the Song Dynasty.

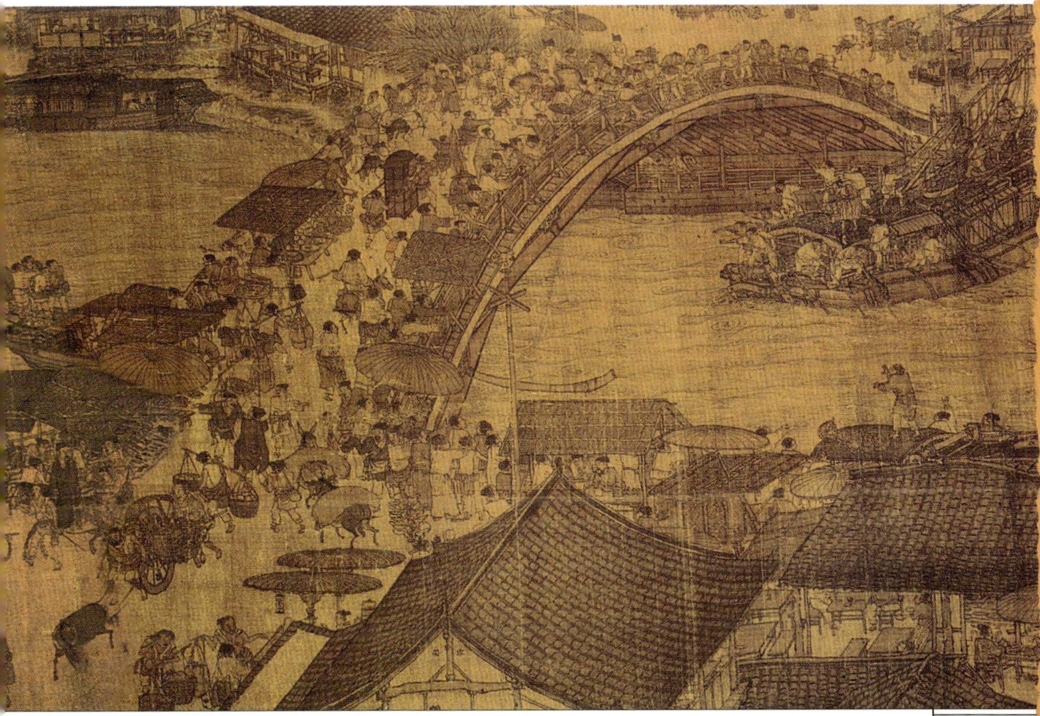

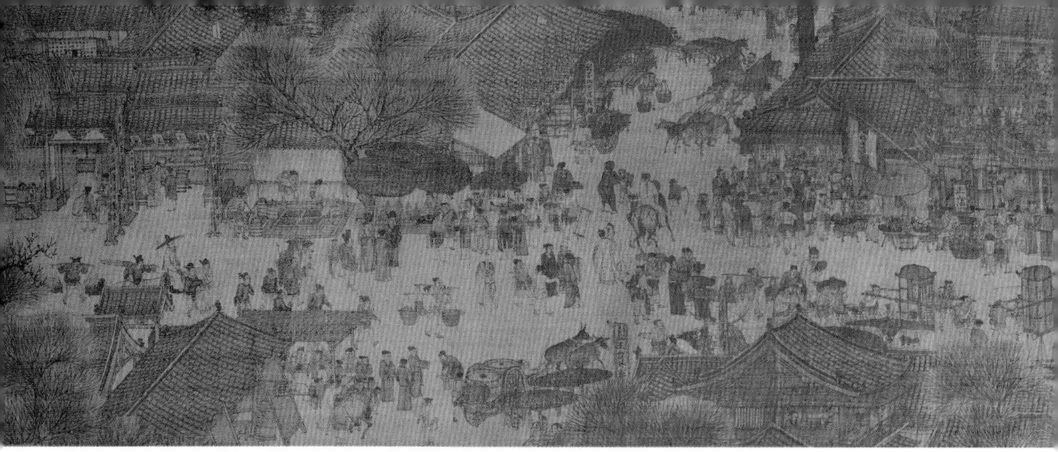
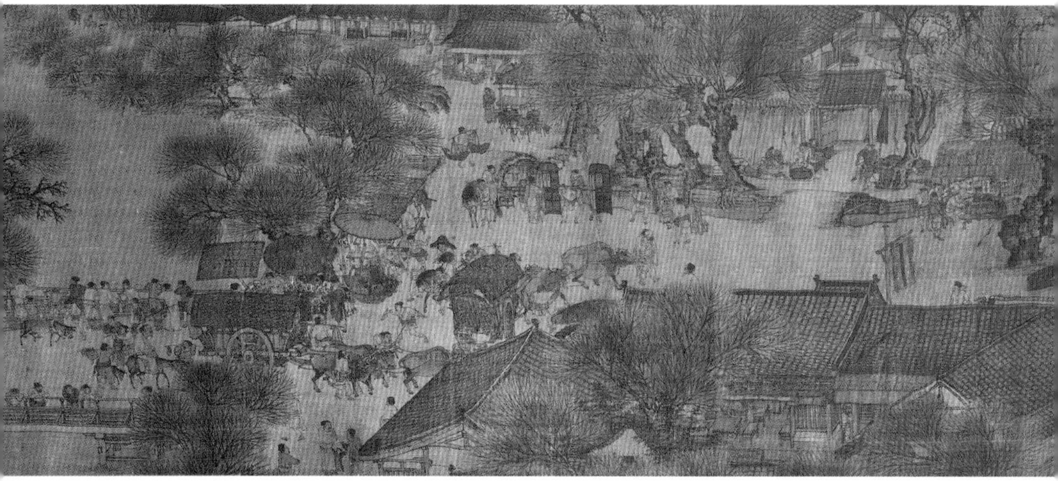
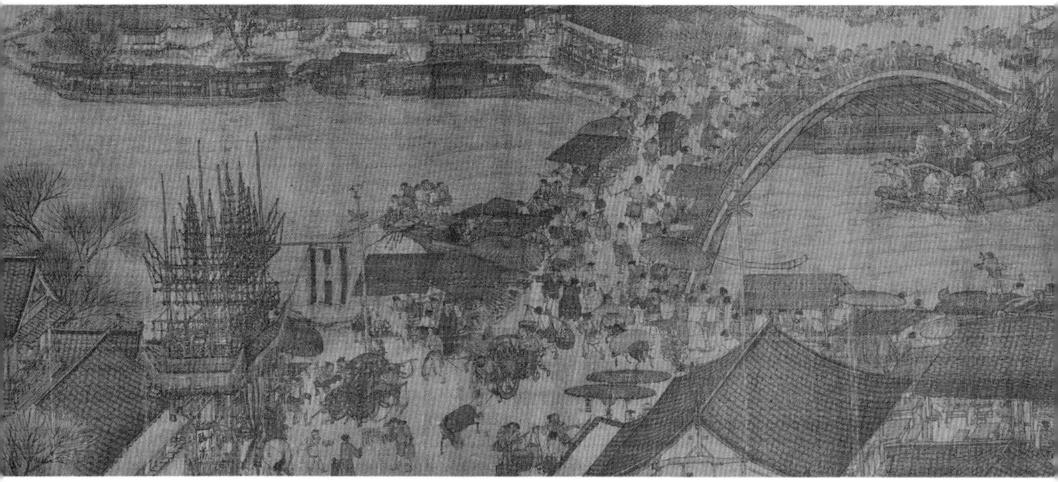
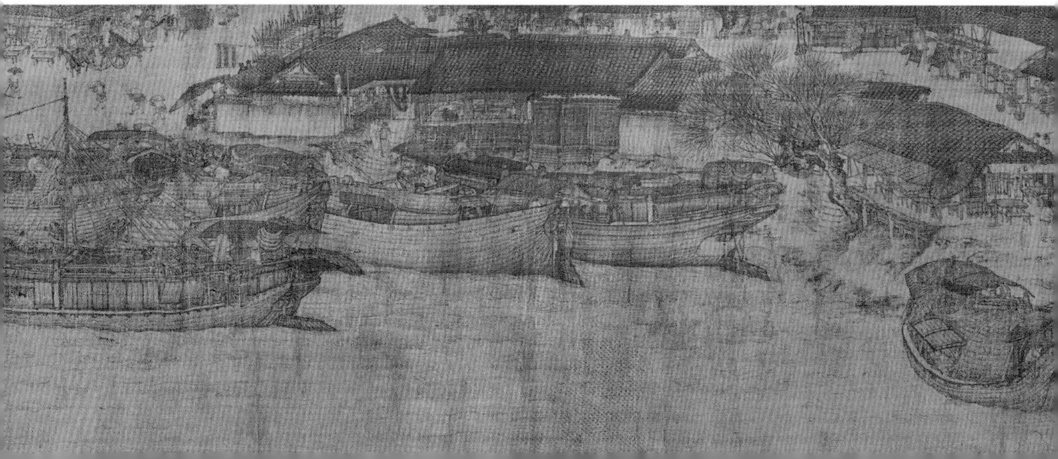

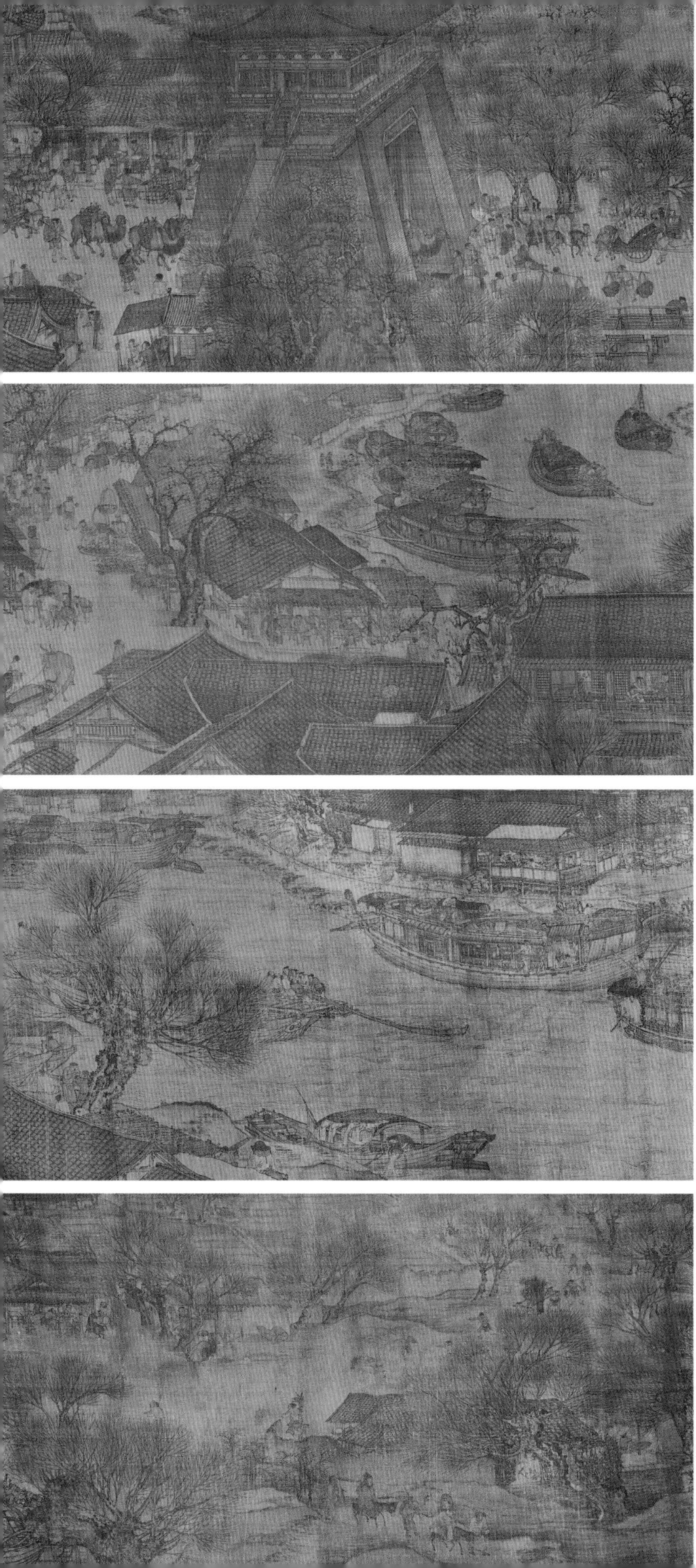

Along the River During Qingming Festival (*Qingming Shang He Tu*) (partial) by Zhang Zeduan of the Northern Song Dynasty

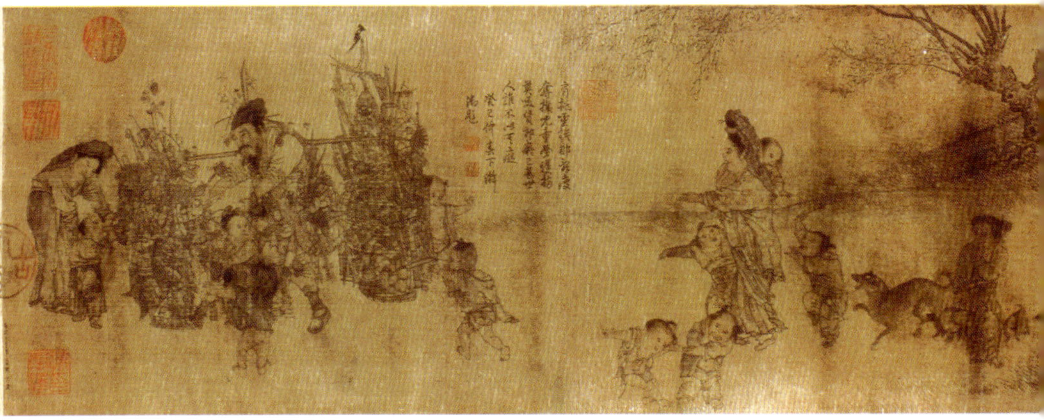

The Hawker (*Huolang Tu*) by Li Song of the Southern Song Dynasty.

The painting presents a scene of the countryside in the Song Dynasty.

bustling life inside and outside the city gate. More than 500 people and several dozen buildings are included in the painting. With the help of a magnifying glass, viewers can see all the details and feel as though they are moving among the crowds, touring the Song capital. The close observations and superb techniques of the painter have turned this artwork into a national heirloom of China and an invaluable gem in the treasure house of world arts.

And here is another genre painting, The Hawker (*Huolang Tu*) by Li Song of the Southern Song Dynasty. When the distribution of goods was not well-developed as it is today, hawkers played an important role in carrying all sorts of goods to all parts of the countryside. Hawkers not only brought daily necessities but also new information to villagers; therefore, their arrival became festive. In the painting, the burden of goods seems so heavy that the hawker has to stoop. The hawker's supply includes all kinds of goods, such as kitchen utensils, toys, fruit and candy. The children are so glad to see the hawker that they hail and run after him. The numerous goods, many of which are of unknown use today, provide invaluable source material of folklore. The figures are created mainly by line drawing, with light colors for added effect. The characters have different poses and gestures, and the goods are depicted in great detail. All this shows the painter's great skills of realistic painting.

Landscape Painting: Indoor Tour of Mountains and Waters

Chinese philosophy emphasizes a close relationship between man and nature. The Chinese believe that by closely observing and experiencing scenes of nature, people can gain morality and wisdom, and they say that benevolent people should often draw inspiration from mountains and water to add to their happiness. This constitutes the philosophical basis for the landscape in Chinese painting.

One should not simply equate the landscape in Chinese painting with that in Western painting. Chinese landscape is not a simple reproduction of natural scenery, but an expression of nature from cultural and aesthetic perspectives. In the eyes of the Chinese, mountains, rivers, lakes and seas have their own lives and spiritual power, and they show different appearances in different seasons and weather conditions, just as humans do.

In Chinese literature and art there is a special term, "indoor tour," which refers to making a virtual tour of mountains and waters by reading literature about nature. But the "indoor tour" may become more wonderful by

Tour in Spring (*You Chun Tu*) by Zhan Ziqian of the Sui Dynasty.

This is the earliest extant Chinese painting with a signature of a painter.

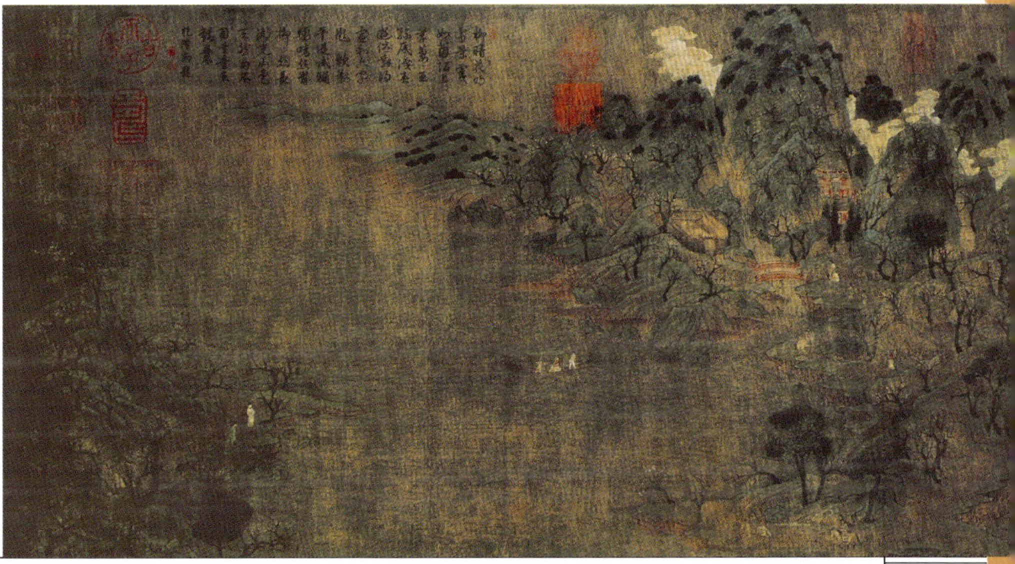

viewing an elegant landscape painting. Here is one of the earliest existing Chinese landscape painting—Tour in Spring (*You Chun Tu*) by painter Zhan Ziqian of the Sui Dynasty. In the painting tourists enjoy themselves in an enchanting spring scenery. Over the hills, peach trees blossom and willow trees overflow with twigs. In the hills men ride on horses, and in the water several women sail in a boat. The mountains and hills are seen from a fine perspective, and a blue-green color dominates the scenery. In Chinese painting there are both blue-green and ink-and-wash landscapes. Mountains on the Fuchun River (*Fuchun Shan Ju Tu*) by painter Huang Gongwang of the Yuan Dynasty is an ink-and-wash landscape. The scroll painting depicts a myriad of scenes on the Fuchun River in Zhejiang Province, east China: woods on the ridges and peaks along the river, trees of different shapes, houses and cottages in the woods, fishing boats, bridges, pavilions and waterfalls.

For landscape painters, nature is their best teacher and closest friend. They have to travel far and wide

All the Strange Peaks in One Draft (*Sou Jin Qifeng Da Caogao*) (partial), a landscape by Shi Tao of the Qing Dynasty.

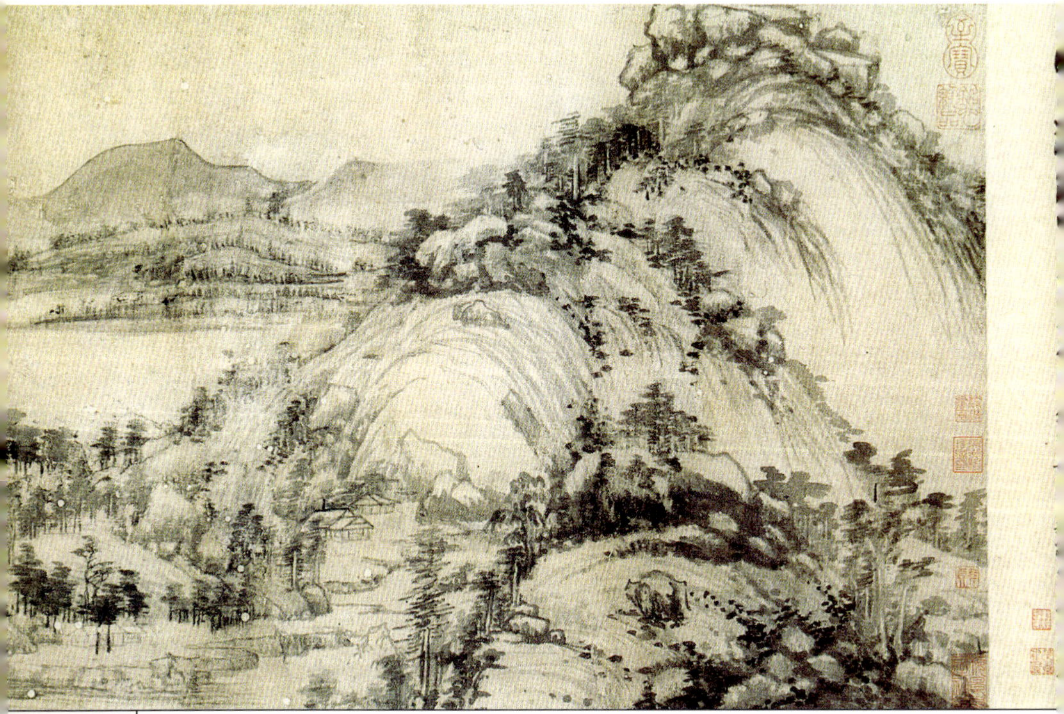

Mountains on the Fuchun River (*Fuchun Shan Ju Tu*) (partial) by Huang Gongwang of the Yuan Dynasty.

The Fuchun River is a well-known tourist attraction in China.

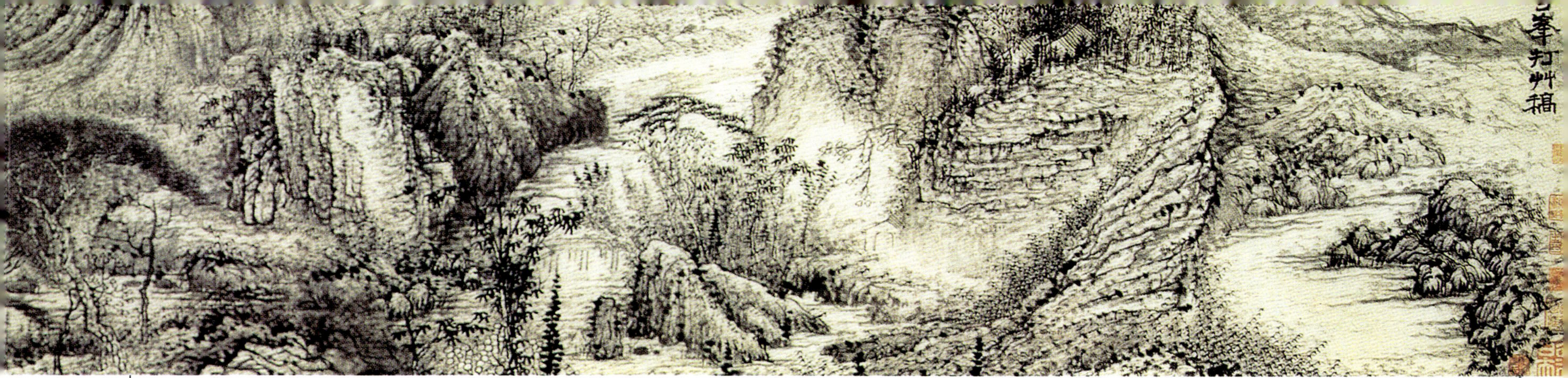

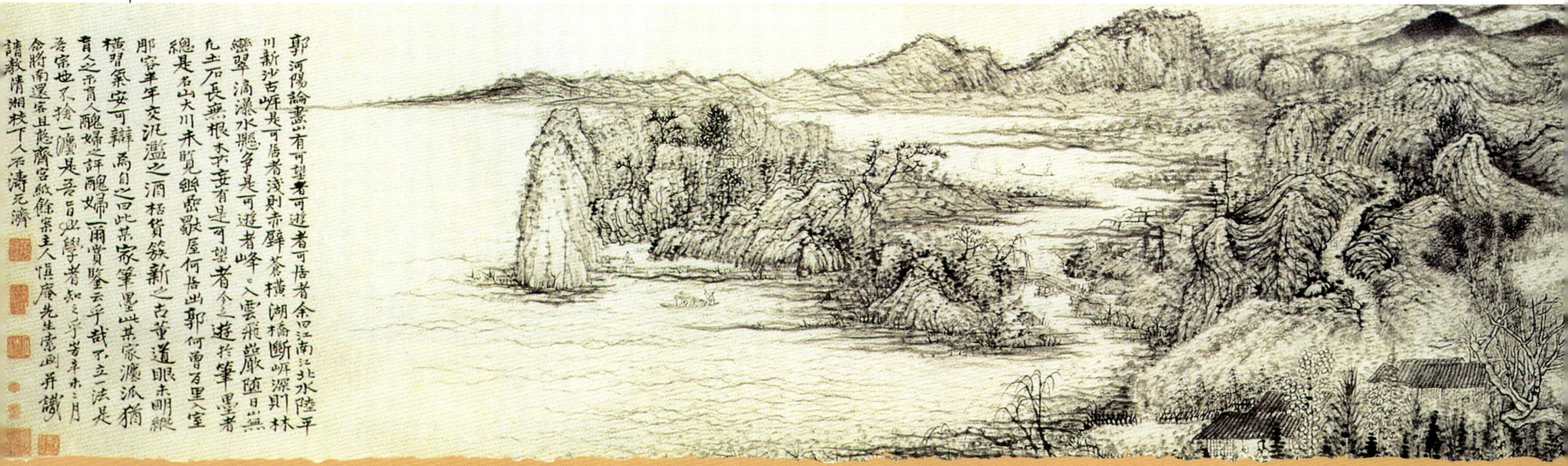

to receive inspiration from famous mountains and rivers. And they cannot simply copy the scenes but synthesize and make abstractions from what they have seen. All the Strange Peaks in One Draft (*Sou Jin Qifeng Da Caogao*), a landscape by Shi Tao of the Qing Dynasty, shows lofty mountains, dense forests, springs, roads, castles, houses, pavilions, bridges and fishing boats. The landscape is densely composed and the bold brushstrokes add vigor. The mountains and waters here must be conceived from numerous mountains and waters the painter had visited, and they not only reflect nature but the interior world of the painter. That is what a Chinese painting requires: imitation of nature guided by the soul. A landscape must show mountains and waters cultivated by the painter in his interior world.

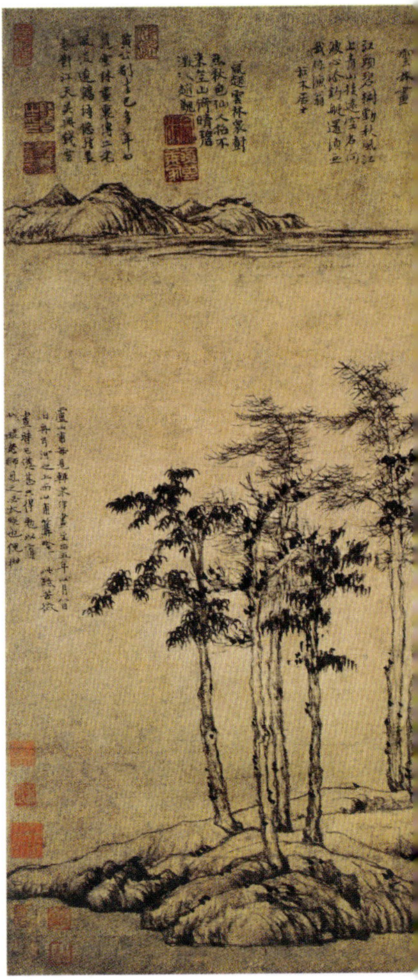

Six Honorable Trees (*Liu Junzi Tu*) by Ni Zan of the Yuan Dynasty.

This painting reflects the mindset of the painter, who disdained high salary and position and yearned for a reclusive life.

If what a landscape gives the viewers is nothing more than the objective image, such a work can only be ranked as secondary. As Chinese painting requires artistic conception, a good landscape must contain rich connotation in its objective image. Take works by Ni Zan of the Yuan Dynasty, for instance. The objects in his works are quite simple; in some cases there are only a few trees or even one tree, one cottage, without any human figures. Such works present an ancient, remote conception, reminding viewers of the painter's lofty sentiments. Artistic conception is an important criterion for judging Chinese paintings.

Flower-and-Bird Painting

In Chinese painting, flower-and-bird painting is a categorical term, which also covers trees, vegetables, fruits, animals, insects, and fish, aside from flowers and birds. This category of painting was established in the Tang Dynasty and developed rapidly in the Five Dynasties Period, when many well-known painters took to it. Painters of the Song Dynasty inherited the tradition of the Five Dynasties Period and boosted the art to its

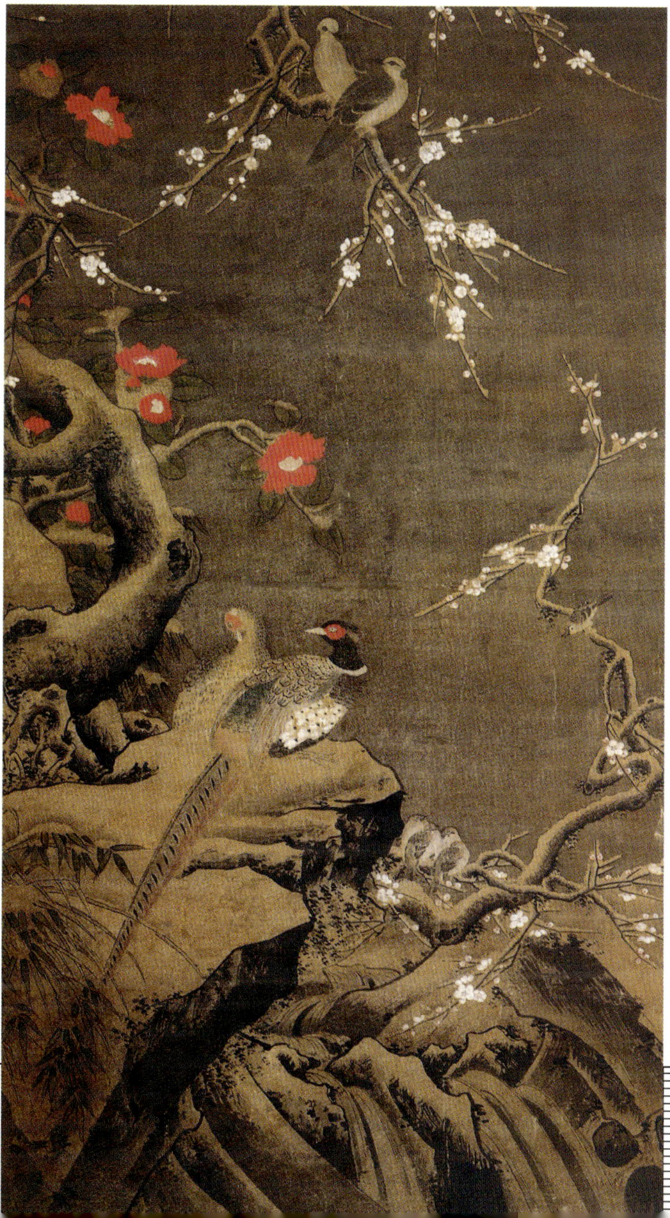

Plum and Golden Pheasants (*Xue Mei Jinji Tu*) by Lu Ji of the Ming Dynasty.

peak. In the Song Period meticulous brush techniques became the norm, and painters often made close observations of objects to get accurate and comprehensive knowledge of them. A legend goes that Ouyang Xiu, a noted scholar of the Song Dynasty, had an ancient painting in his collection, on which was a cat under a cluster of peony flowers. One day, Ouyang showed this painting to one of his friends, and the friend judged from the shapes of images that it was a scene at noon. He explained that the petals of flowers were fully extended but the color was somehow dull, and the cat under the cluster had dark eyes but narrowed pupils like a line —all these indicated the time was noon. Close observation reveal that in the morning petals are covered with dew and the color is bright, while the pupils of cat's eyes are round in the morning or evening but narrowed to a line at noon. Meticulous flower-and-bird painting calls for a faithful presentation of objects. In this Two Sparrows and a Hare (*Shuang Niao Xi Tu Tu*), the painter depicts a scene in the garden in late autumn. A sparrow standing on a branch twitters at the hare, and the hare turns its head at the sparrow. Another sparrow closes its wings to land on a branch. The withered twigs, dried grass and slender bamboos wave in the wind, and viewers can almost hear their rustling.

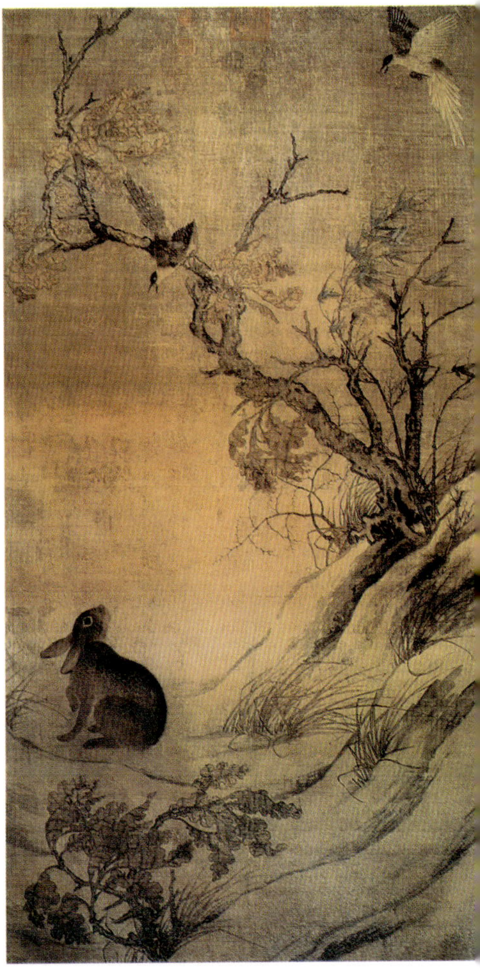

Two Sparrows and a Hare (*Shuang Niao Xi Tu Tu*) by Cui Bai of the Song Dynasty.

Emerging roughly in the same period as meticulous flower-and-bird painting was a sketching-thoughts style of this art. Painters of this style paid more attention to brushstrokes and their expressive role in revealing the painter's mind. The objects they presented were more

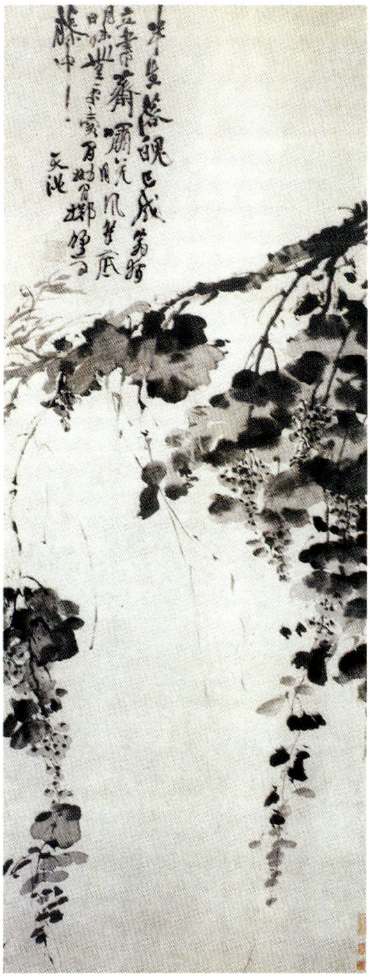

Grapes in Ink (*Mo Putao Tu*) by Xu Wei of the Ming Dynasty.

Fish (*You Yu Tu*) by Zhu Da of the Qing Dynasty.

The fish has an exaggerated bizarre eye.

subjective than objective, more distant from the real objects in nature. In Grapes in Ink (*Mo Putao Tu*), painter Xu Wei of the Ming Dynasty used the ink-and-wash technique to paint the leaves, vines and grapes. At first sight, viewers may find the grapes dissimilar to real ones, but soon they recognize the crystal-like grapes through the ink and wash. The painter was not trying to show the likeness of grapes but to depict his own thoughts after going through all the hardships and struggles. Zhu Da, a celebrated artist of the Qing Dynasty, painted peculiar exaggerations to the eyes of fish and birds in his works. The bizarre eyes were very big and, in some cases, square. Zhu was from the royal family of the Ming Dynasty, and when Qing rulers replaced the Ming court, Zhu was deeply distressed. He lent his thoughts of grief and defiance to his works, making them caricature paintings in Oriental arts.

Noble Symbols in Flower-and-Bird Painting

Chinese painting is highly symbolic, and favorite objects in flower-and-bird painting include the plum, orchid, bamboo and chrysanthemum. In Chinese tradition, these plants are said to have a noble character, like refined gentlemen. In Chinese philosophy, the term gentlemen refers to intellectuals of high integrity, second only to sages. As the plum blossoms in winter amid snow, it is used to signify dauntlessness. The orchid is a symbol of purity and integrity. The bamboo suggests the spirit of the scholar, which is modest and upright. The chrysanthemum blooms in late autumn, defying strong winds and frost, like a proud gentleman. These themes are often found in other forms of literature and art, as well as in paintings. In these plants Chinese artists show their respect for and pursuit of noble moral values.

Painter Zheng Sixiao of the Song Dynasty was well-known for his orchid paintings. After the Northern Song Dynasty was destroyed, orchid plants in Zheng's paintings all bared their roots or appeared rootless. When people asked him why, he said in anguish, "My country

Plum Blossom (*Mei Hua tu*) by Wu Zhen of the Yuan Dynasty.

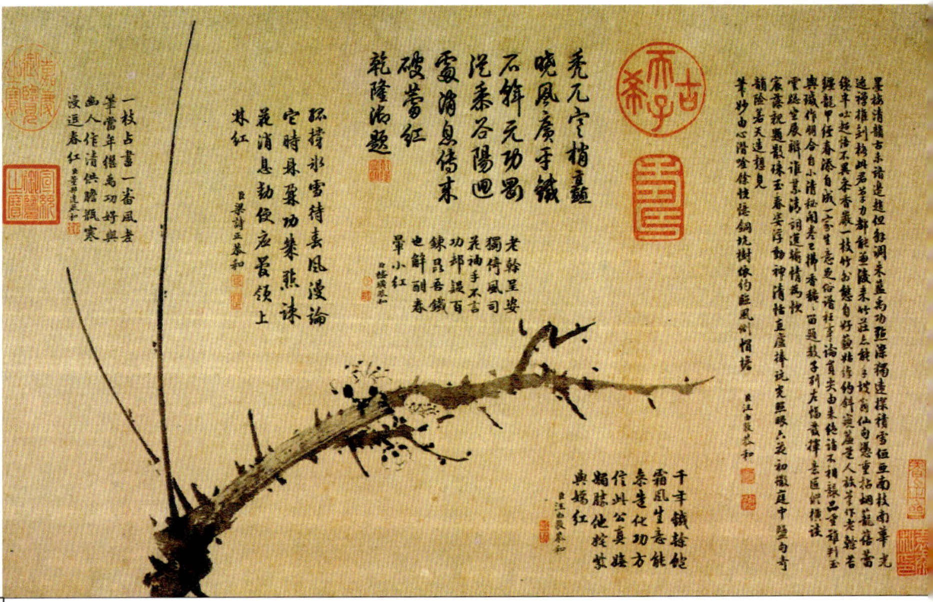

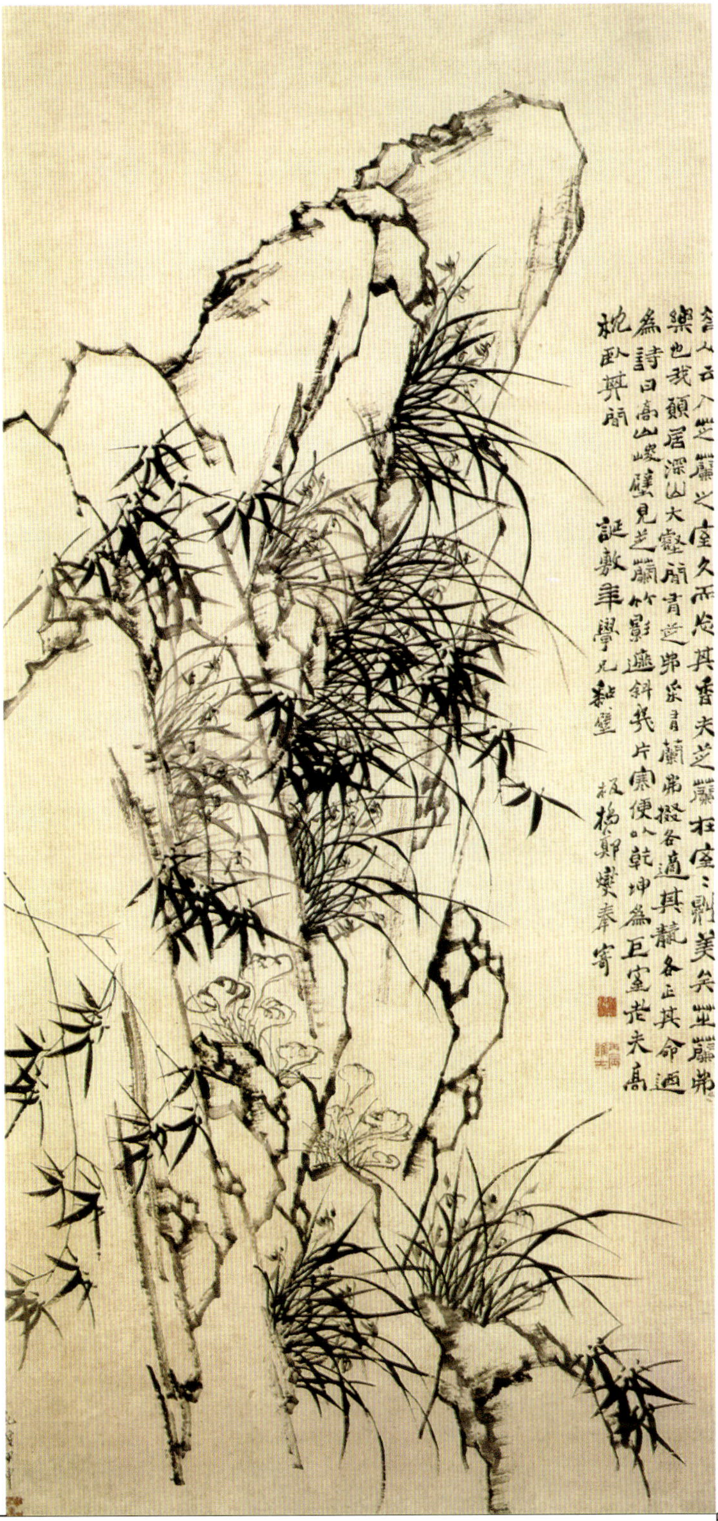

Orchid and Bamboo (*Lan Zhu Tu*) by Zheng Banqiao of the Qing Dynasty.

Zheng was one of the Eight Unconventional Artists of Yangzhou in the Qing Dynasty. His noble character won him the admiration of the public.

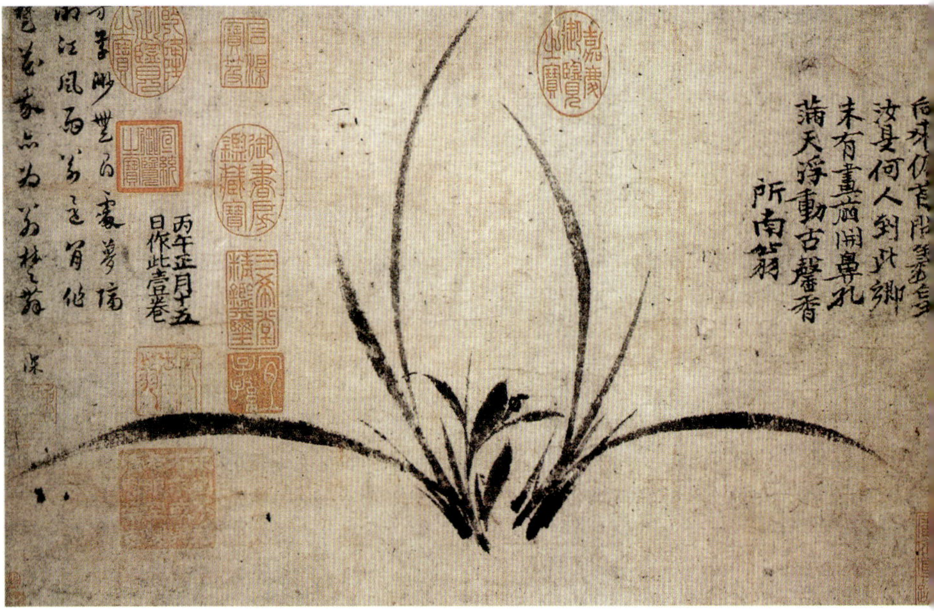

Orchid (*Mo Lan Tu*) by Zheng Sixiao of the Song Dynasty.

The painter was a well-known patriot in Chinese history.

and family are all lost; how can I find any soil for my orchid plants!" In this way Zheng showed his patriotism and loyalty to Song. Zheng Banqiao of the Qing Dynasty was best known in China for his ink-and-wash bamboo paintings. He had served as a local official. Witnessing the suffering of regular people, he decided to resign rather than go along with corrupt superiors and colleagues. This is a salient feature of Chinese *literati* paintings—the use of these symbolic plants to express their noble feelings.

Dunhuang Frescoes: Treasures of Chinese Art

When you come to China, you may travel along the famous Silk Road that linked China with central Asia and Europe in ancient times to visit Dunhuang, where the Mogao grottoes keep numerous frescoes, sculptures and other artworks from the 4th to 14th centuries. The works, including magnificent and elegant masterpieces, constitute treasures of ancient Chinese art. Among the frescoes are a large number of paintings featuring Buddhist stories, folktales and decorations, with the Buddhist narrative paintings being the most colorful and auspicious.

To win followers in the public, Buddhists tried to popularize their doctrines by all means, including visual images. The narrative paintings in the grottoes were intended to influence viewers with Buddhist doctrine. With rich content and moving scenarios, the paintings are

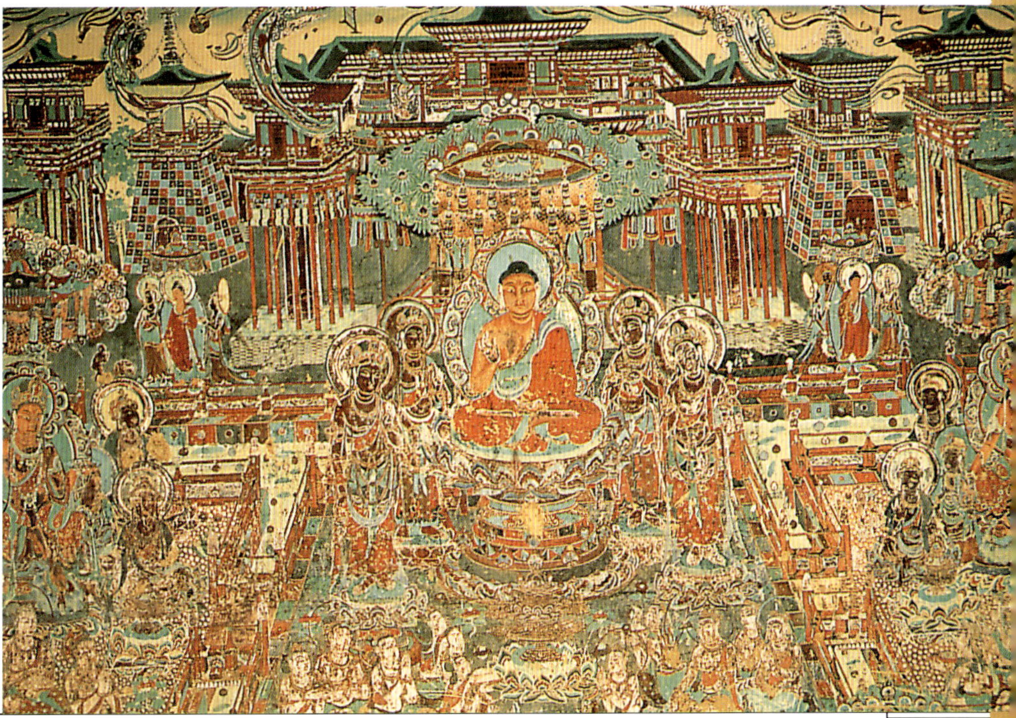

The frescoes in Mogao grottoes of Dunhuang are mostly about Buddhist stories.

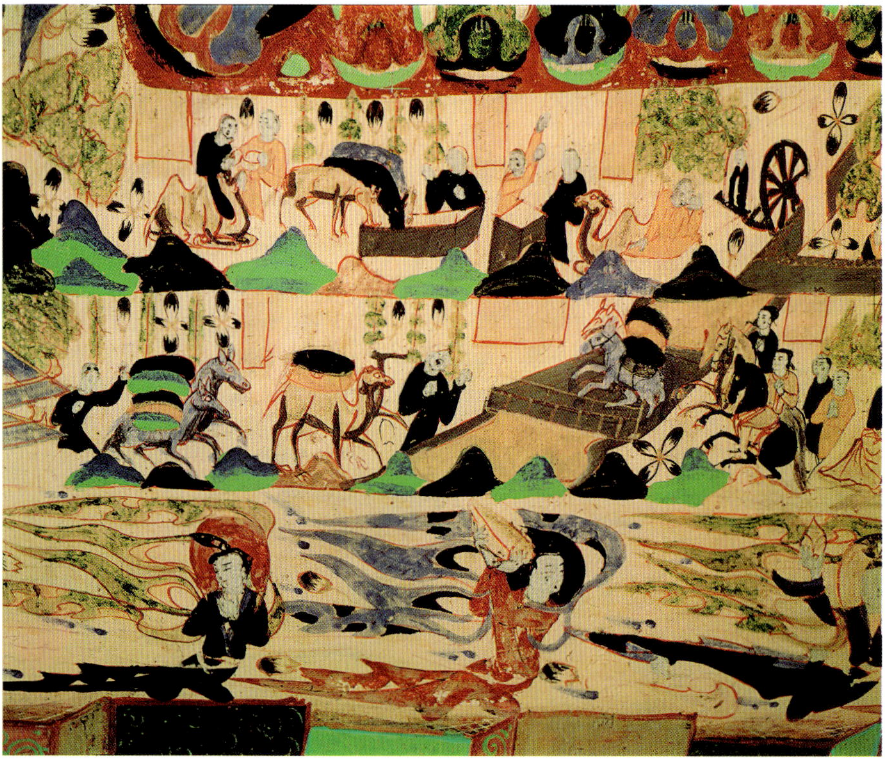

The fresco in No.296 of Mogao grottoes in Dunhuang shows scenes on the ancient Silk Road.

realistic as well as romantic.

Flying Apsarases, or celestial nymphs in Buddhism, constitute a symbol of Dunhuang frescoes. In more than 500 grottoes in the area, there are numerous flying Apsarases. In waving skirts and with flying ribbons in hand, they dance freely in the sky, some standing on clouds, some rising heads jutting, some holding flowers and others carrying plates. The images have inspired Chinese artists, who have created works out of these eternal entertainers for the gods and blessed souls.

Since the Dunhuang frescoes were discovered in the late 19th century, the place has been a sacred place for artists, and many of them have received inspiration from the paintings. Zhang Daqian, a noted Chinese painter remained in Dunhuang for three years under difficult conditions, devotedly copying the murals. Later, Zhang applied what he learned in Dunhuang into his creations and developed his airy style. This Beauty by

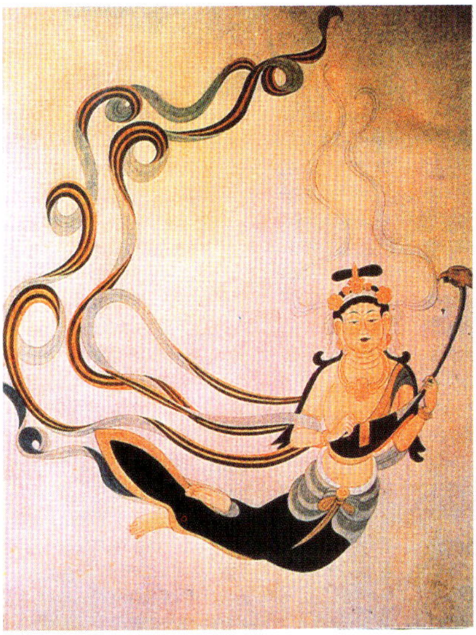

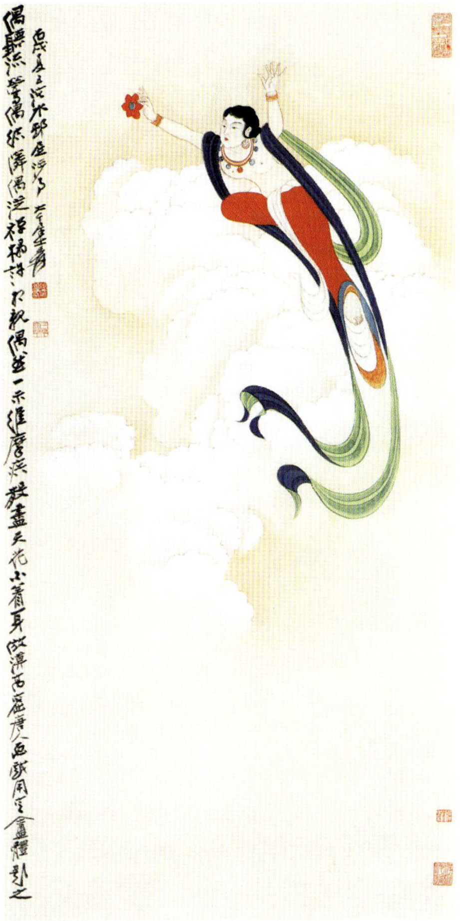

Flying Apsarases, or celestial nymphs in Buddhism, in No.25 of Yulin grottoes, painted during the Five Dynasties Period.

The celestial nymphs are so well known that that have constituted a symbol of Dunhuang paintings.

The Celestial Nymph by Zhang Daqian (1899 –1983)

This work is clearly of the style of Dunhuang frescoes.

Zhang carries the brand of Dunhuang frescoes. In 1956 Zhang held a personal exhibit at the Louvre Museum in Paris, and met with the great painter Pablo Picasso. The Spanish painter disclosed to Zhang his great admiration of Chinese painting, and asked Zhang to comment on his own works done with Chinese brushes. What a pity for Picasso: he had never visited Dunhuang!

Paintings and Poems: Sister Arts

In China, paintings are often known as wordless poems and poems, paintings that speak to the viewer. Such a comparison is also found in the West, and people believe that poetry and painting are sister arts. Su Shi, a great intellectual of the Song Dynasty, praised the works of Wang Wei, a great artist of the Tang Dynasty, saying that his poems were picturesque while his paintings, poetic. One of Wang Wei's poems is about painting, which reads to the effect:

Mountains are colorful seen from afar
No water's rippling can be heard even by its side
Flowers remain when spring is gone
And no viewer can frighten a bird into flight.

This poem is like a riddle, and the answer to it is the title: Painting.

Indeed, poetry is an important criterion in the evaluation of Chinese paintings. Many painters take their themes from poems of the Tang Dynasty, and some of them directly indicate that the painting depicts a poem by poet so-and-so. An often-quoted story goes: in the 1950s, well-known novelist Lao She once asked painter Qi Baishi to base a painting on a verse: "Frogs croak ten miles along a mountain spring." What an undertaking to show frogs croaking in a painting! After careful consideration, Qi used tadpoles to show the poetic conception: from the dark rocks a spring flows, and several tadpoles swim in the stream. No frog can be seen in the picture, yet viewers are able to imagine frogs croaking all the way down the stream.

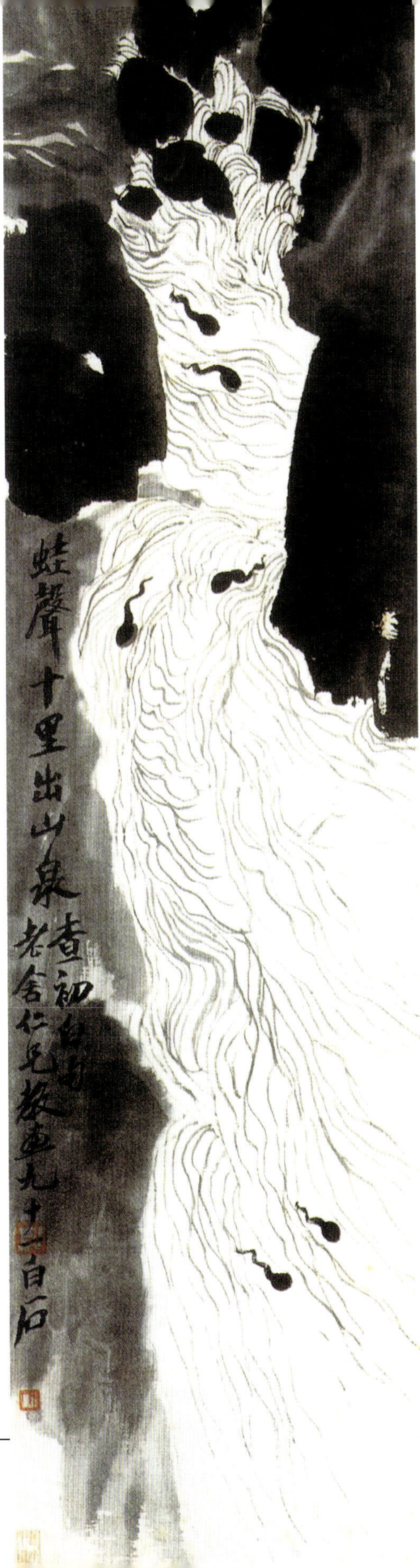

Frogs Croak Ten Miles Along a Mountain Spring (*Washeng Shili Chu Shanquan*) by Qi Baishi (1864–1957)

The painter ingeniously created a graphic image of the verse.

Meticulous Style and Sketching-Thoughts Style

Chinese painting can be divided into two categories according to the applied techniques: meticulous style and sketching-thoughts style.

In the meticulous style, objects are presented in meticulous lines on glue-processed silk or Xuan paper. And meticulous painting can again be divided into four groups: line drawing, light-color, heavy-color, and

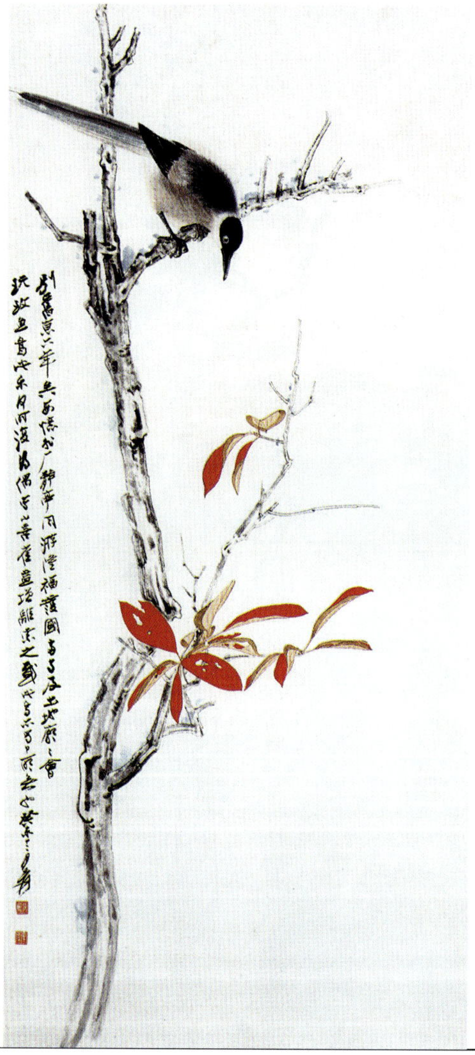

Magpie and Red Leaves by Zhang Daqian (1899–1983)

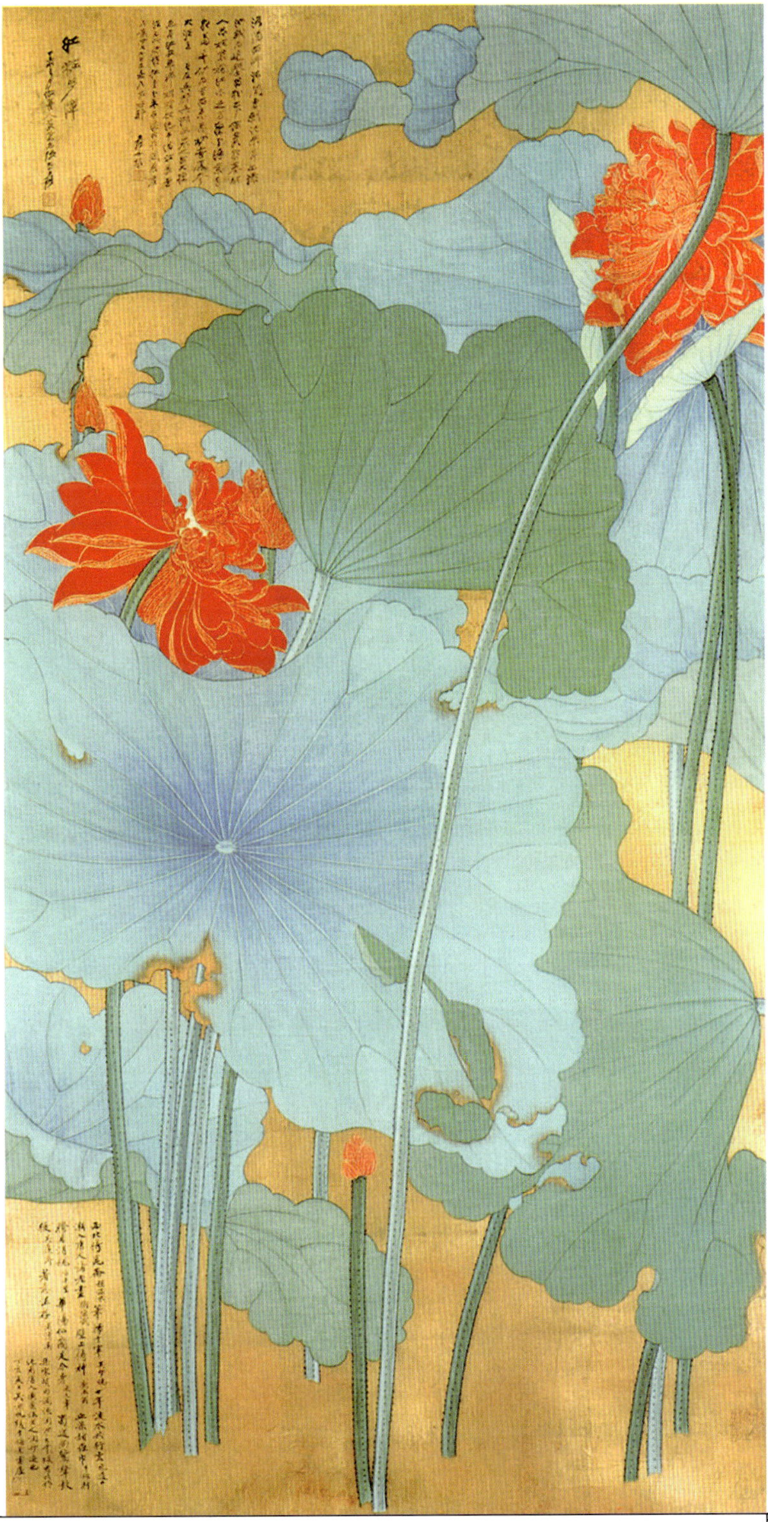

Lotus Flowers (*Hongzhuang Buzhang*) by Zhang Daqian (1899–1983)

This is a typical work of the meticulous heavy color style.

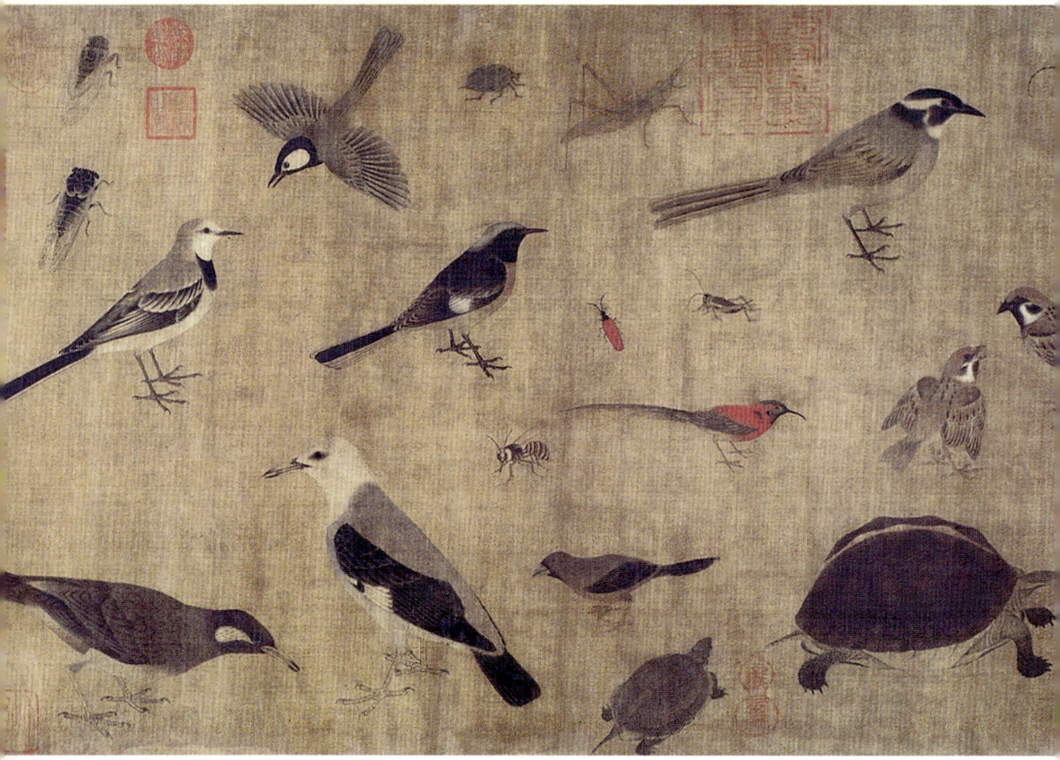

lineless watercolor.

Meticulous painting calls for being faithful to life. The following story shows the high level of Chinese painters in this field. In the Five Dynasties Period, painter Huang Quan made several meticulous paintings of birds for the emperor to hang in the palace. Once when the emperor was preparing to go hunting with his falcons, one of them saw the paintings and swooped down on them in a stunningly swift move—the painter had deceived even the falcon.

In sketching-thoughts style, painters use a few bold brushstrokes to work out the image in a highly generalized and exaggerated manner and to achieve a profound artistic conception. Such paintings are usually done on raw Xuan paper, and painters create images more vivid than those of the meticulous style in swift brushstrokes to express their feelings. Such paintings can be divided into three groups: high sketching-thoughts

Birds, Tortoises and Insects by Huang Quan of the Five Dynasties Period.

The painter created 24 vivid images of birds, tortoises and insects in this small space of silk painting.

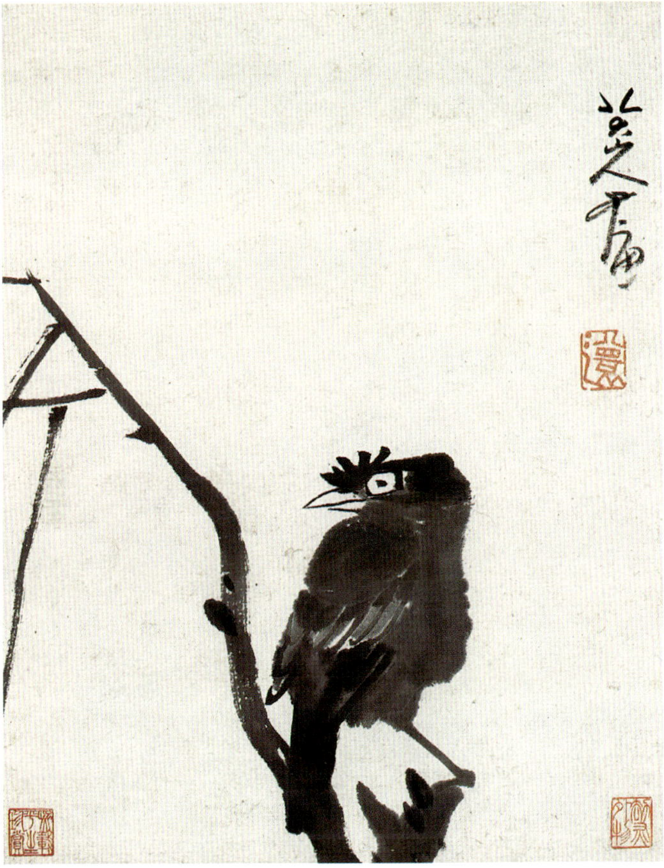

Flower-bird painting by Zhu Da of the Qing Dynasty.

Though not faithful to life, the painting is close to artistic reality. In Chinese art, this is known as "unlike likeness."

style, regular sketching-thoughts style and semi-sketching-thoughts style.

In sketching-thoughts style, painters pay greater attention to capturing the spirit rather than appearance. For them, the artistic truth is more important than being faithful to life. Painter Wang Wei of the Tang Dynasty once made a painting of a green banana plant in white snow. How could a tropical plant from the south survive heavy snow in the north? Such a concept defies logic but fully expresses the painter's philosophical faith. Foreigners who meet Chinese paintings for the first time often wonder why many Chinese painters present plum blossoms and peonies in black ink. Yes, black flowers are not realistic, but, artistically, they are genuine and more helpful for painters to create vivid images.

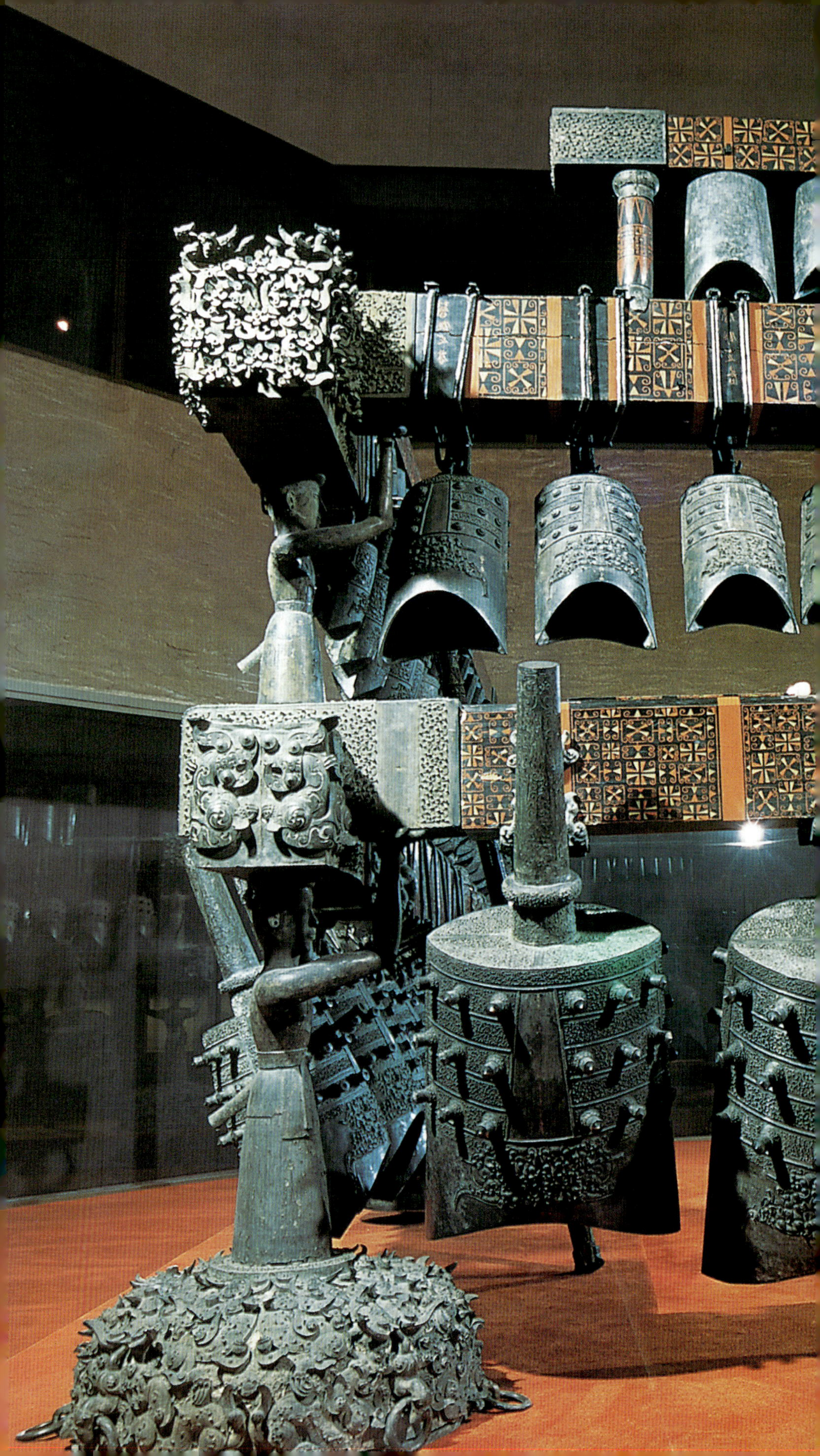

Music

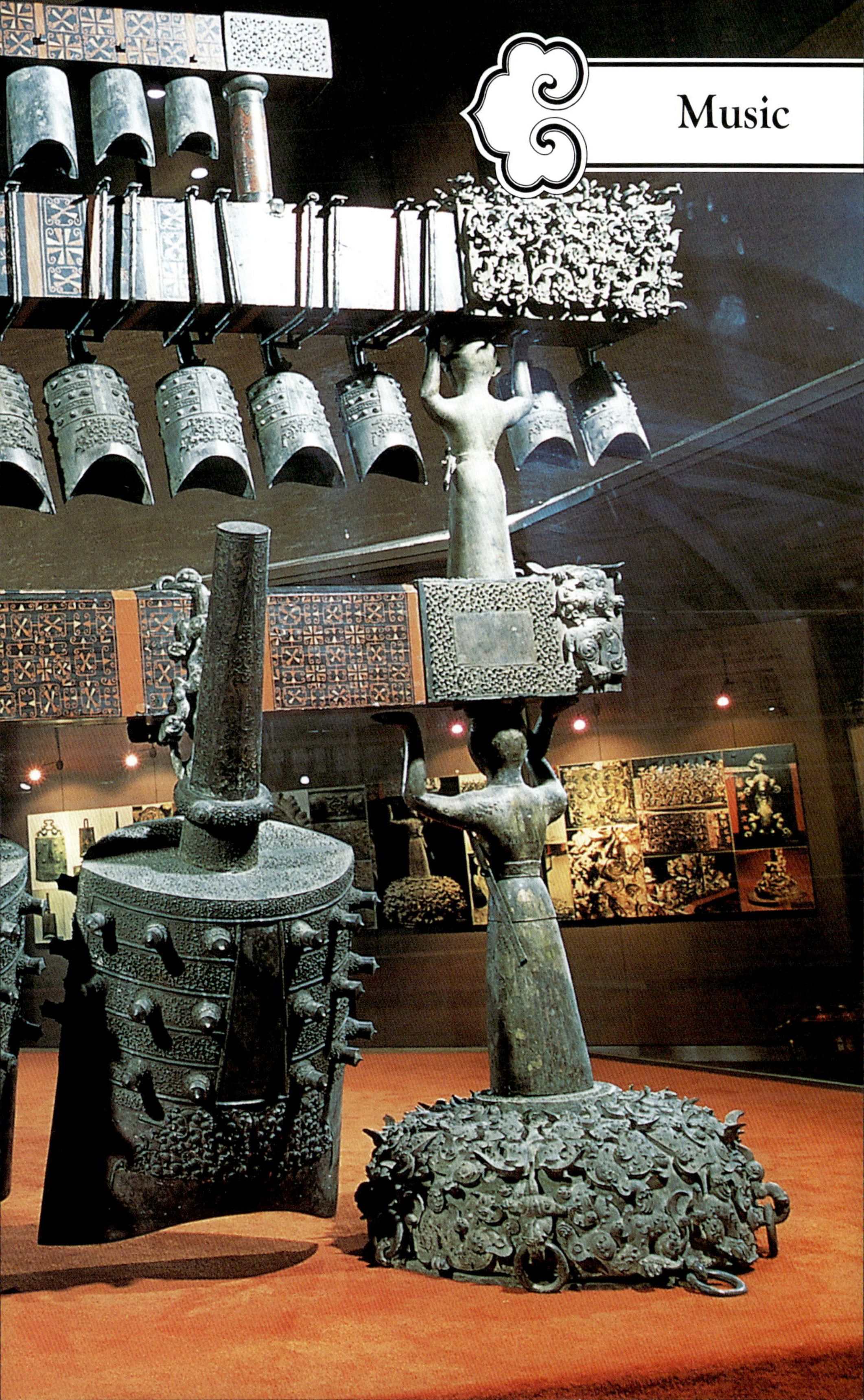

Chinese Music: An Art of Harmony

Chinese national music is an important messenger of traditional Chinese culture, with harmony as its salient feature. This feature has been playing an important role in Chinese culture as well as its political life.

Traditional Chinese culture stresses harmony, including peace of mind, unity in human relations, and harmony between man and nature. The Chinese believe that music originated from the heart's understanding of nature. A very early Chinese musical classic says that music comes from the heart when moved by nature and music itself is an expression from the heart. In Confucian philosophy, music nourishes the mind and enables regular people to become sages, and it also tempers the heart and regulates human relations to achieve social stability.

The above introduction shows that music helps to cultivate personality, improve governance, and foster social stability. *Shang Shu* (The Book of Documents), one of the earliest books of history in China, says that when the eight musical instruments achieve harmony,

Figurines of musicians from the Tang Dynasty.

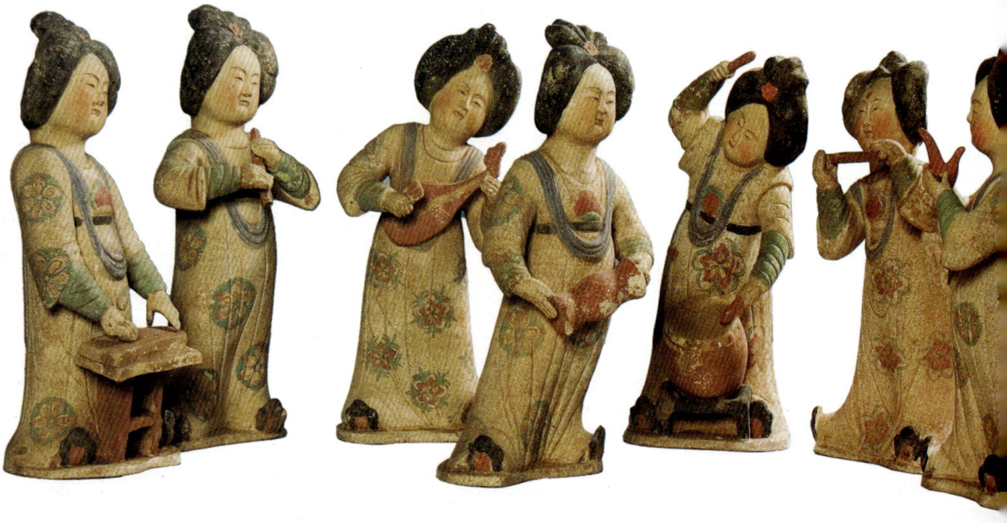

then god and man can live in peace. (The eight musical instruments refer to those made of eight materials: metal, stone, earth or clay, leather, silk, wood, gourd, and bamboo.) Artistically, harmony means neutralization, simplicity and moderation, or proportion, unity and concordance in musical works. It rejects sharp contrasts of musical elements or abrupt highs and lows. In all its forms, Chinese music is a pursuit of harmony. In this sense, an understanding of Chinese national music will lead to a real understanding of the spirit of Chinese culture, and vice versa.

Ritual, Music and Civilization

Chinese music has a long history. In their hunting, sacrificial and other activities the primitive people sang the first folk songs, and introduced the history of Chinese music. In 1986, archaeologists unearthed 21 bone flutes in a Neolithic site in Jiahu village, Wuyang County of Henan Province, and determined that they date back 8,000 to 9,000 years. Musicologists tested them and found to their surprise that the flutes conform to the regular five-tone scale. As such one can imagine that the beginning of music in China must be far earlier than the making of these wind instruments.

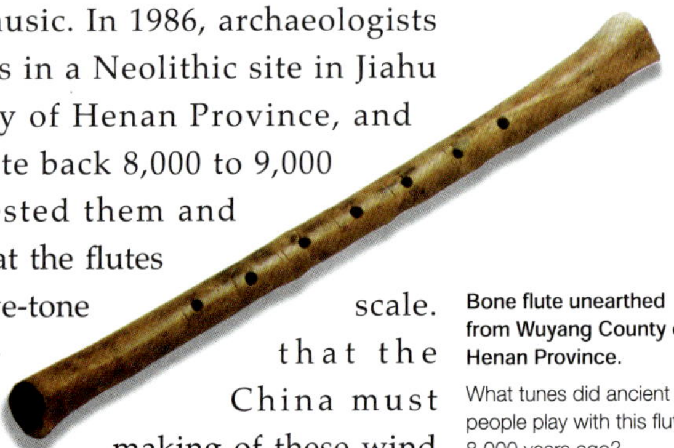

Bone flute unearthed from Wuyang County of Henan Province.

What tunes did ancient people play with this flute 8,000 years ago?

In the Shang Dynasty Chinese music had the bell and drum as the dominant instruments, and this lasted till the Qin Dynasty, the first unified empire in China. The chime bells and chime stones produced booming sounds and special rhythms. Accompanied by drums, they created a noble, solemn atmosphere. Such music was called "the elegant music," to be played at sacrificial ceremonies in the royal courts. Melodies of this elegant music were extremely appealing. It is said that when Confucius heard one of the most famous melodies in the state of Qi, he was so intoxicated that for several months he "forgot" the taste of meat. Sometimes these melodies were accompanied with words, and the graceful lyrics were later compiled

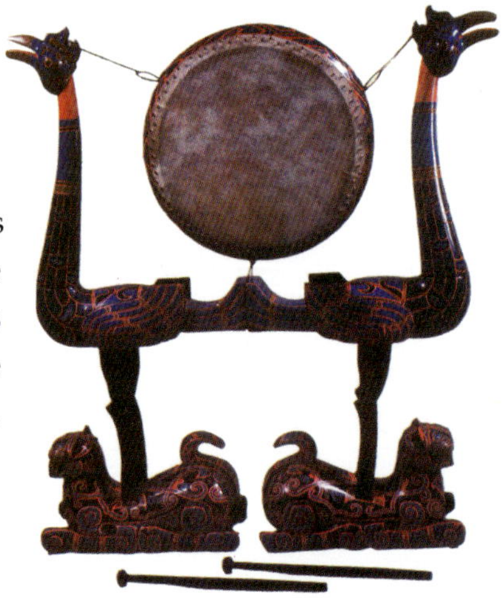

A drum on a tiger-and-bird rack unearthed from a tomb of the Chu state, the Warring States Period.

This instrument shows the imagination and craftsmanship of Chu people.

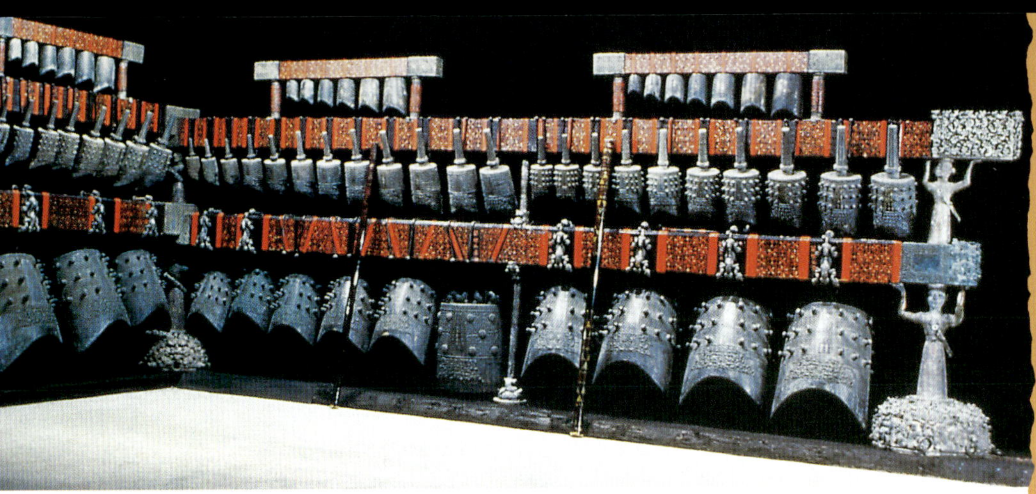

Chime bells unearthed in 1978 from the tomb of Marquis Yi of the state of Zeng in Suixian County, Hubei Province in central China.

into *Shi Jing* (the Book of Songs), the earliest collection of Chinese poems and the origin of Chinese literature.

The typical instrument for the bell-and-drum music was the chime bells, an important percussion instrument of ancient China. The bells were made of bronze, and were hung in an orderly manner on a rack according to size. The bells produce distinct, penetrating sounds. Chime bells from different dynasties are of various shapes and numbers. In ancient times they were important instruments of royal court music, to be played at expeditions, banquets, court ceremonies and sacrificial rites. They can be played alone or with other musical instruments, and they can also be used to accompany singing and dancing. Now chime bells are mainly used in Chinese orchestras. On today's stage, such instruments that date back several thousand years add a strong sense of history.

According to historical records, the making of chime bells began in the Shang Dynasty and reached its peak in the Warring States Period. In 1978 a set of 65 chime bells

Chime stones

Chime stones were used to play solemn music for kings and aristocrats.

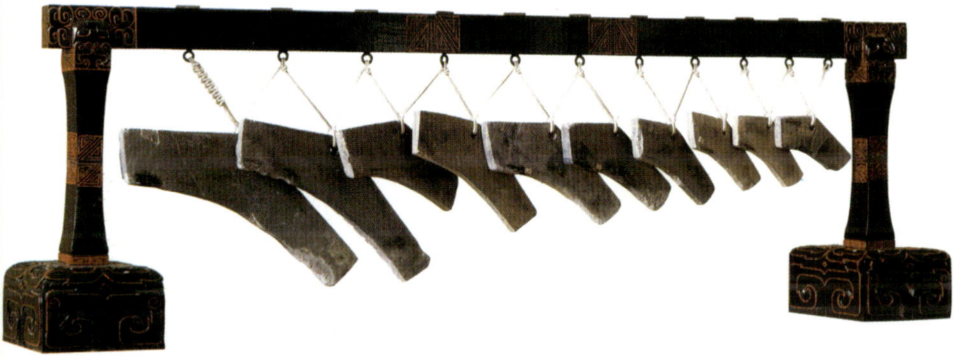

were unearthed from the tomb of Marquis Yi of the state of Zeng in Suixian County, Hubei Province in central China. On all the bronze bells were found inscriptions on musical tones in the seal script, totaling more than 2,800 characters. Studying the inscriptions, experts found that the Chinese had adopted equal temperament as early as the 5th century BC, or 1,800 years earlier than its appearance in Europe. Some international musicologists compared the chime bells of Marquis Yi with the Great Wall in China, the pyramids in Egypt and the Hanging Gardens of Babylon, praising the bells as "the eighth wonder of the ancient world."

In the Qin and Han dynasties song-and-dance music became the main form of Chinese music, and this trend lasted till the following Sui and Tang dynasties and the Five Dynasties Period. Before the Sui Period the Han ethnic group contributed the most to Chinese music, but after that came a great musical exchange between the Han and other ethnic groups, both in and outside China, and Chinese song-and-dance music reached its peak. In the Qin and Han Periods the royal court had an imperial Music Bureau to manage musical activities. At its height the Music Bureau was staffed with more than 600 musicians; they collected folk songs, composed works and performed. After the Qin and Han dynasties the chime bells and chime stones were replaced by the *yu* pipe and *se* stringed instrument, which were more suited to music of fast and strong rhythms. In the late years of the Eastern Han Dynasty, the *yu* and *se* instruments were again replaced by the *zheng* zither and the flute. At that time the *pipa*

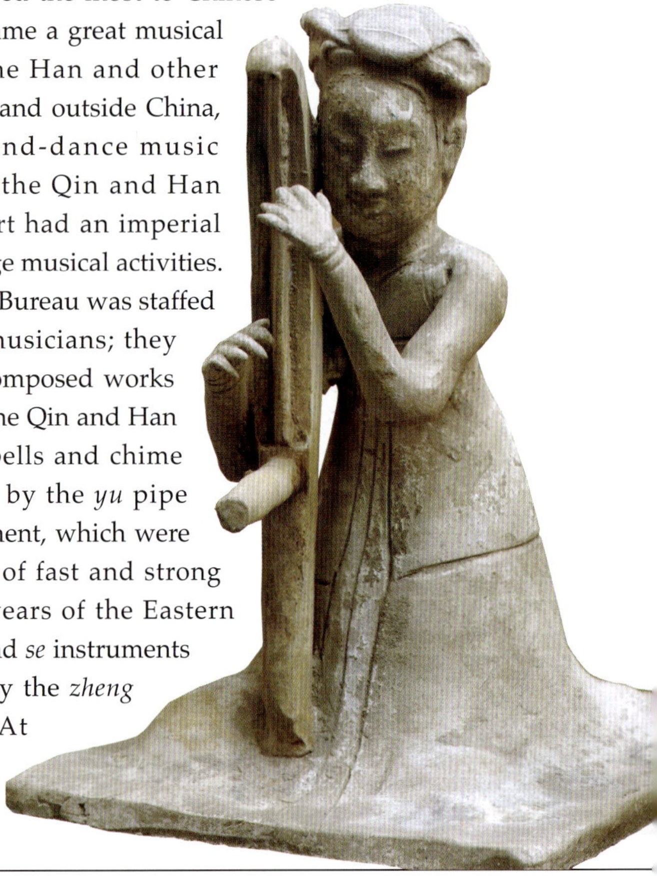

A figurine of musician playing the *konghou* harp from the Sui Dynasty.

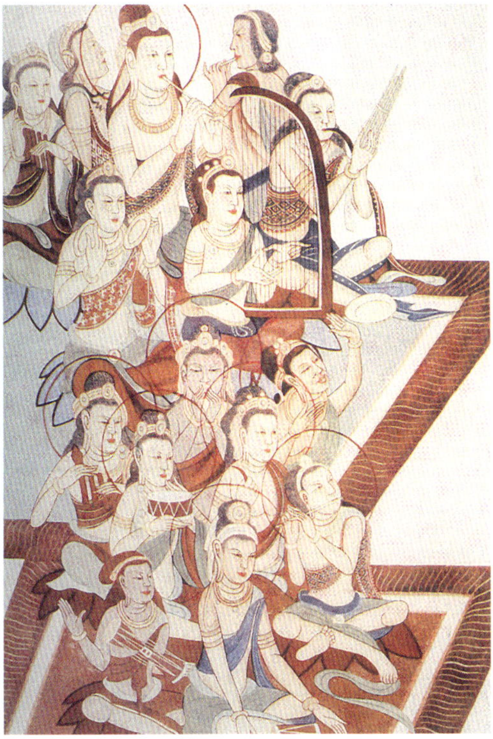

A band of the Tang Dynasty shown in the frescoes of Mogao grottoes in Dunhuang.

The Tang was one of the most prosperous dynasties in Chinese history. This fresco shows the well-developed arts of the era.

lute and *konghou* harp were introduced from central Asia to China, and they later became important instruments of Chinese music.

Probably beginning in the Northern and Southern Dynasties era, foreign and ethnic minority elements were introduced to the music of the Han ethnic group, and by the Sui and Tang dynasties Chinese music became an amalgamation of various ethnic groups, including those in Korea, India and central Asia. In the Tang Dynasty artists created works that integrated instrumental, singing and dancing, and the most famous was *Ni Shang Yu Yi Qu* (Song of Fairies), which described how the emperor met fairies on the moon. A poet wrote that when the Song of Fairies was performed on a large boat, the boat had sailed 15 *li* (1 *li* = 0.5 km) before the performance ended. From the Tang orchestras in the frescoes of Dunhuang grottoes, the spectacular performances can only be imagined.

In the Sui and Tang dynasties a new form of folk songs developed, which reached its height in the Song Dynasty. The words of the folk songs, *ci*, became the mainstream of the Song literature. As the lyrics were of various lengths, they are also known as the long and short verses. Such folk songs were quite popular in the Song period, and poet Liu Yong was one of the best lyricists of that time, even admired by the emperor. There was then such a saying: wherever there is a well, there are people singing Liu Yong's songs.

Chinese music entered a new stage in the Song Dynasty. Before this, music was mainly played in royal

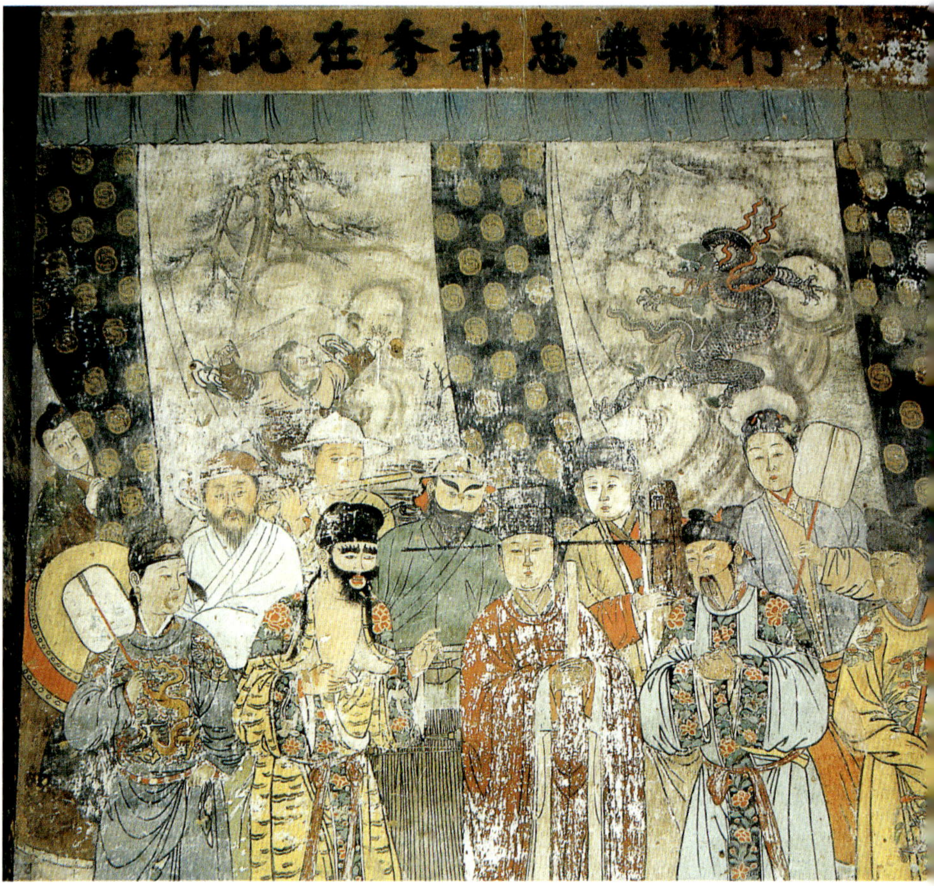

courts and was known as "court music." In the Song Dynasty, commerce grew and cities expanded. Urban residents began to have their own entertainment facilities, where musical performances were given. People called such music "populace music." In this period a new form of art emerged, which integrated talking with singing. Such an art form later developed into drama in the Yuan Dynasty. In the Song, Yuan, Ming and Qing dynasties, Chinese music and traditional Chinese operas were partly merged.

A fresco in the Yingwang Temple in Hongtong County of Shanxi Province.

The fresco painted during the Ming Dynasty shows a scene of the zaju drama of the Yuan Dynasty.

Since the 20th century Chinese music has again experienced a new merger with foreign music and made new developments.

Guqin: The Oldest Plucked String Instrument of China

Guqin is the oldest plucked string instrument of China, with a history of more than 3,000 years. In the Book of Songs, the earliest collection of Chinese poems, there are quite a few descriptions of this instrument. Playing *guqin* tops the four arts that ancient Chinese *literati* were required to master: *qin* (*guqin*), *qi* (*weichi* or go), *shu* (calligraphy), and *hua* (painting). In the study of an ancient Chinese man of letters, there usually were a sword hanging on the wall and a *guqin* lying on the table. The sword symbolizes courage and the owner's determination to dedicate himself to the country, and the *guqin*, his artistic talent and sensitivity. The ancient Chinese appreciated scholars who were adept in both literary and military arts.

The *guqin* is a Chinese zither with seven strings stretched over its 1.2-meter sound box, which produce mellow, silvery and varied sounds. Ancient people regarded the playing of *guqin* as a ceremonial event. The player would first bathe,

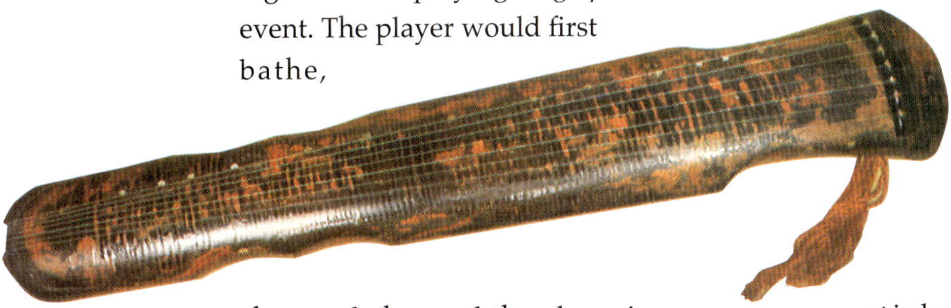

A well-known *qin* string instrument from the Tang Dynasty.

This instrument has been played by a large number of celebrities in history.

change clothes and then burn incense sticks before sitting on his haunches to play. The instrument was placed on his legs or on a table, and he plucked the strings with his left hand and pressed them with his right to produce accurate tones in accordance with the marks on the sound box. The *guqin* is highly expressive, capable of voicing all the emotions and depicting all scenes of nature. It can be played solo or in an ensemble, and can accompany singing. In the some 700 ancient musical works of *guqin* now still in existence, mostly written by

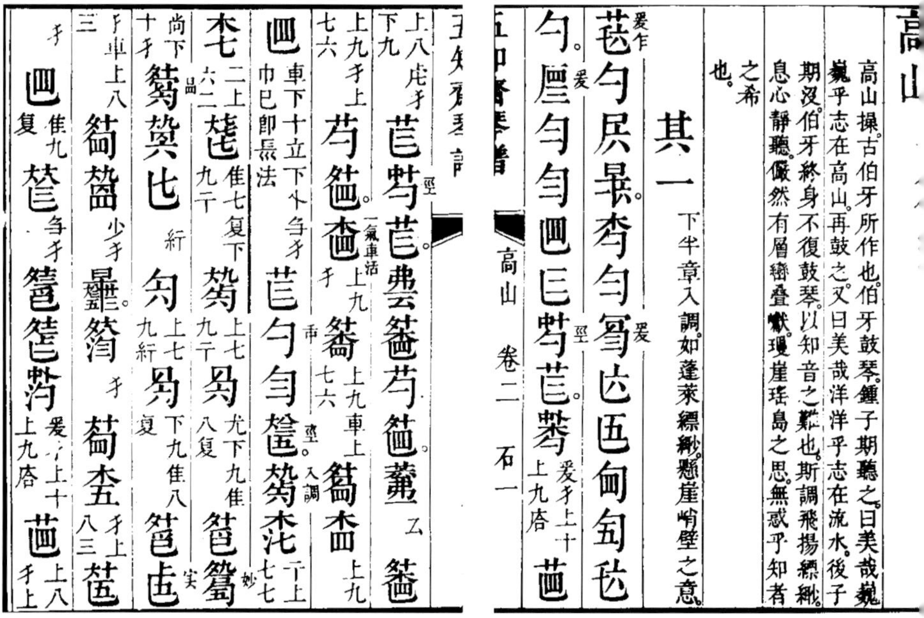

An ancient Chinese *guqin* music book.

This score of High Mountains records in Chinese characters and special signs the fingering of the music.

scholars, almost half were meant for accompaniment. Ancient Chinese scholars made substantial contributions to the development of *guqin* music.

In traditional Chinese culture, the *guqin* was often found in scholars' communications, love stories or even activities of military strategists. The instrument is also mentioned in a number of Chinese proverbs.

In November 2003 the United Nations Educational, Scientific and Cultural Organization (UNESCO) included the art of *guqin* music to be among the 28 masterpieces of the Oral and Intangible Heritage of Humanity in its second proclamation.

High Mountains and Flowing Streams: *Guqin* Music in Outer Space

In 1977 the United States launched the Voyager spacecraft to explore intelligent extraterrestrial life. The spacecraft carried a gold phonograph record containing sounds and images that portrayed the diversity of life and culture on earth. Among its 27 musical works is ancient Chinese *guqin* music, High Mountains and Flowing Streams (*Gao Shan Liu Shui*), attributed to Bo Ya, a noted *guqin* musician in ancient China. This music was recommended for the gold record because of its interpretation of the exchange between man and universe, as a representative of Chinese culture and arts.

There is a moving story about a great *guqin* player and a great appreciator behind this piece of music. Legend has it that when musician Bo Ya was traveling in central China, he played the *guqin* on a moonlit night. The music attracted Zhong Ziqi, a laborer who was good at playing *guqin* music. When Bo Ya thought of mountains as he plucked the strings, Ziqi exclaimed, "Oh so lofty, it must be Mount Tai!" And when the music changed as Bo Ya

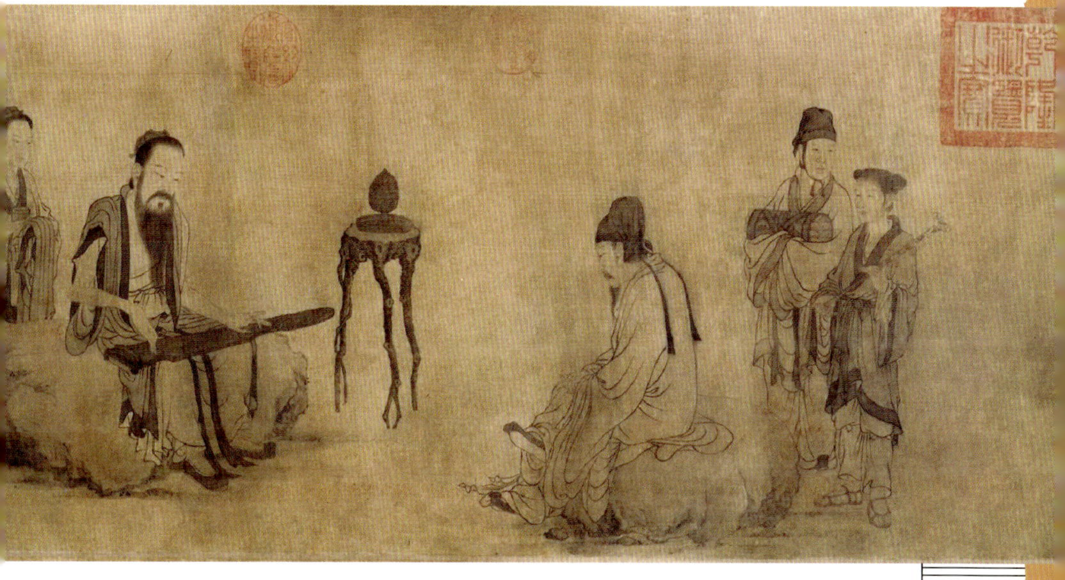

Bo Ya and Zhong Ziqi enjoying *guqin* music.

There is a moving story about BoYa, great *guqin* player and Zhong Ziqi, a great appreciator, behind the music of High Mountains and Flowing Streams.

thought of flowing streams, Ziqi again cried, "Oh so overwhelming, you're intending to represent a river!" Bo Ya was so glad that someone understood his music so well that he promised to meet Ziqi again six months later. But when Bo Ya visited next, he learned that Ziqi had died. In deep grief, Bo Ya visited Ziqi's tomb and played the music again for his friend. When the composition reached its end, Bo Ya destroyed his *guqin*, determined never to play it again, as he believed nobody else would ever understand his music as well as Ziqi had.

This enlightenment of the composition and the story behind it implies the ancient Chinese philosophy of integration of man and nature, and has enabled it to be passed down from generation to generation for more than 2,000 years. The Confucian doctrine links benevolence and morals to lofty mountains and wisdom to flowing water. This *guqin* music of High Mountains and Flowing Streams may help in understanding the character and wisdom of the Chinese.

Pipa: "Like Pouring Large and Small Pearls Onto a Plate of Jade"

In the Mogao grottoes in Dunhuang are a large number of flying Apsarases in the frescoes, and many hold a *pipa*, an ancient, four-stringed musical instrument.

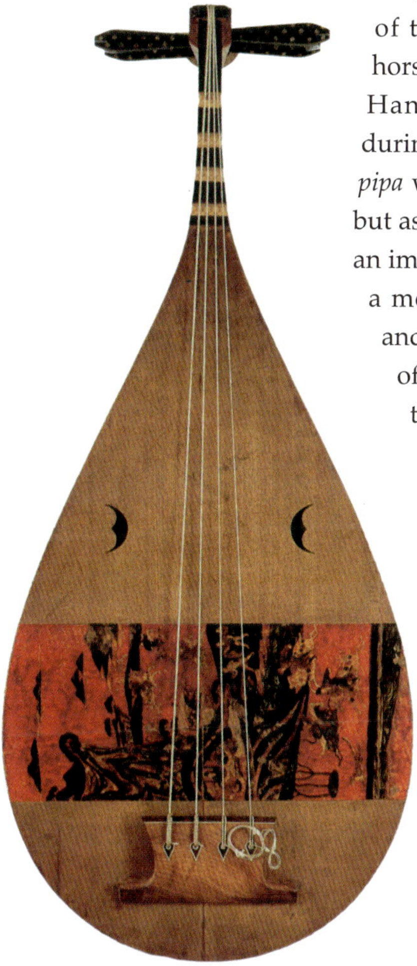

The *pipa* used to be a string instrument of the nomadic people, to be played on horseback. It became popular in the Eastern Han Dynasty and got its name probably during the Wei and Jin dynasties. At first the *pipa* was used for accompaniment in singing, but as players developed their skills it became an important solo instrument. The *pipa* is now a member of Chinese national orchestras, and a major instrument for some branches of music in south China, such as those in the lower reaches of the Yangtze River and in Guangdong Province, including local operas and ballads.

The *pipa* is highly expressive. By plucking and touching the strings in different ways, a successful player can render various scenes: fighting troops, the rain in spring, a woman weeping and a tyrant roaring. People often describe the sounds of *pipa* as "pouring large and small pearls onto a plate of jade." And this verse comes from a famous poem by poet Bai Juyi of the Tang Dynasty. Bai wrote in his Song of the *Pipa* (*Pipa Xing*):

A *pipa* instrument of the Tang Dynasty, now in the collection of a museum in Nara city of Japan.

The large strings hummed like rain,
The small strings whispered like a secret,
Hummed, whispered—and then were intermingled,

Like pouring large and small pearls onto a plate of jade.

Among the existing, well-known *pipa* compositions, the Ambush on All Sides (*Shimian Maifu*) tells a story of a war between rivaling troops, the Snow Ushers in Spring (*Yangchun Baixue*) shows scenes in spring, and A Moonlit Night on the River in Spring (*Chun Jiang Hua Yue Ye*) is based on a Tang poem of the same theme. Almost every *pipa* composition has a moving story behind it, and by listening to the *pipa* music, much can be learned about Chinese culture.

The audience enjoying a *pipa* solo in the ancient painting of The Feast of Han Xizai (*Han Xizai Ye Yan Tu*).

Obviously the player had charmed the audience.

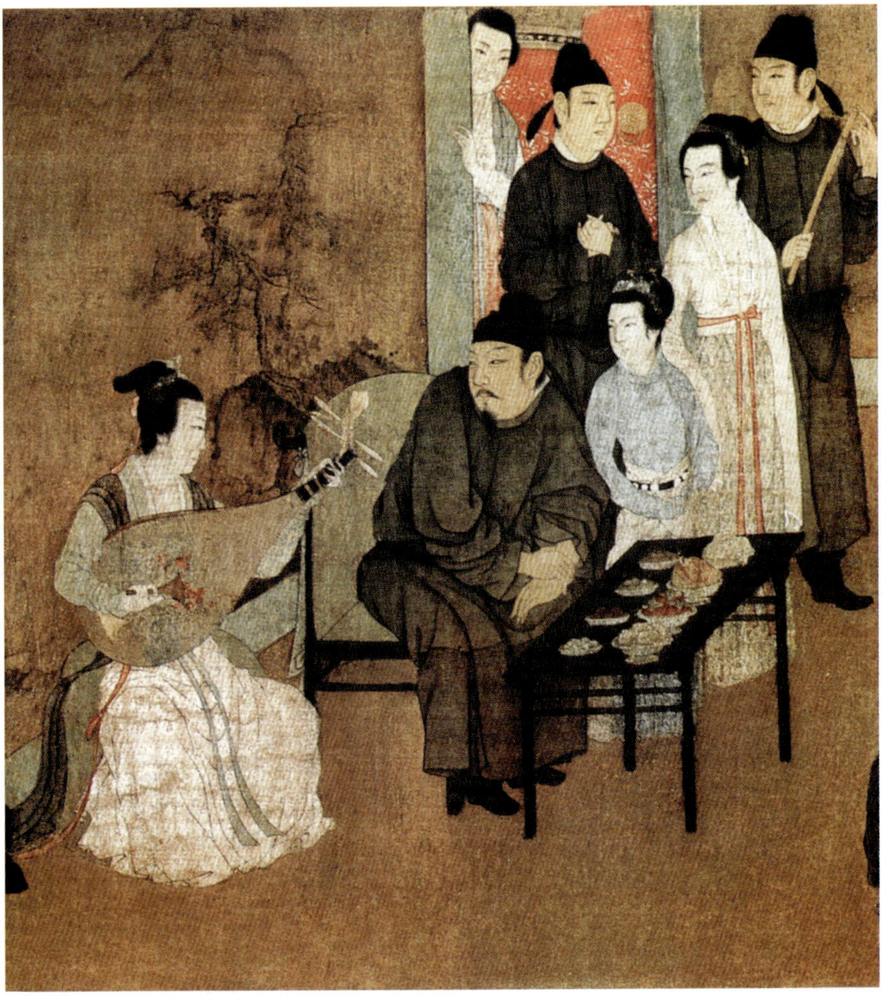

Zheng: Another Chinese Zither

Zheng is another Chinese zither that dates back more than 2,000 years, and it is also known as *guzheng* (*gu* means ancient in Chinese). The instrument got its name from onomatopoeia, imitating its sounds. The *zheng* has a long history, rich national flavor and a large number of traditional compositions, able to express ancient and elegant sentiments.

The *zheng* has a rectangular sound box, usually made

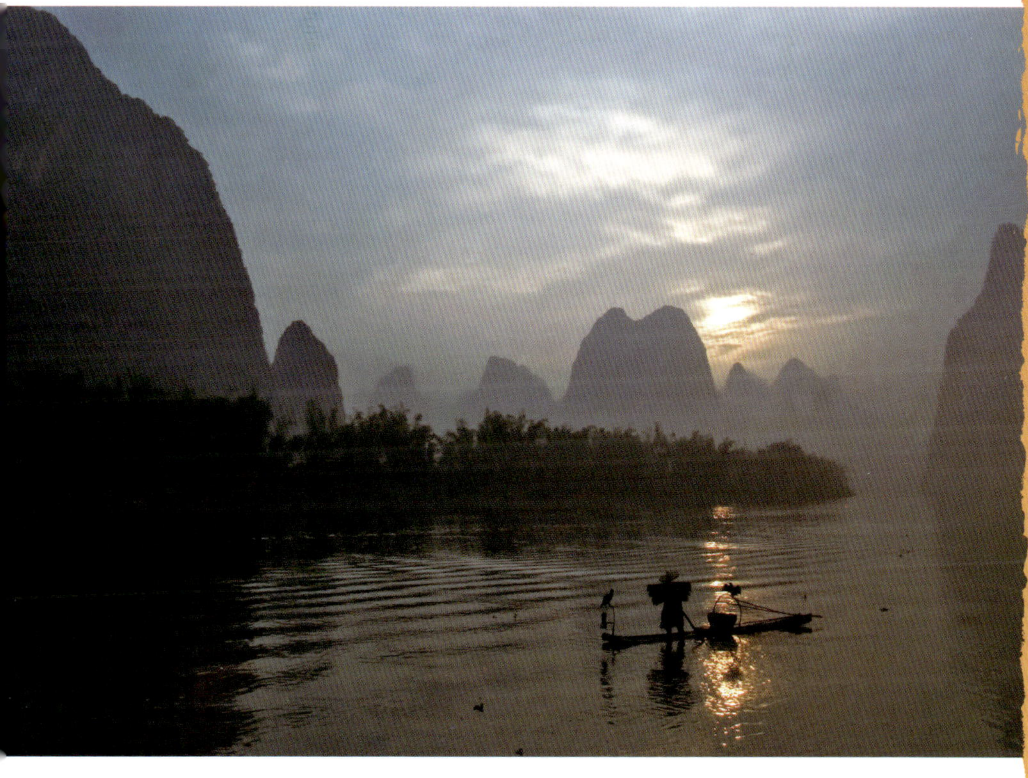

Fishermen Return at Dusk (*Yu Zhou Chang Wan*)

This picture shows the scene of a popular composition of solo *zheng* music.

of phoenix tree wood, with movable bridges and 16 –25 strings over an arc surface of the sound box. The movable bridge can regulate the pitch, extending the *zheng*'s range to four eight-tone scales. Its undertone is vigorous, its alt, clear, and its median, mellow. The player touches the strings with the left hand in varying ways,

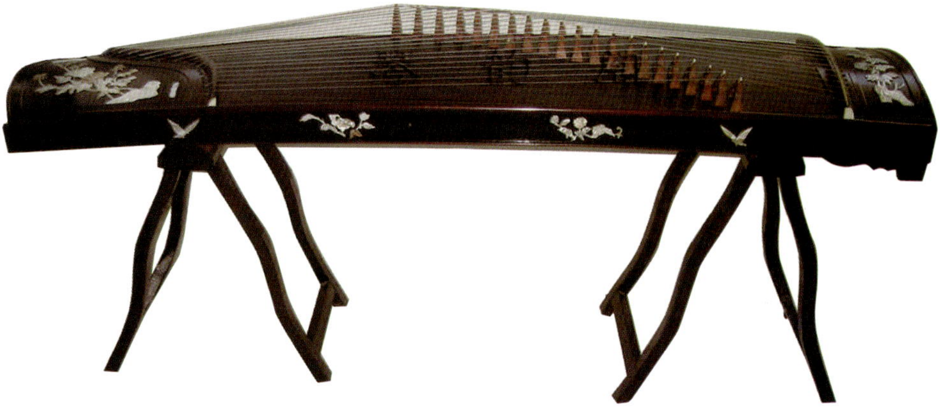

Zheng, a Chinese zither.

The *zheng* zither appeared quite often in literary works in ancient China.

making it most expressive for both elegance and vigor. As the *zheng* is tuned in the five-tone scale, it is typical of Chinese music. The instrument can produce both solo and accompaniment compositions.

Fishermen Return at Dusk (*Yu Zhou Chang Wan*) is a popular composition of solo *zheng* music. The work describes beautiful scenery on the lake, fishing boats returning home in the evening and the sentiments of happy fishermen.

Erhu and Spring Water Reflects the Moon

Erhu, a two-stringed bow-and-string instrument, is one of the most popular Chinese instruments in the *Hu-qin* family (*Hu* stands for "foreign" or "the northern folk" in Chinese, and "*qin*" is a general name for all kinds of string instruments). The *erhu* has been in use since the Tang Dynasty, and it is now played both solo and in an ensemble as an important element of the string band. The *erhu* music is suitable for expression of both deep sorrow and vigor. Among the *erhu* compositions a well-known one is the Spring Water Reflects the Moon (*Er Quan Ying Yue*).

Hua Yanjun (1893–1950), the composer, was a native of Wuxi City in Jiangsu Province, east China. He was also known by his infant name A-Bing. This genius of a folk artist went blind in his middle age, and he had to make a living as a migrant performer, when China was in turmoil and the Chinese people had hard lives. Most of the works A-Bing played were also composed by him. One of his masterpieces, The Spring Water Reflects the Moon, was a presentation of his own miserable life. The music represents a memory of happy times, complaints about the miseries of society, and an expression of the composer's dauntlessness. The famous conductor Seiji

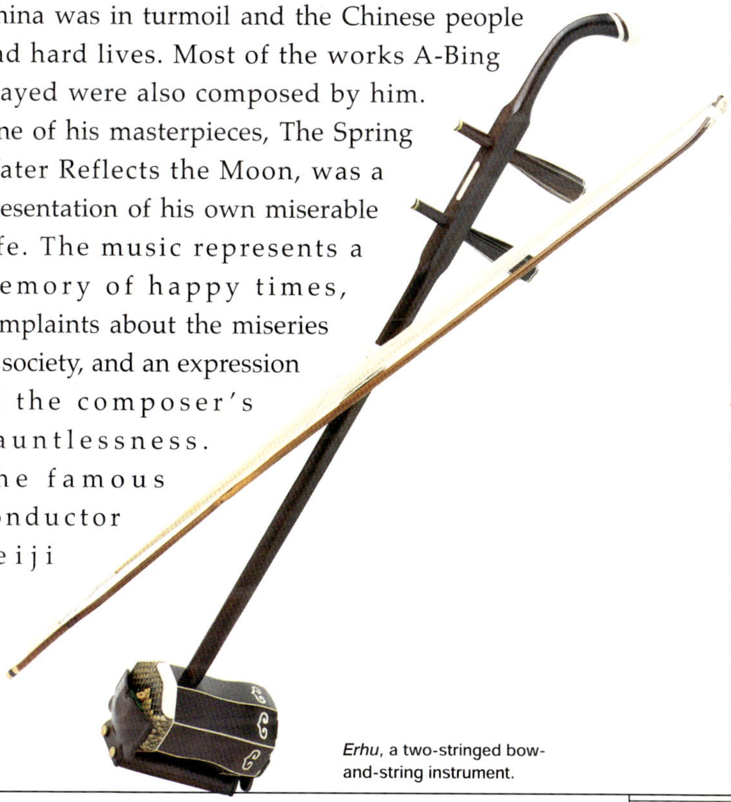

Erhu, a two-stringed bow-and-string instrument.

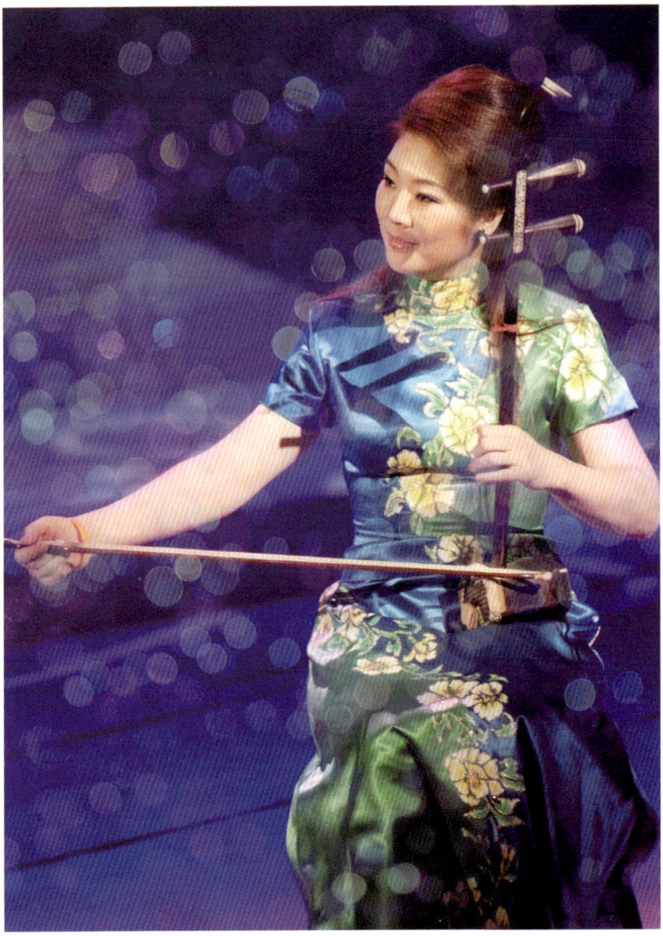

Erhu players giving a performance.

Ozawa was moved to tears when he heard this *erhu* composition for the first time, and he said, "We should be on our knees on hearing such a piece of music!"

A-Bing moved China and the world at large with his *erhu* music. The Spring Water Reflects the Moon has become one of the most popular Chinese traditional compositions. A-Bing's life and his achievements remind us of another great musician—German composer Beethoven. Both of them suffered great misery, and both have left lasting works for humanity.

The Butterfly Lovers: A Violin Concerto

In the 20th century Western music was introduced to China and it has been growing, blossoming and bearing fruit ever since. The violin concerto *Liang Zhu* (*The Butterfly Lovers*) is just such a wonderful flower grown in Chinese soil, a successful integration of Western music and its traditional Chinese counterpart.

There is a sad love story behind this musical work,

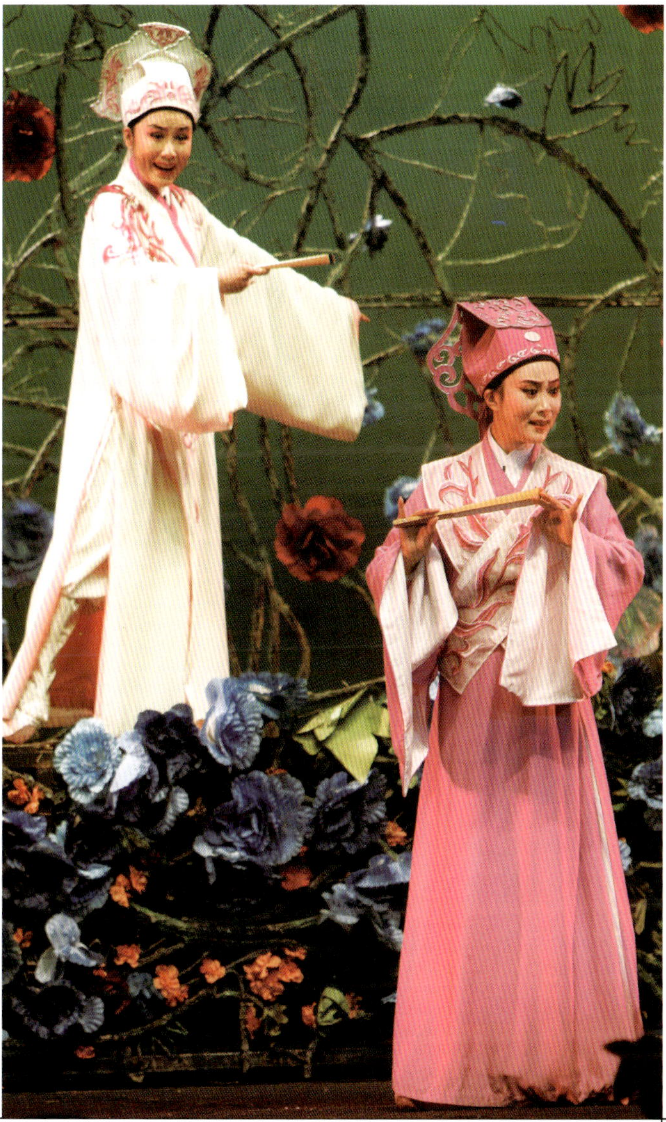

A scene from *Liang Zhu* (*The Butterfly Lovers*).

a Chinese version of Romeo and Juliet, but a thousand years earlier than Shakespeare's. Zhu Yingtai, a girl from a rich family, disguises her gender and enters a school in Hangzhou, where she meets Liang Shanbo, an intelligent student from a poor family, and they become good friends during their three years in school. Later, they fall in love when Liang realizes Zhu is a girl. But Zhu's father tries to force Zhu to marry another young man from a rich family. Utterly sorrowful, Liang soon dies of an illness. When Zhu learns about Liang's death, she goes to his tomb and weeps. Suddenly the tomb splits open, and Zhu throws herself in. Then, the two lovers turn into a pair of butterflies, and they dance together amid the flowers, never to part again.

He Zhanhao and Chen Gang, two talented students at the Shanghai Conservatory of Music, composed this concerto in 1959, and it became one of the most popular musical works in contemporary China. The composers, borrowing arias from the Shaoxing opera in Zhejiang Province, applied the techniques of both symphony and Chinese folk operas to create this narrative music in presenting the moving story to the audience. This creative symphonic work has eminently Chinese national characteristics, and is a great success recognized by musicians the world over.

What a Beautiful Jasmine Flower

Folk songs are oral works created by average people to express their sentiments. As China is a vast country with a long history and a large number of ethnic groups, Chinese folk songs vary from north to south and from east to west. In south China, the climate is mild, the soil is fertile, there are numerous rivers and lakes, and the scenery is beautiful. Folk songs created in such an environment are elegant. In comparison, in northwest China the climate is frigid and there are lofty mountains and vast loess plateaus, where people struggle against nature for survival. There, folk songs are loud and straightforward. The style of the south is compared to flowers and spring rains, while that of the northwest, horses and autumn winds.

Here are the words of Jasmine Flower (*Moli Hua*), a folk song in Jiangsu Province, east China:

What a beautiful jasmine flower,
What a beautiful jasmine flower—
An entire garden blooming is not as fragrant as she is.
I think of picking one jasmine to keep by my side
Yet I'm afraid her guardian will berate me.
What a beautiful jasmine flower,
What a beautiful jasmine flower—

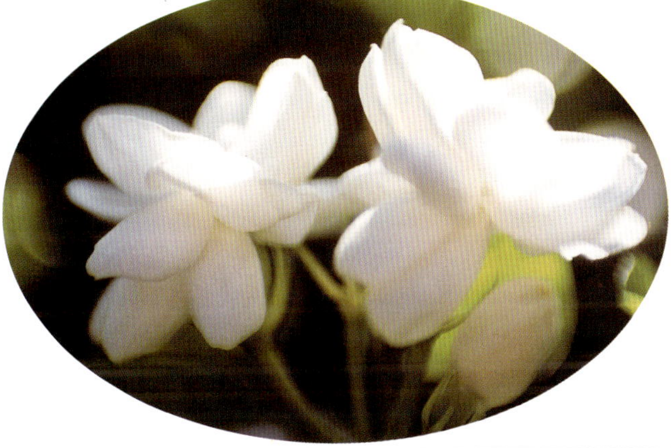

Jasmine Flower (*Moli Hua*)

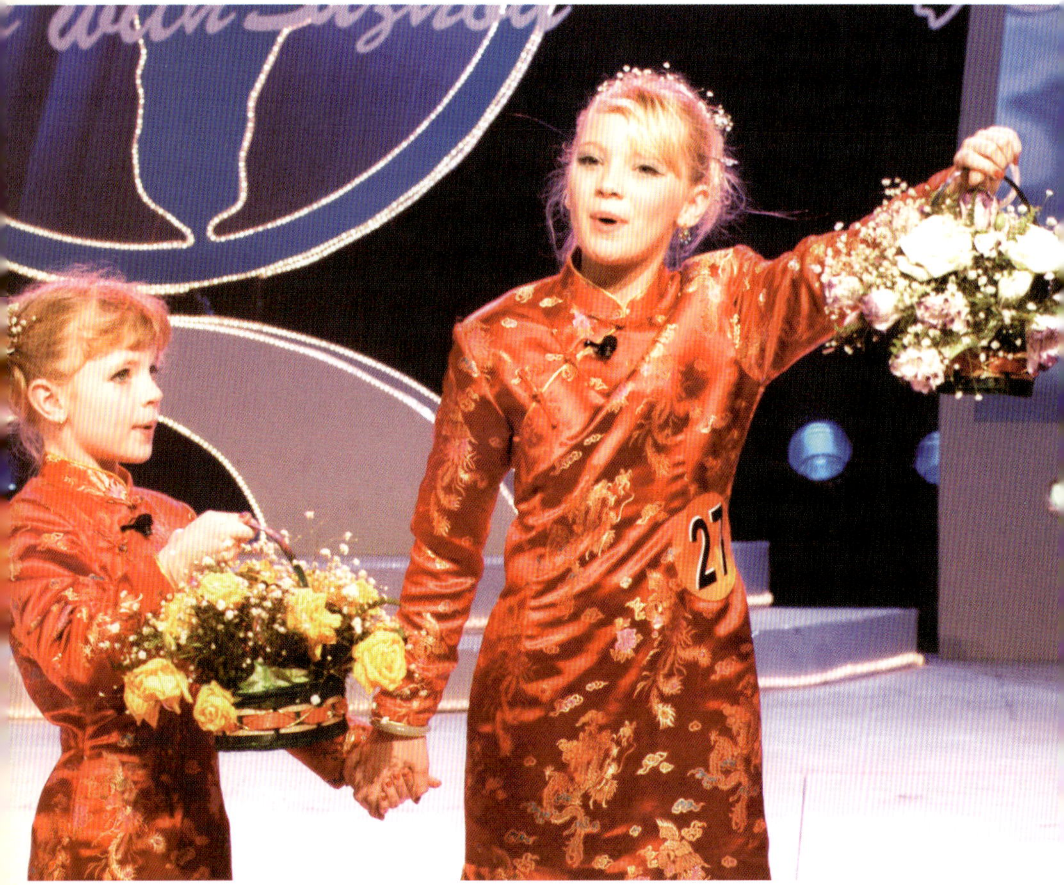

Two American girls singing the Jasmine Flower.

When she's in bloom snow is not as white as she is.
I think of picking one jasmine to keep by my side
Yet I'm afraid of teasing and mockery.
What a beautiful jasmine flower,
What a beautiful jasmine flower—
The entire garden cannot hold a candle to her.
I think of picking one jasmine to keep by my side
Yet I'm afraid she will not bud the year after.

This Jasmine Flower is typical of the folk songs from the lower reaches of the Yangtze River. It is elegant and expressive. This folk tune was adopted by Italian composer Giacomo Puccini in his opera *Turandot*, a fictitious princess of the Yuan Dynasty in China. This tune was used as a major musical component, and all the roles in the opera were in Yuan costume. These factors lent a Chinese flavor to an opera composed and performed by foreigners. In 1926, the opera debuted in Italy, and the Chinese folk song was thus introduced to the world.

The tune of Jasmine Flower has been played on many important occasions in recent years: at the handover ceremony for Hong Kong's return to China on the night of June 30, 1997 before the Chinese and British leaders appeared; on the lawn in the White House of the United States when President Bill Clinton welcomed Chinese President Jiang Zemin in autumn 1997; in the Great Hall of the People in Beijing when President Clinton paid a return visit to China in 1998; at the handover ceremony for Macao's return to China when the delegation of the Chinese government arrived on the night of December 19, 1999; and at a ceremony revealing the emblem of the 2008 Beijing Olympic Games in the Temple of Heaven in Beijing on August 3, 2003. This tune has become a symbol of the Chinese people for peace and friendship.

Shanqu Folk Song

Shanqu is a form of Chinese folk song that is popular in northwest Shanxi and north Shaanxi Provinces. The lyric of Migrating West (*Zou Xikou*), a typical *Shanqu*, goes like this:

My brother you're migrating west
And I your sister can't hold you
Hand in hand I see you to the gate
Holding you by the sleeve I also hold back my tears
What a pity I can't go with you
And I can only wish you back home at an early date

In China, apart from siblings, lovers or even young couples may also address each other as brother and sister. In the old days poor peasants in northwest Shanxi used

A folk musician from northern Shaanxi Province playing Migrating West (*Zou Xikou*).

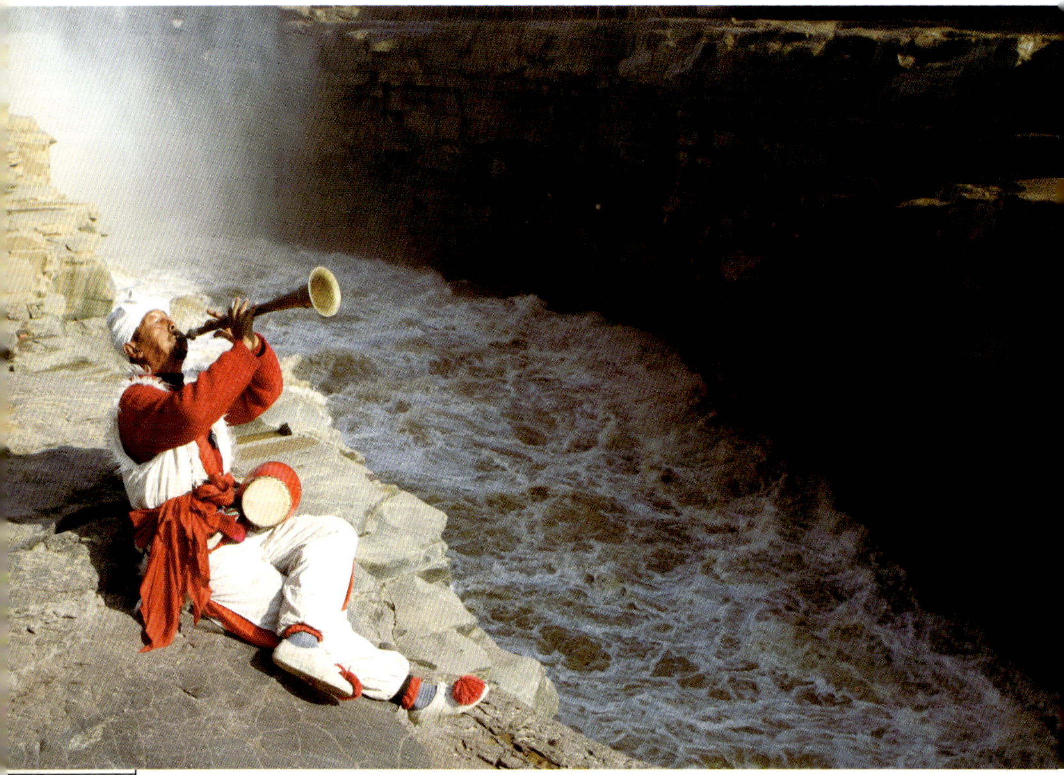

to flee famine by crossing the Yellow River and migrating west to Inner Mongolia. Quite a few of the migrants would stay there for years, to return home only once in several years, and some died of hardship being away from home. Every time they left, they risked parting from their dear ones forever. Every year in spring when male migrants left in groups, people sang this sad folk song at the ferries on the Yellow River. They sang, they yelled, and they expressed their grief in this song.

Muqam and Folk Long Song

China's Ministry of Culture adopted in 2006 this emblem of China Intangible Cultural Heritage: The outer ring symbolizes endless circulation, and the square inside implies great space for intangible cultural heritage. The pattern in the center, a fish pattern, comes from the earliest extant pottery in China, in which a Chinese character文 (culture) can be recognized. As fish live in water, it also implies intangible cultural heritage will circulate forever like water. The two abstracted hands around the fish pattern signify careful protection of intangible cultural heritage.

Emblem of China Intangible Cultural Heritage.

On November 25, 2005 UNESCO announced the third proclamation of 43 masterpieces of the Oral and Intangible Cultural Heritage of Humanity. Among them are the Art of Chinese Xinjiang Uyghur Muqam (China) and Urtiin Duu—Mongolian traditional folk Long Song (Mongolia and China).

The Xinjiang Uyghur Muqam is the general term for a variety of Muqam practices widespread among the Uyghur communities, which form one of the largest ethnic minorities of China. Xinjiang Uyghur Muqam is a composite of songs, dances, folk and classical music, and characterized by diversity of content, dance styles, musical morphology and instruments used. This form of art is found in 19 countries and regions in central, south and west Asia, and in north Africa. Throughout history, the Xinjiang region has been marked by a high degree of cultural exchange between East and West, in particular due to its location on the hub of the Silk Road.

Urtiin duu (long-song), or "Mongolian folk long-song," is so named due to its slow, flowing melody with *rubato*

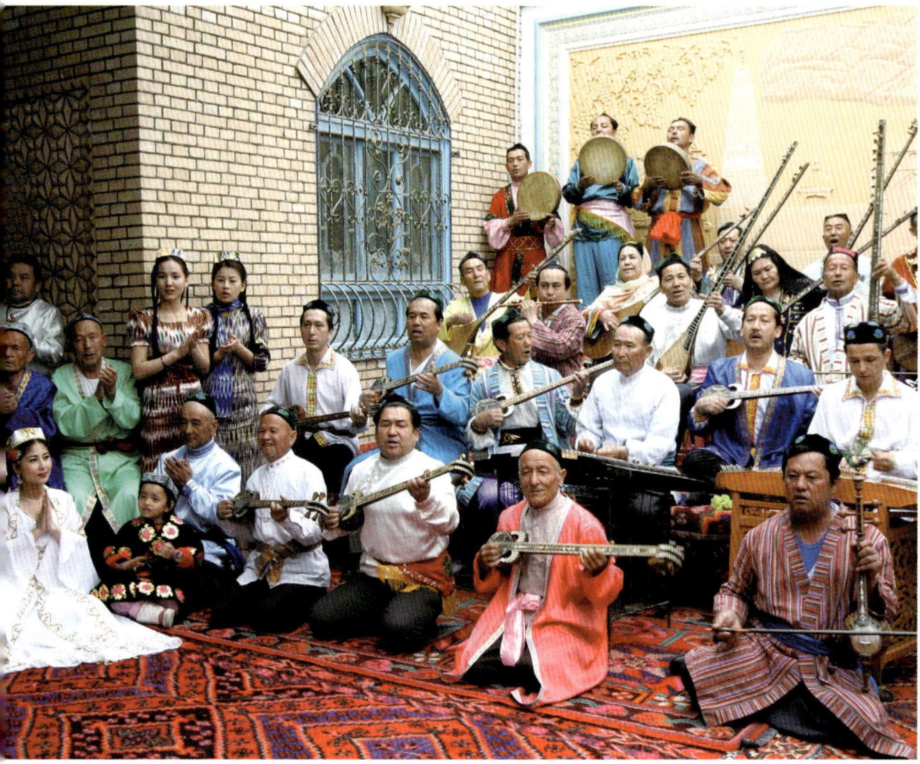

A Muqam performance.
Xinjiang Uyghur Muqam is a composite of songs, dances, folk and classical music.

tempo, and its relatively long text, each syllable of which is extended over several notes. *Urtiin duu* is a lyrical chant made of 32 verses with a highly ornamented melody praising the beauty of the steppe, mountains and rivers, the love for parents or close friends, expressing reflections on human destiny. Performances and compositions of *Urtiin duu* are closely linked to the nomadic, pastoral way of life.

As a grand, ritualistic expression associated with important celebrations and festivities, *Urtiin duu* plays a distinct and honored role in Mongolian society. It is performed at weddings, the inauguration of a new home, birth of a child, branding of foals or other social and religious festivities. *Urtiin duu* performances as well as contemporary compositions still play a major role in the social and cultural lives of nomads living in Mongolia and in the Inner Mongolia Autonomous Region of China.

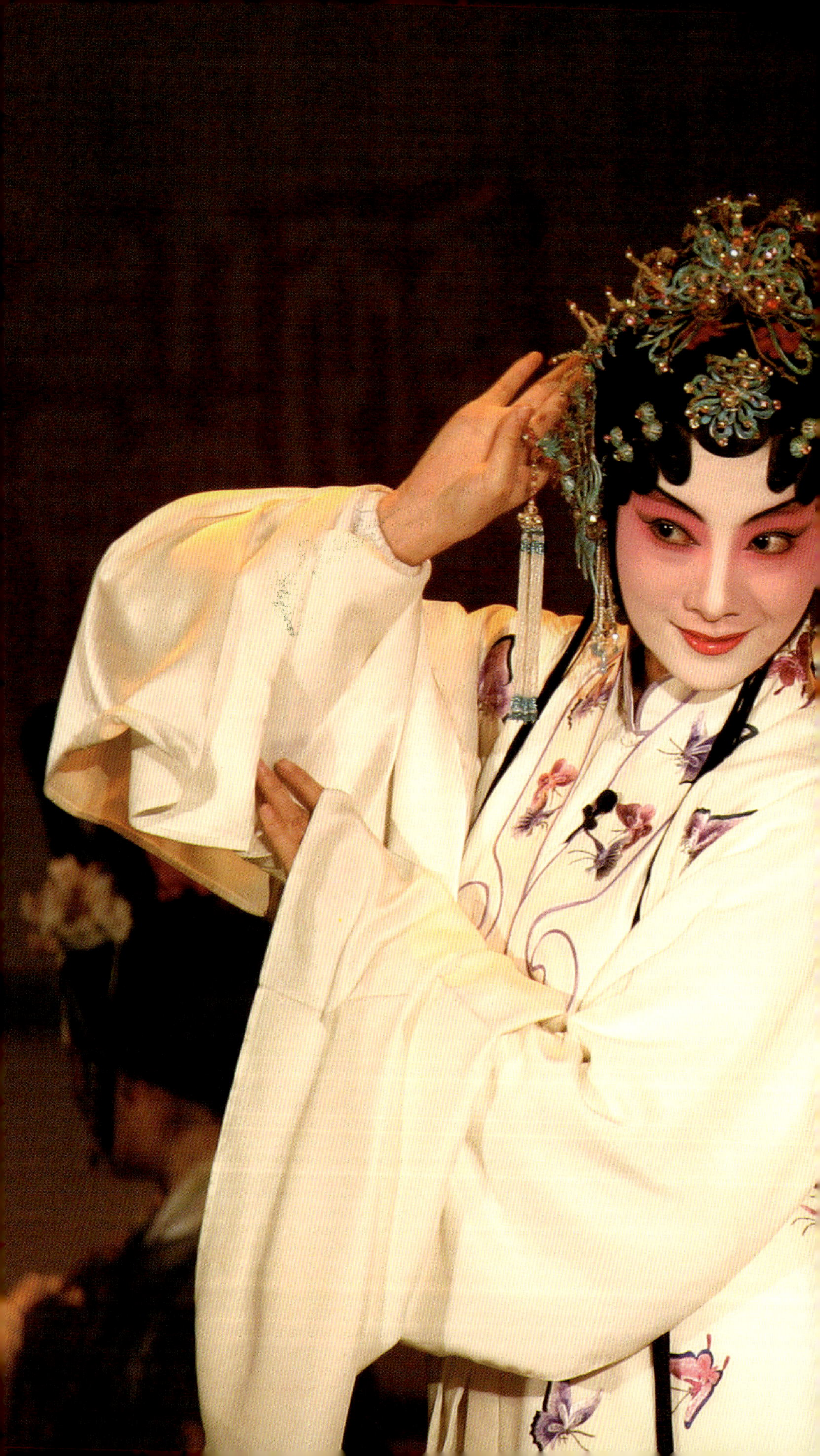

Opera

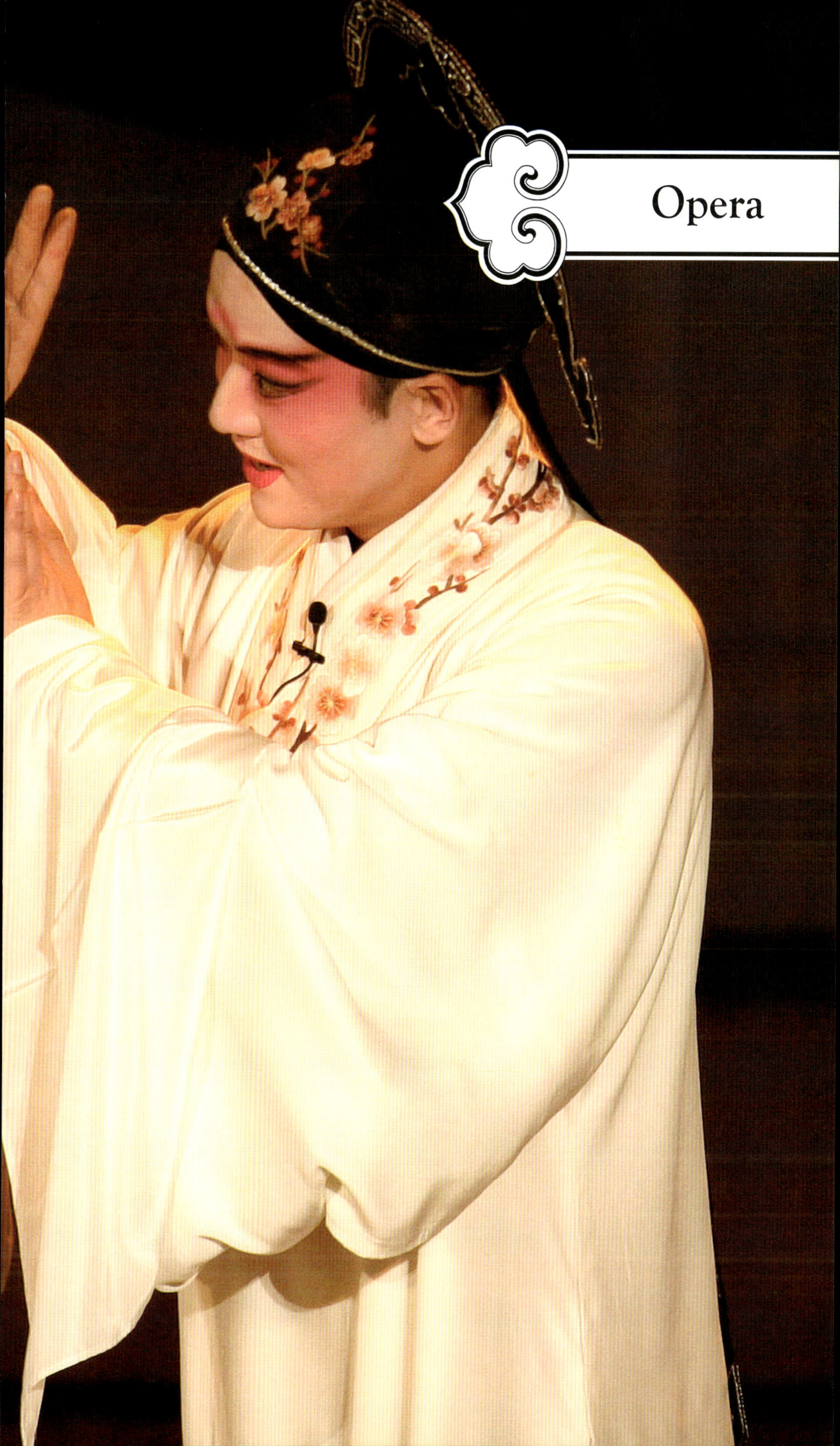

Four Basic Skills: The World as a Stage

Chinese opera is a stylized art form that incorporates literature, music, dance, painting, martial arts, acrobatics, performing and other elements. The three major ancient dramatic cultures of the world include the Greek tragicomedy, the Indian Sanskrit play and Chinese opera, all of which enjoy a great and glorious history. However, the Indian Sanskrit play has already faded into history, and the former flourishing of the Greek tragicomedy can only be imagined by what remains of the once-grand theaters. Luckily, Chinese opera has survived and been refined both in form and content, with more than 300 types and thousands of playlists. Today, both in large cities and in rural areas, various types of operas are performed often, vividly depicting the fluctuations in life. Chinese opera inspires audiences into reflecting on the great changes in history, perhaps bringing to mind the metaphor that the stage is a miniature world and the world, a grand stage. Chinese opera is a stylized performing art, which relies heavily on role-playing, mu-

A theater during the reign of Emperor Guangxu of the Qing Dynasty.

Peking Opera was fashionable during this period, and the theater-goers included nobles, officials and the ordinary people alike.

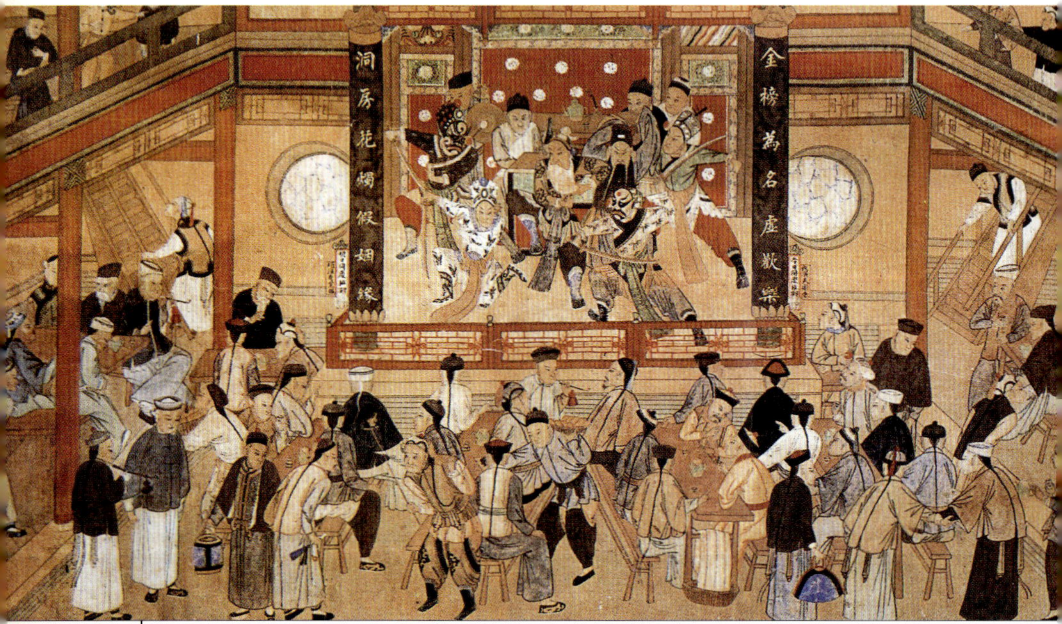

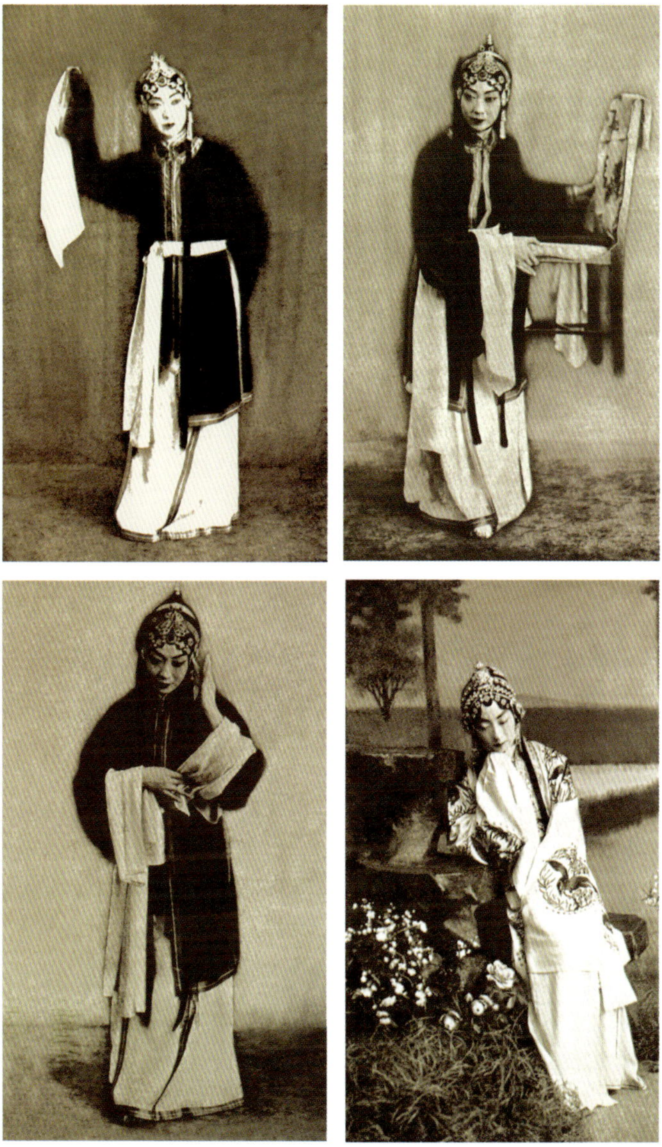

Chinese opera is a highly stylized art form.

The pictures illustrate four postures: looking, picking-up, thinking, lying, all performed by Mei Lanfang.

sical dialogue and dance movements to express the plot. To sum up, the music-dance structure usually includes four major skills: singing, reciting, posing and fighting. Singing is the major way for the characters to communicate their feelings or to narrate the story, and it is designed to fulfill the necessary characterization and emotional development. With graceful musical images to add to the audience's pleasure, singing is usually the decisive

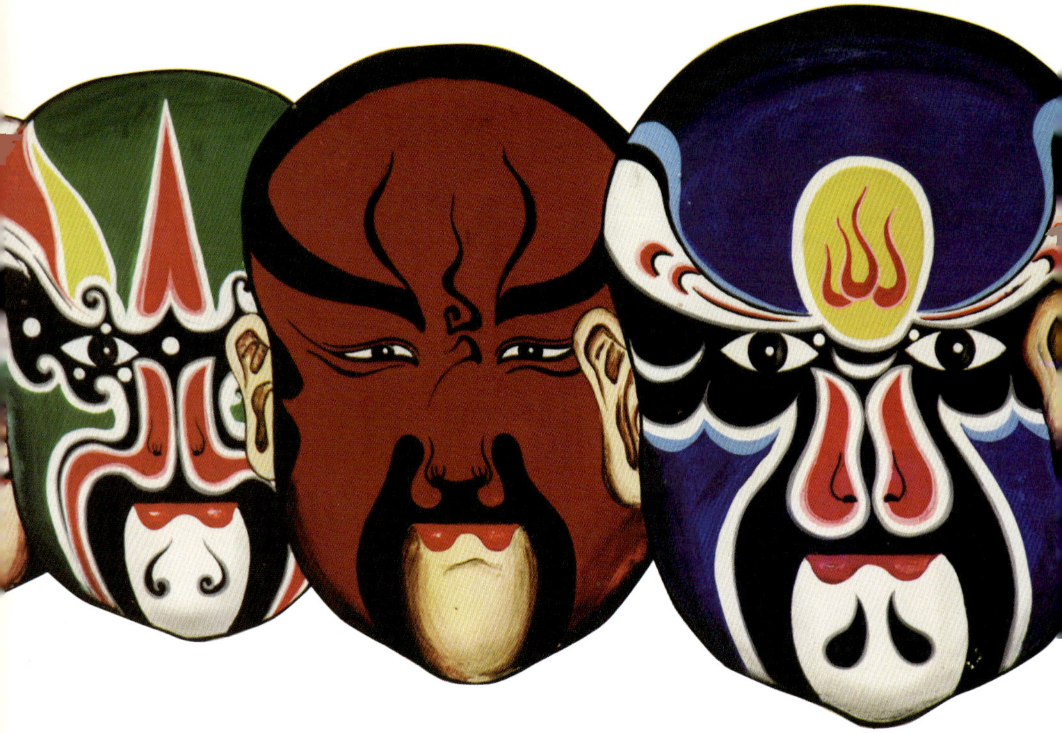

Types of facial makeup in Chinese opera.

Facial makeup is the unique plastic art of Chinese opera, and it makes use of colors and designs to express in exaggerated forms the loyalty and treachery, good and evil, beauty and ugliness, and dispositional characteristics. During the course of its development, there have emerged several basic stereotypes of facial makeup.

factor in making or marring the actor's performance, and different ways of singing, even with the same opera playlist have led to the formation of different schools. Recitation—the dialogue or monologue of the characters—has adopted a poetic and musical language of drama. The actors adapt their reciting first to the particular play and then to the features of the character and the development of the plot so as to convey the delicate and elusive changes in rhythm and, thereby, to be melodious and realistic. Posing, a general term for the gestures, facial expressions, manner and poise, constitutes the main part of the performance and of stage movement. Fighting includes dance movement or the artistic adaptation of traditional martial arts and is represented by imitating either a duel or a scene of war. The organic combination of the four skills forms the most striking feature of Chinese opera.

Although Chinese opera pays tribute to reality and the sense of life, it is not so in the actual performance. "戏(*xi*),"the Chinese character for drama, can mean literally "being fictitious." The time and space of dramatic performance are often imagined. The stage therefore can be a moving space: the entrance and exit of the actor can signify changes in time and place. For example, an actor walking around the stage playing a general (and four additional walk-on roles) might be indicating the change of one site to another, which might be hundreds of miles away. A lady's gesture of lighting a lamp may mean the darkening of the day; the gesture of blowing it out after singing for a while may mean the dawning of the day, and the two gestures may suggest the passing of a whole day and night, which happens quickly in real time. The characters and their movements can also be imagined. Take the walk-on roles as an example. Although actors in these roles always appear on stage with similar face, costume and movement, they represent different characters in different plays. Meanwhile, although there are usually just four walk-on roles, they can represent thousands upon thousands of men and horses. The movements are also imagined. If the actor wants to climb stairs, he just needs to raise his clothes and one foot—no stairs are shown on stage. This device can also be found in the use of stage props. When the curtain is drawn, there might be

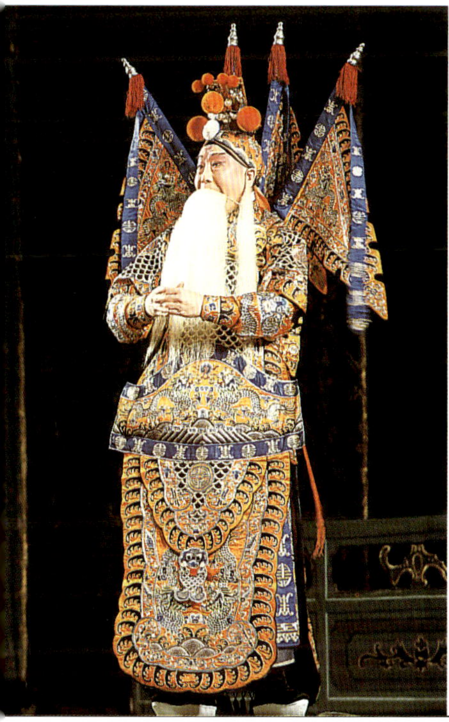

Laosheng

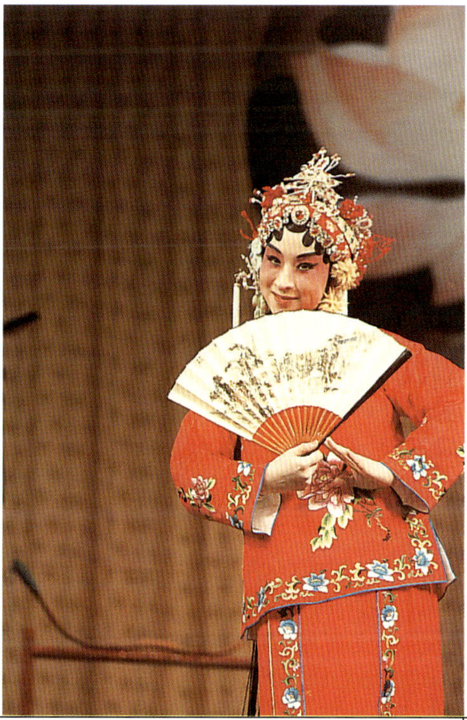

Huadan

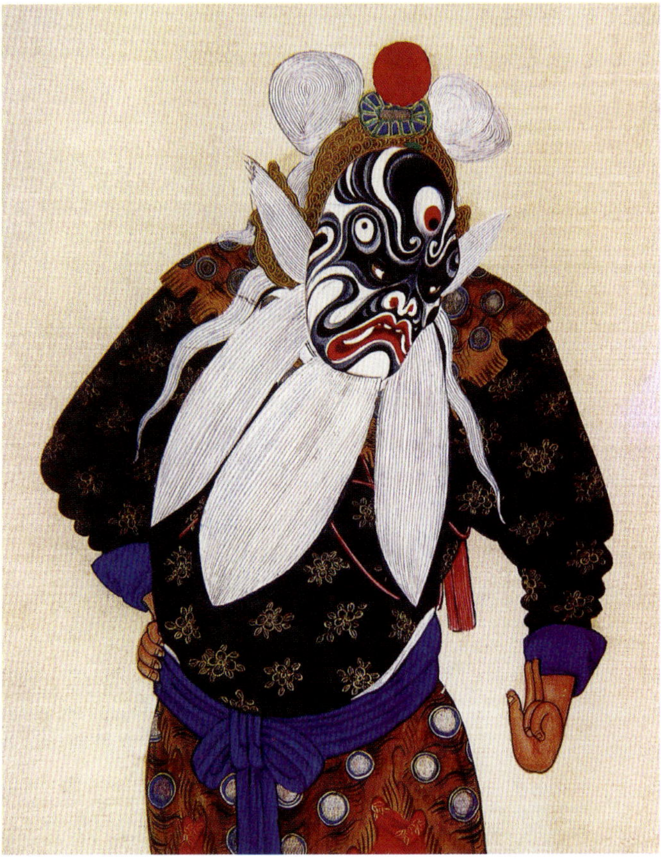

Jing

only one table and two chairs. But do not overlook these two seemingly unimportant objects. The color of the table-curtain denotes the rank of the character, and the arrangement of the table and chairs suggests the scene. A horsewhip might symbolize a fine horse, and two oars might symbolize a boat. As for a river and clouds, which are not easy to represent, two small flags on the table, painted with images of water and clouds, might be used. Waving the flags might symbolize the rising wind, the scudding clouds and swelling rivers.

Chinese opera takes on a strong stylization, which can be seen first in the makeup of the characters, especially in the types of facial makeup. A popular song, "Singing the Types of Facial Makeup," is so well known that even many foreign friends sing it with great enthusiasm.

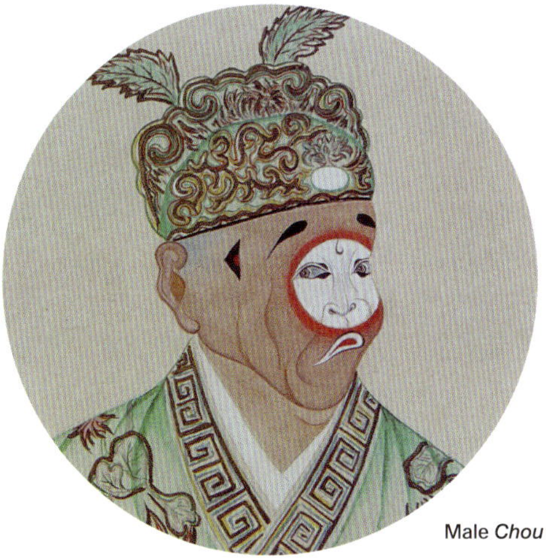

Male *Chou*

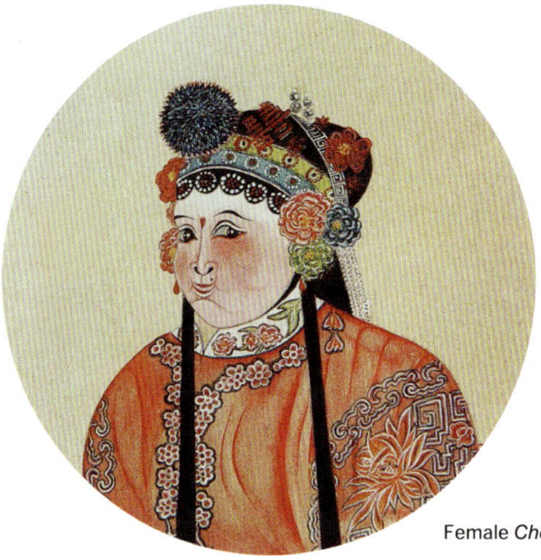

Female *Chou*

You can easily identify the status and disposition of the characters from their facial makeup. The makeup for the honest and kind-hearted characters is carefully painted to enhance their solemnity and sense of justice while the makeup for crafty, evil characters is designed to be as ugly as possible. The color of the makeup is also emblematic of the character's disposition: red is used for honest and faithful officials, white is used to paint treacherous officials, blue is used to paint irritable characters and black is used for upright, unselfish characters. Thus, the audience can easily discern the character's temperament from the clearly classified and vividly painted makeup. For example, the makeup for Guan Yu, a renowned general in the period of the Three Kingdoms who was famous for his valor and faithfulness, is painted red, while the makeup for Cao Cao, a famous political figure in the same period can only be painted white because he's described as a crafty, evil villain in *The Romance of the Three Kingdoms*, one of the most widely circulated novels in China. In fact, Cao Cao is in Chinese history an important statesman of great talent and penetrating vision. Paradoxically, despite later historians' effort to do Cao Cao justice, he is still painted white. For many Chinese, the impressions formed from the facial makeup cannot be easily changed, and white therefore has come to be the color that stands for craftiness and evilness on stage.

Let's get acquainted with the roles in Chinese opera. The types of the roles ("*Hangdang*" in technical terms) usually include *Sheng, Dan, Jing* and *Chou,* which can be subdivided according to gender, age and disposition. On stage, these roles have their own appropriate attire and facial makeup, which might present certain difficulties for newcomers to Chinese opera.

Sheng, male roles, are characterized by the handsome features of the facial makeup and can be subdivided according to age and status of the characters into *Laosheng, Xiaosheng, Wusheng* and so on. *Dan,* female roles, can be subdivided according to their age and status into *Qingyi, Huadan, Daomadan, Laodan* and so on. *Jing* refers to the male roles where the actor wears paint on his face. *Chou* refers to amusing, humorous or ugly roles and can be played by males and females.

With this basic knowledge of Chinese opera, differentiating the roles on stage and "entering" the play is easier. Now, please look at the stage photos and try to figure out their dispositions by the facial makeup and costumes.

The History: Over 2,000 Years

Chinese opera originated in ancient song and dance. Around 800 BC, there emerged "优(*you*)," who were kept by the nobles for their own entertainment. These people, usually males, good at singing, dancing and impersonations, developed into the earliest actors of Chinese opera. According to an age-old and widely spread story about a famous actor, Meng, these people could sometimes exert influence through their performance. Sun Shu'ao, one of the Chu Kingdom's high officials and on whom the king of Chu relied heavily, died and his poverty-stricken children went hungry. Seeing this, actor Meng dressed up as Sun and imitated him. Startled, even the king thought Sun had come back to life. In showing his sentiment for Sun, the king ordered Meng to hold Sun's former position but Meng refused, saying that he could not see any good in being an official because although Sun had been honest during his lifetime in performing his duties and did not seek any private fortune, Sun's family still went hungry. Realizing the actor's true intent, the king sent his solicitude to Sun's family immediately and raised Sun's boy to a high-ranking level. This story might have been the beginning of the stage performance of opera in China, and the phrase "actor Meng in costume" was thereafter used to refer to the performance of opera.

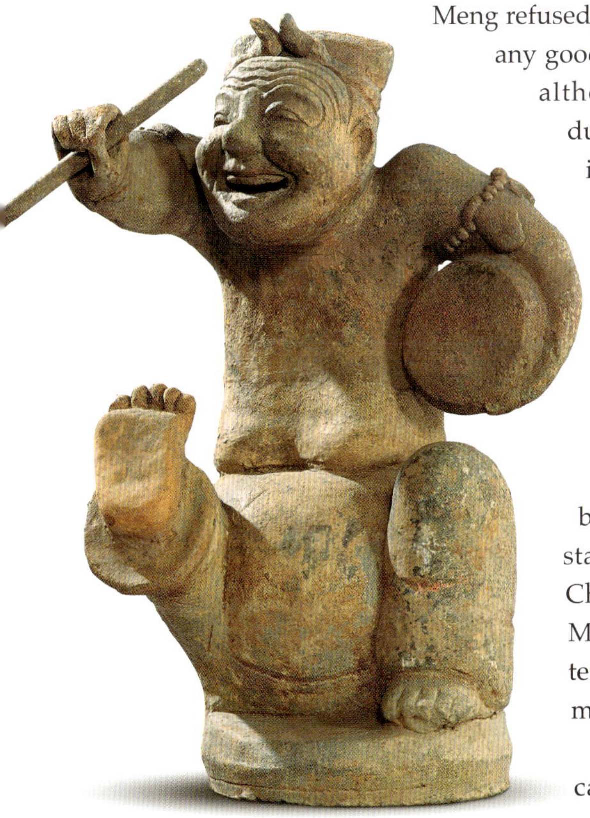

Talking-singing figurine with a drum, East Han Dynasty.

In the Tang Dynasty there came into existence "*Canjun*

opera," characterized by its humor. "*Canjun*" was originally a rank for minor officials and there was indeed a certain "*canjun*" who was punished for being corrupt. In order to use him as an example to the others and to thereby stop all possible corruption, the emperor ordered one "*you* (actor)" to dress up as "that *canjun*" and another actor to mock and satirize him. So, two actors were first involved in the performance. Later the number of the actors gradually increased and the performance became more and more complex. The main purpose, however, was still to satirize and reprimand through amusing gestures and remarks.

Emperor Xuanzong of the Tang Dynasty, although a man of daring strategy, had a musical temperament and was very fond of singing and dancing. He established a special institute called "the Pear Garden (*Liyuan*)" as a place to train actors. Moreover, he selected actors personally, gave them guidance and even performed on stage himself. This theatrical troupe was actually the first opera school in China. Actors in later times referred to this theatrical circle as "the Pear Garden" and called themselves students of the garden. In the past, a statue of the founder of the opera could usually be found in theaters where the actors could pay their respects. Guess who the founder was? Emperor Xuanzong!

Along with great development of the urban economy in the Song Dynasty appeared recreational places frequented by city people. The folk songs, dances, the genre of talking and singing, and comic plays showed tendencies of merging, and "a variety play (*Zaju*)" came into being, which became further refined in the Yuan Dynasty; "Yuan *Zaju*" embodied the peak in Chinese opera history. In the Yuan Dynasty, since scholars were the least respected in society and their social status was no higher than that of beggars, they had no opportunity to become officials through an academic route and had to focus their talents on artistic endeavors. Thanks to their personal misfortune, the Yuan *Zaju* reached unprecedented heights and from this came a number of

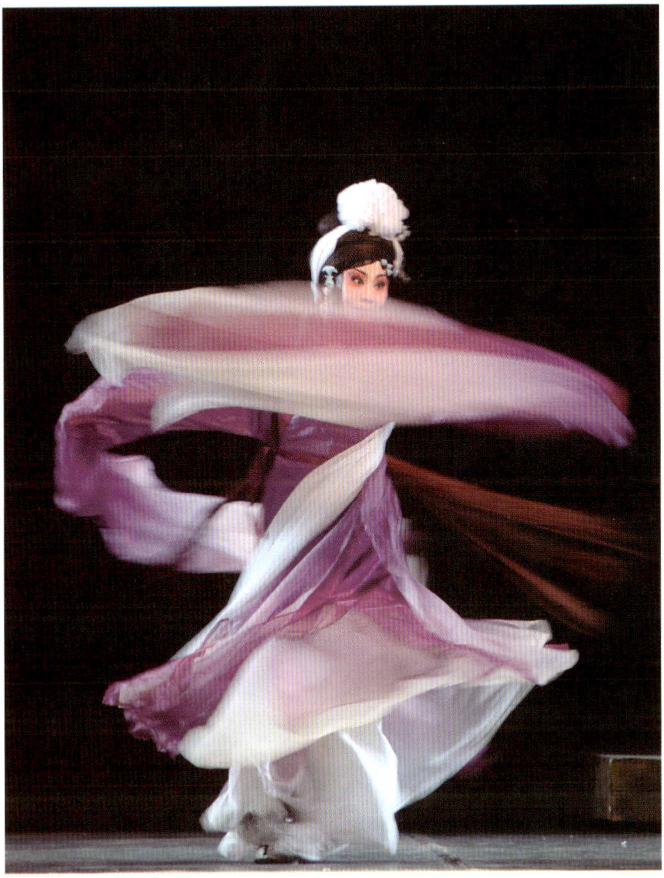

Stage photo of *Dou E Yuan*

master playwrights. Take Guan Hanqing for instance. His tragedy, *Dou E Yuan* (*The Injustice to Dou E*), is perhaps the best-known play in China for its stirring effect. Wang Shifu created the well-known "*Xi Xiang Ji* (*The West Chamber Romance*)," which provides a vivid description of the intensely sentimental feelings of young love and continues to be a favorite play. Another playwright, Ji Junxiang, though not so well-known in his native land, was widely known in the Western world for his play, *Chao's Orphan*. This play is perhaps the first to be introduced to the Western audience: in the 18th century, a French priest translated and introduced it to Europe; later the famous French author F.M.A. Voltaire adapted it into *The Chinese Orphan* and put it on stage in Paris; afterwards, the famous German poet and thinker, J.W.

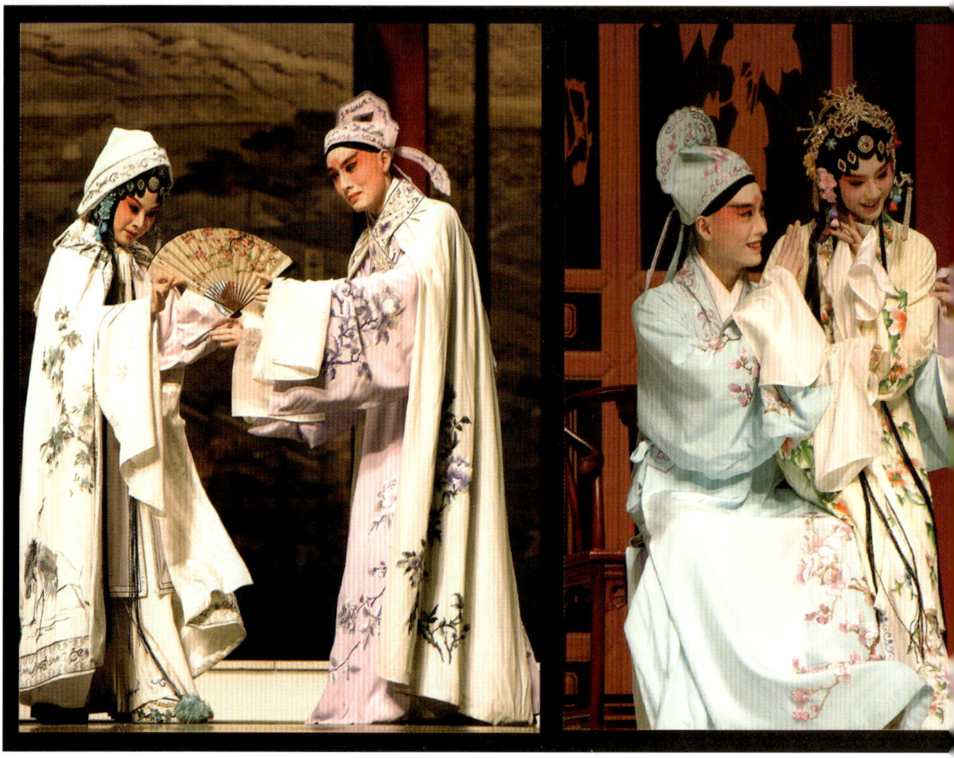

Stage photo of *The Peach Blossom Fan*

von Goethe adapted it into a tragedy, *Elpenor*. Therefore, *Chao's Orphan* is perhaps the only Chinese play to be accepted by 18th century Europe; in addition, it shares a similar plot with Shakespeare's *Hamlet*.

Variations in the dramatic art occurred in the Ming and Qing dynasties, and "*Chuanqi* (romance)" replaced "*Zaju*" as the new, dominant mode of drama. "*Chuanqi* (传奇)," which taken literally means "strange and odd stories" —complicated and elusive yet moving stories that take place among human beings, ghosts and gods. *Chuanqi* usually have elegant verses and greater scales, and many masterpieces have been created in this form. The performances became more skillful and were usually conducted in *Kunqu* opera. Tang Xianzu, one of the greatest playwrights in the Ming Dynasty, wrote the famous drama, *The Peony Pavilion*. Kong Shangren, a playwright in the beginning of the Qing Dynasty, wrote the famous *The Peach Blossom Fan*, which is set along the Qinhuai

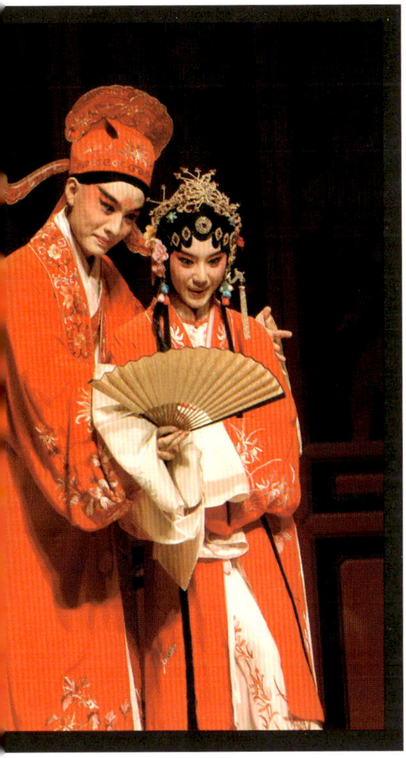

River in Nanjing. Located in the most prosperous part of Nanjing, an important city ever since the Three Kingdoms, the Qinhuai River has witnessed many personal joys, sorrows and national fluctuations, and provides a suitable setting for a moving love story between a singing girl and a renowned scholar. Facing a national life-and-death situation, the two lovers cannot control their own fates and are doomed to great sorrow. With fractured families and a collapsing dynasty, the two lovers end up in Taoist temples, greatly disillusioned with life and engaged in religious pursuits. Apart from the theme of love, this play has another theme, the breaking down of a dynasty, which expresses the author's deep contemplation of history and national destiny. In fact, the combination of entertainment and education, with special emphasis on moral inculcation and cultivating a sense of national duty, is a striking feature of Chinese opera.

Kunqu Opera: Orchid in the Garden of Operas

In May 2001, the United Nations Educational, Scientific and Cultural Organization (UNESCO) issued the first list of "the Oral and Intangible Heritage Masterpieces of Humanity," and *Kunqu* opera, being one, made China one of the 19 countries to be bestowed with this honor. *Kunqu,* also named *"kunqiang"* or *"kunju,"* is named after its birthplace, the Mountain Kun, in Jiangsu Province. With a history of more than 600 years, it is credited with "the forerunner and the master of all forms of opera in China." *Kunqu* is noted for its smooth and elegant style, fine and exquisite expression, song-and-dance-based performance, and also for its specifically designed movements. Regarded as a prime example of Chinese opera, *Kunqu* has benefited many local operas.

If you are familiar with the Chinese orchid, then it can function as a good metaphor to describe the features of *Kunqu.* The orchid usually grows in a quiet valley among mountains, has only a few leaves and is subtle in its blooming. Its enigmatic and pleasing scent may surprise you. If you grow this orchid, you will have an opportunity to experience its fresh fragrance. Because of

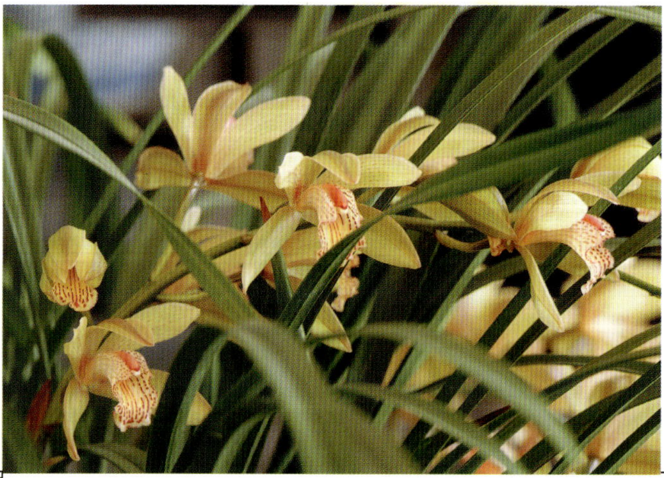

The graceful orchid

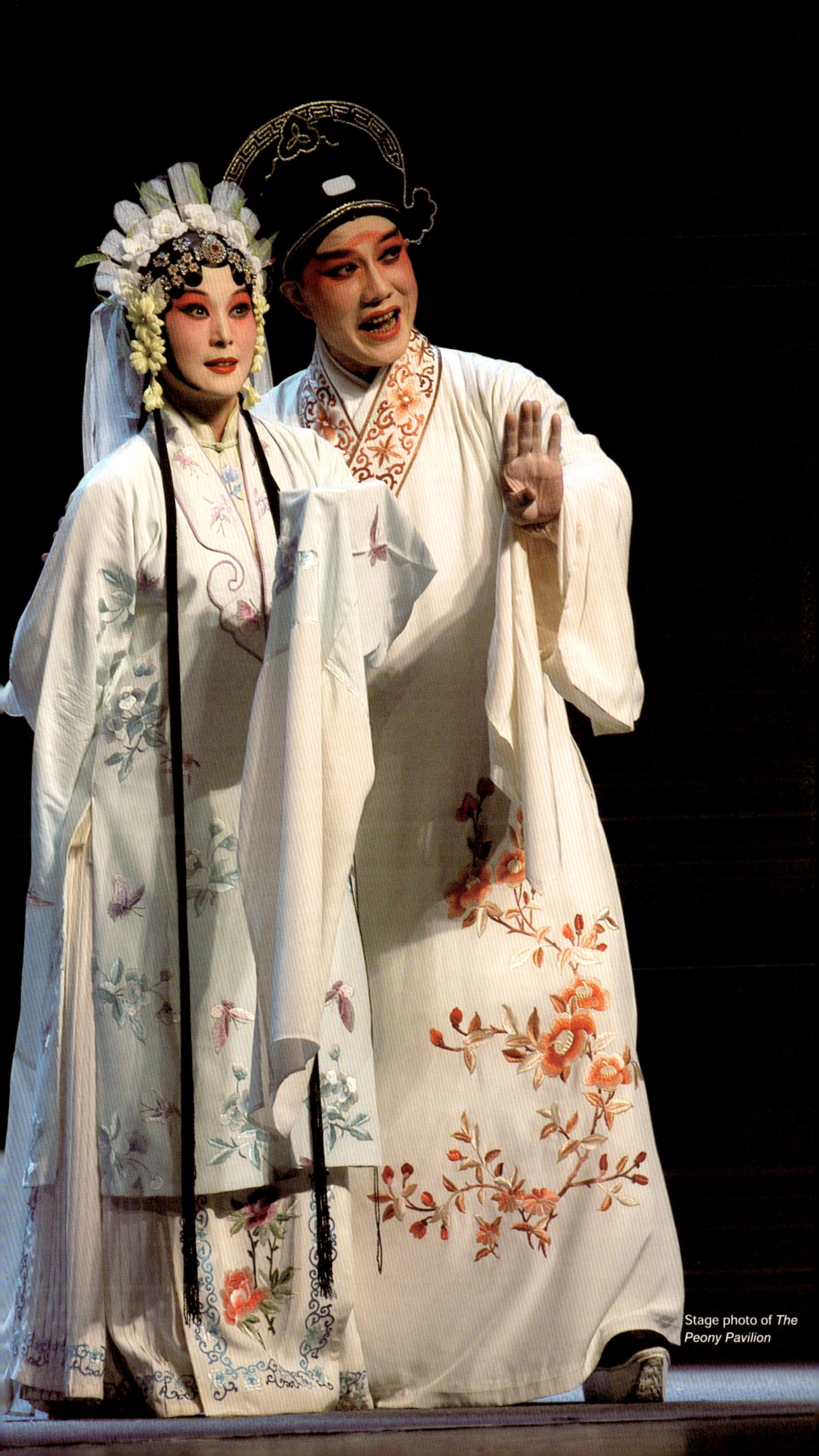

Stage photo of *The Peony Pavilion*

these qualities, the Chinese orchid has often been called "the gentleman among flowers." *Kunqu* might seem odd now, but keeping this metaphor in mind, you will come to enjoy its unique beauty through observing and appreciating its beauty, for *Kunqu* has been called "the orchid among various forms of operas," which, like the orchid, also has an elegant, innate beauty.

The Peony Pavilion, on stage in China for over 400 years, retains its vitality. A young lady from a wealthy and noble family dreams of meeting a handsome young scholar by chance, but she becomes lovesick afterwards. Her love for the young man in her dreams is so strong that she falls seriously ill and dies a quick, reluctant death. Years later, her dreamed-of lover visits her burial site and falls in love with her ghost. The pure, strong love between them brings her back to life and the lovers eventually marry. This is an intensely romantic tragicomedy of love, in which the strength of love between young people, absurd though it may be, is fully expressed. Since its existence, this play has attracted countless young passionate lovers. According to the written history of the Ming Dynasty, an actress playing the heroine was so moved by the love story that she identified completely with the heroine and died in great sorrow.

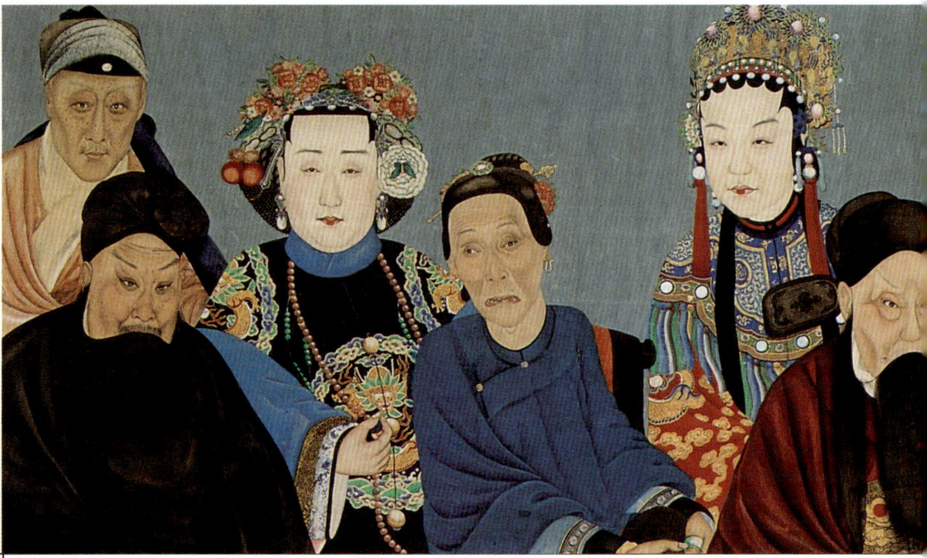

Peking Opera: The National Drama

The mention of Chinese opera might remind foreign friends immediately of Peking opera, which to them is almost the same as the Chinese opera. This is a sure indication of the influence of Peking opera in China and even in the world. This impression, though not quite exact, is not far from the truth: Peking opera, which epitomizes Chinese culture and art, is certainly the essence of China. If martial arts can be viewed as the "national arts," then Peking opera can be viewed as the "national drama."

Peking opera became known around 1840 in Peking (Beijing); hence, its name. In actuality, its development was based on certain southern operas, which accounts for its popularity among not only the northern but also southern audiences. Of the 300 or more lists of Chinese opera, Peking opera, though with the shortest history, is the most influential, attracts the largest audience and offers the most lists. Peking opera is also well-liked by foreign friends, which, in their eyes, like the Great Wall, is a symbol of Chinese culture and civilization.

Like other types of opera, Peking opera pays special

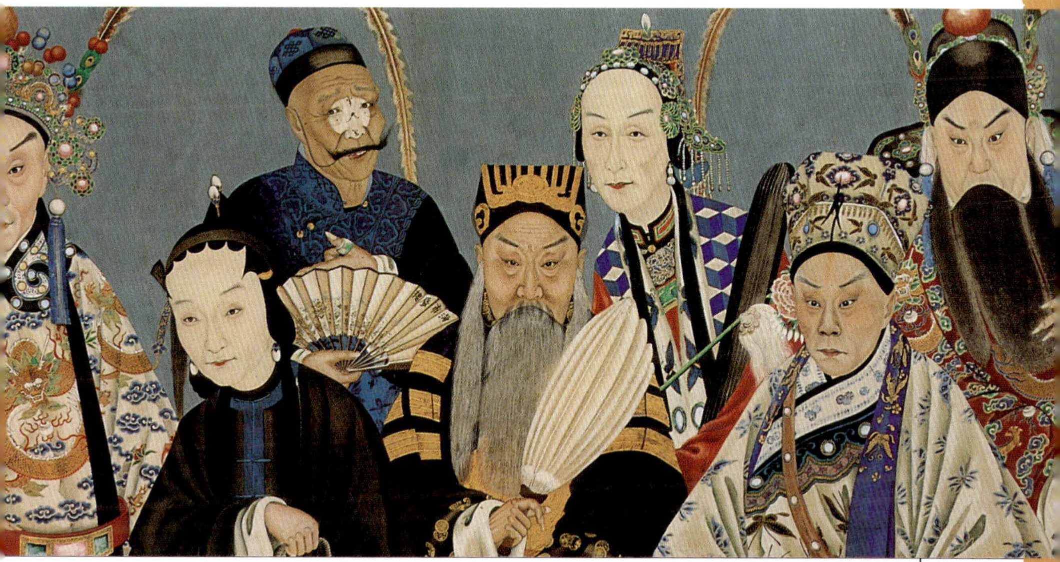

Part of the painting, *Tongguang Shisan Jue*, which describes the 13 most famous actors of Peking opera during the Tongzhi and Guangxu periods in the Qing Dynasty.

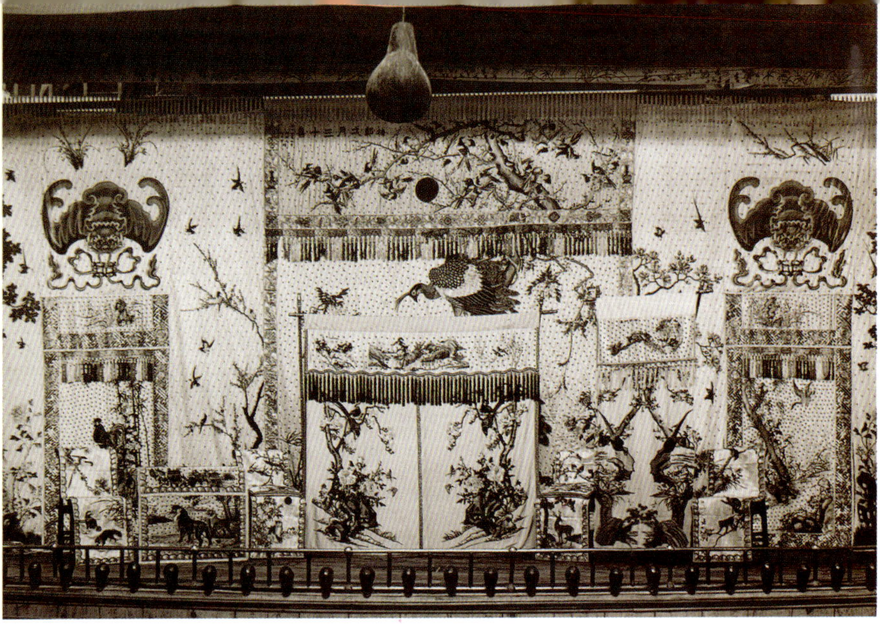

The stage setting of Peking Opera.

attention to singing, reciting, posing and fighting, the four major criteria that audiences use in evaluating and enjoying the performance. Singing here refers to the "*Changqiang*" of Peking opera, including operatic tunes and lyrics. The former was modeled on the "*Xipi*" of *Huiju* opera and on "*Erhuang*" of *Hanju* opera, and was called "*Pihuang*," which is characterized by boldness, resounding and tonality, and also by the gentle exquisiteness of Chinese folk songs. The latter, greatly influenced by ancient Chinese poetry, is refined and elegant, and has high literary value. The last words of every sentence form a rhyme so that the singing displays pleasing cadence, rhythm and melody. According to the sex and age of the characters, the actors and actresses use different voices. Old male and female characters sing in their genuine voice, which is much like their daily voice; young female characters use falsetto, which is sharp and piercing; and middle-aged males use both kinds of voice.

Apart from singing, the characters must perform "*Daobai* (spoken performance)," which belongs to the reciting part of the opera. "*Bai*," which means "speaking" in ancient Chinese, is divided into "*Jingbai*" and "*Yunbai.*" The former means literally a performance language based on the Peking dialect, but with necessary artistic modification, exaggeration and beautification. The latter, "*Yunbai*," by contrast, assimilates more ancient speech sounds and certain sounds of the southern dialects and takes on greater rhythmic quality while maintaining a distance from everyday pronunciation. When viewing a Peking opera, judge for yourself: if the characters' pronunciation sounds like standard Chinese pronunciation, it is "*Jingbai;*" otherwise, it is "*Yunbai.*"

Foreign friends who have just begun familiarizing themselves with Peking opera might feel strange about the exaggeration and stylization of the actors' and actresses' body movements, for they are very different from those in ordinary life. This, however, constitutes one major feature of Peking opera, and is what the actors' and actresses' "posing" aims for. For example, the "orchid-shaped finger gesture" of the "*Dan,*" with the thumb placed on the side of the first part of the middle finger, the index finger straight ahead, the ring and little fingers slightly up, makes the hand look like an orchid and this displays feminine charm and grace. Moreover, the "posing" in Peking opera demands that every gesture and every body movement be performed to the rhythm of the accompanying music. The "fighting" in Peking opera, subdivided into fighting empty-handed and fighting with weapons, is derived from Chinese martial arts, but undergoes certain beautification and takes on obvious stylization.

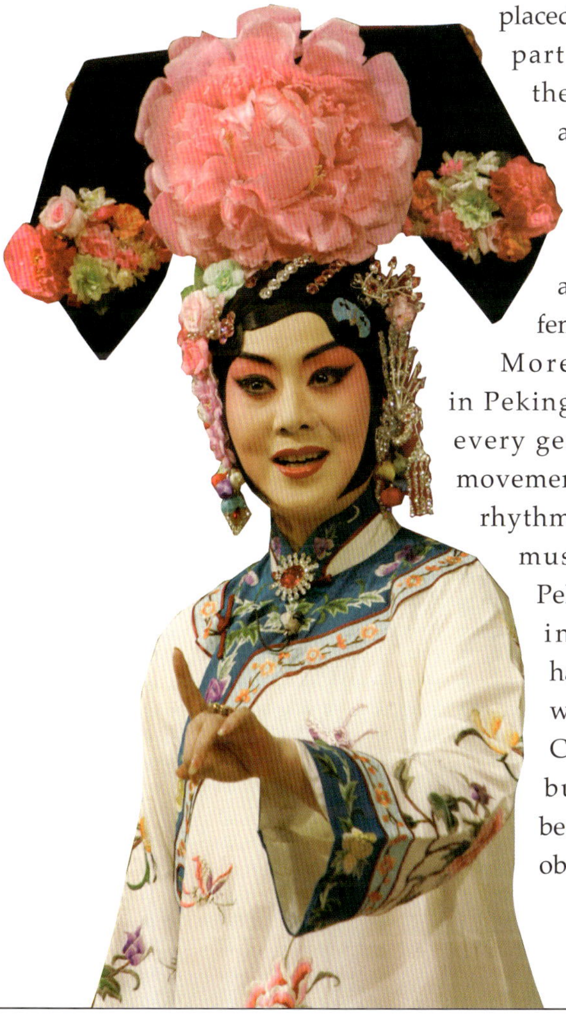

Orchid-shaped finger gesture of the *Dan*

Mei Lanfang: Introducing Peking Opera to the World

As far as Peking opera is concerned, Mei Lanfang (1894–1961) is a household name. Ranking the first of the "Four Famous *Dan*" roles and born into a renowned Beijing family with a tradition of performing opera, he is without doubt an outstanding artist in Peking opera. With more than half a century's practice on stage, and with an eye on legacy and innovation, he embodied the essence of Chinese opera, created many unforgettable vivid artistic images and accumulated many excellent lists of plays. More important, he improved the singing and performing of "*Dan*" of Peking opera and established a new school of performance, the Mei School, giving it a unique and a masterly foundation of performance.

The Mei School has been acclaimed as a milestone

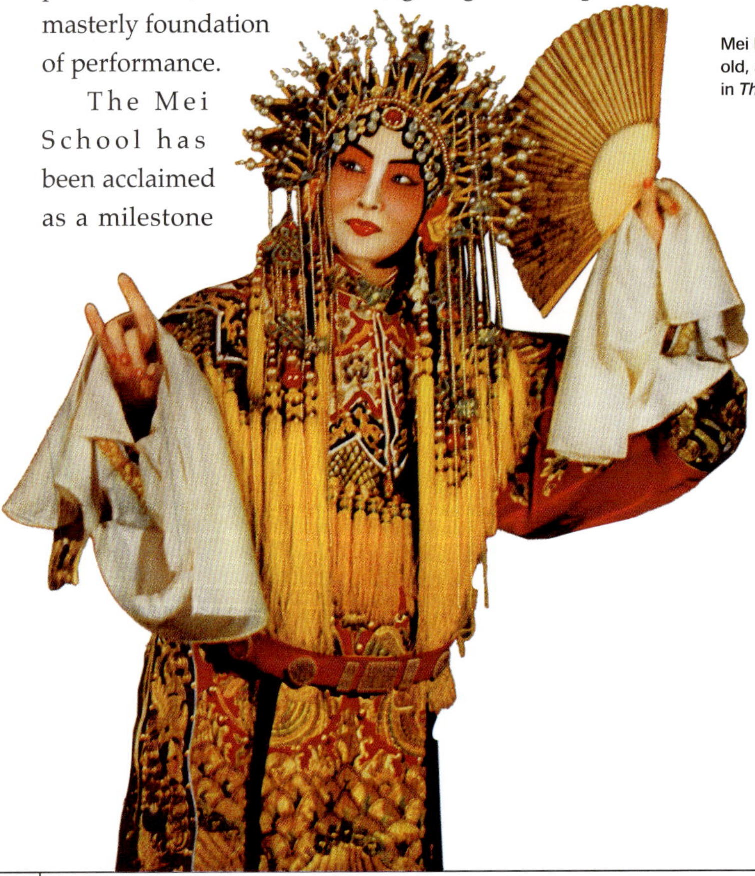

Mei Lanfang, already old, acting as Lady Yang in *The Drunken Beauty.*

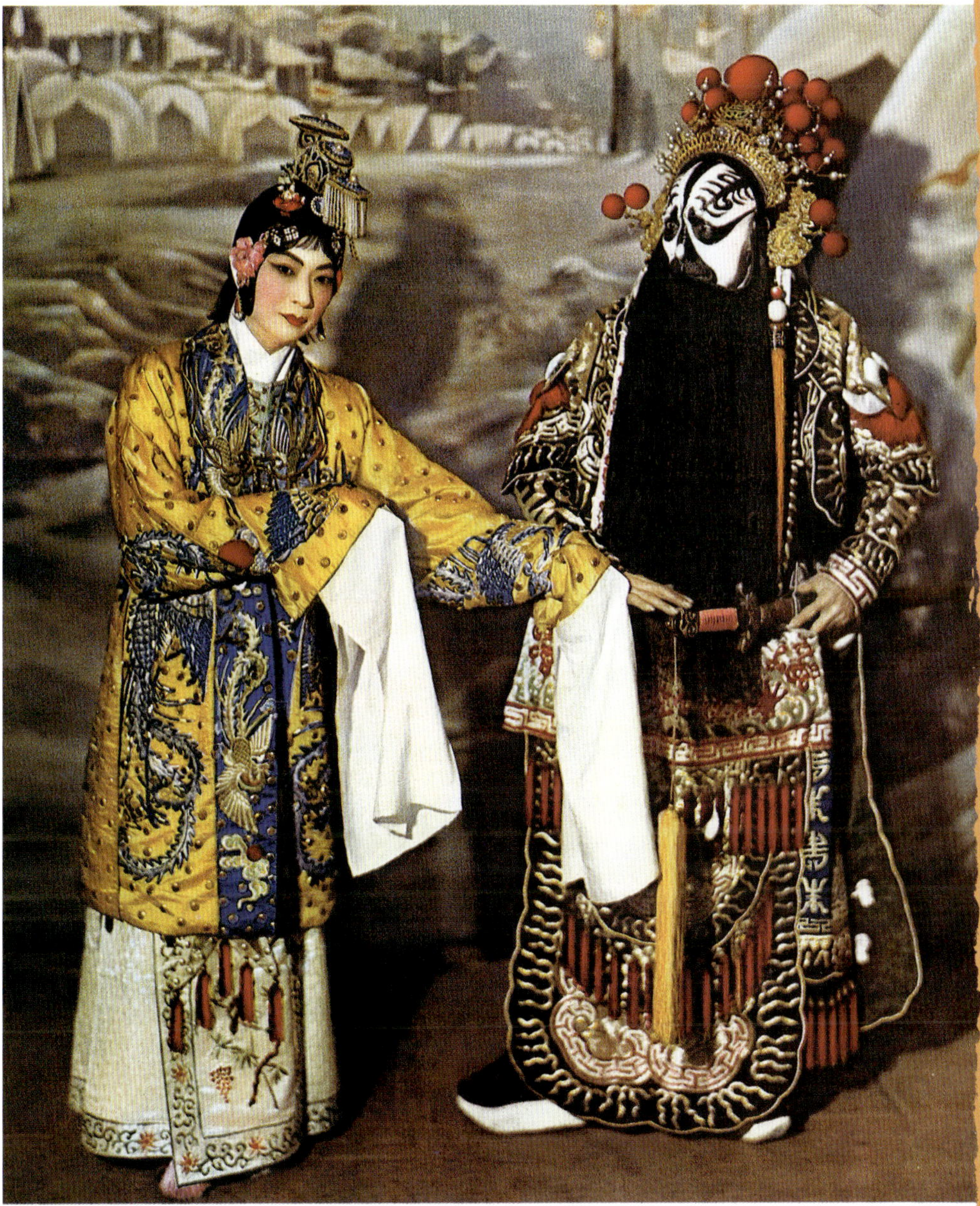

Mei Lanfang and Yang Xiaolou, another very famous Peking opera artist, in *King Xiang Yu's Farewell to His Beloved* (*Farewell My Concubine*).

in the development of Peking opera. If you have a chance to visit Beijing, you are strongly urged to visit No. 9, Huguosi Street in Xicheng District, where the Mei Lanfang Museum is located. The cultural relics on display will help you to better understand the mind and art of this great artist.

Mei Lanfang enjoys worldwide fame, mainly because of his performances in a number of foreign countries. He visited Japan three times (1919, 1924, 1956), the United States of America once (1930) and the former Soviet Union twice (1935, 1952). These performances won him great fame and he was even regarded as the incarnation of beauty, but, more important, his activities improved the understanding of Peking opera to foreign audiences, making it one of the important branches of the world's dramatic arts. In 1935 on his visit to the Soviet Union he met the famous Soviet dramatist Konstantin Stanislavsky and the famous German dramatist Bertolt Brecht, both of whom expressed their high appreciation of his amazing and incredible performance. Also, they both agreed that Mei's performance was what they had been looking for in their art and thereby provided a fruitful supplement to their respective methods of performance. Because each of them had their own conception of art, and stood for different schools of drama, the three different schools represented by them are viewed as the three significant systems of drama in the world.

Of Mei's masterpieces, two are widely known: *The Drunken Beauty* and *King Xiang Yu's Farewell to His Beloved* (*Farewell My Concubine*). The latter depicts a portrayal of Xiang Yu, one of the famous heroes in Chinese history, his concubine, Yuji, and centers around Xiang's military failure. The tragedy of a hero is often twofold: the failure of his career and the end of his life. Meanwhile, this failure also means great pain and terror to his beloved. In this play, Mei Lanfang acts as Yuji, and, according to the plot, he needs to express exactly and exquisitely the feminine pain and sense of terror so as to reflect the hero's grief under dire circumstances. Mei's talent as a performer is completely displayed in this masterpiece, making Yuji one of the most attractive characters on the Chinese opera stage.

Local Operas: The Significance of Gongs and Drums

Since free development of different forms and styles of Chinese opera has long been the case, many local types of opera have existed along with Peking opera in much of the country. Many, such as *Yuju, Yueju* and *Huangmeiju*, have enjoyed nationwide popularity because of famous plays or actors.

Yuju, also called "Henan clapper opera," prevails in Henan, Hebei, Shandong and other provinces. In 1998, the Disney Company produced its 36th classic motion picture movie, Mulan, which is modeled upon an age-old story about a girl who disguises herself as a young man and serves in the imperial army in place of her father. Her bravery wins victory for the nation and fame for herself. The story was first made into a long poem and later adapted into a *Yuju* play for stage performance. Hua Mulan thus became a household image in China. Chang Xiangyu, the famous actress in *Yuju* opera, succeeded in embodying the persistence, confidence, gracefulness and shyness of this heroine. One of the famous arias in

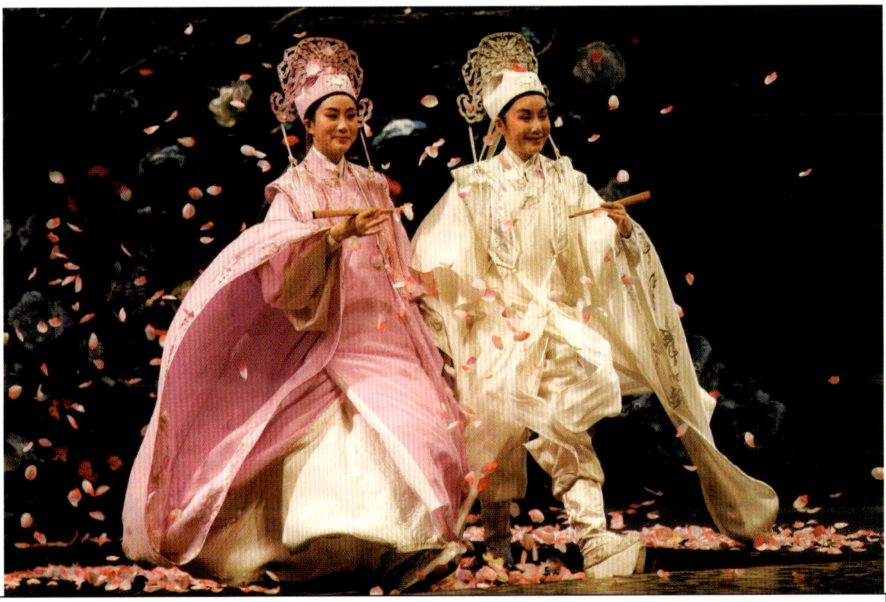

Stage photo of the famous "Changing into Butterflies," an act of *Liang Shanbo and Zhu Yingtai (The Butterfly Lovers), Yueju opera.*

the play, *Who Can Say Women Are Inferior?* eulogizes the virtues of the hardworking endurance and persistence of the kind-hearted Chinese women, and is so well-liked by audiences that many foreign friends who are fond of Chinese culture can sing part or all of this aria.

Yueju is the opera prevalent mainly in Zhejiang and surrounding provinces. It is famous for its graceful performance and the most widely known play is *Liang Shanbo and Zhu Yingtai* (*The Butterfly Lovers*). This play, which we have already talked about in our discussion of music, depicts the moving love between the two young people. The section where these two lovers change into beautiful butterflies and fly freely among flowers is the most moving part.

Huangmei opera, prevalent mainly in Anhui Province, has produced two famous plays, *The Goddess's Marriage* and *The Cowherd and the Weaving Girl*. Both plays depict love between goddess and man and are familiar in China. One aria in the former play lauds a beautiful girl who, in pursuit of pure, innocent love, is willing to relinquish her status as goddess in order to live with a good-natured farmer. Even in the remote areas of China, this song can be frequently heard.

Chuanju opera, mainly prevalent in Sichuan and

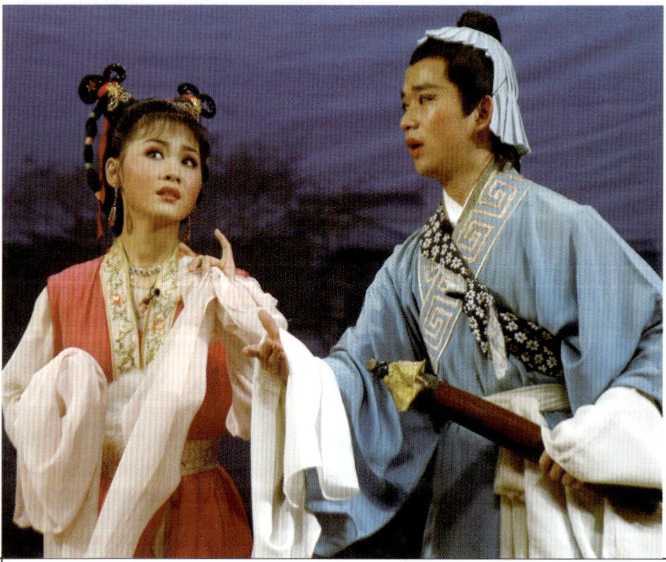

Stage photo of *The Goddess's Marriage*, *Huangmei* opera.

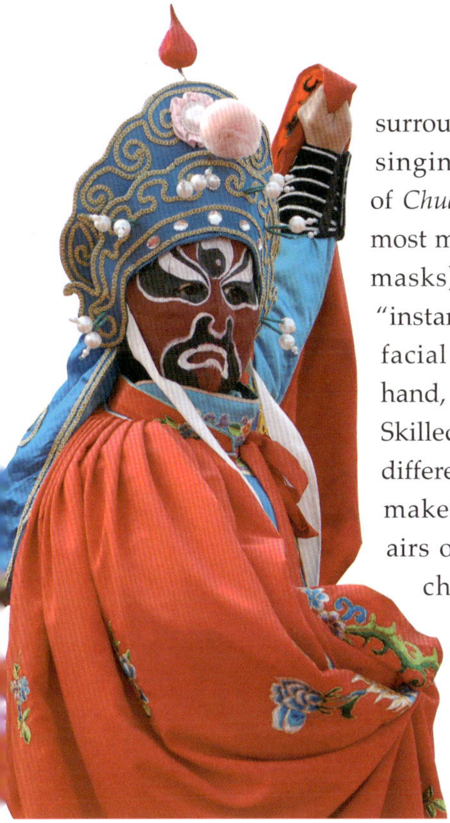

surrounding areas, is famous for its resounding singing, humor and rich flavor. Many types of *Chuanju* have their own special "tricks," the most miraculous of which is "*bianlian* (changing masks)," leaving audiences amazed. It is an "instant" art, where the actors can change the facial makeup within a moment of raising a hand, flicking the sleeve, or swaying the head. Skilled actors can produce more than a dozen different looks in less than 20 seconds. Different makeup can stand for different expressions, airs or moods so that sudden changes in the characters' mental states, for example, horror, despair, anger or even treachery, can be represented. The purpose of adopting this technique is to imitate the dynamic changes of the characters' interior world.

Changing masks in *Chuanju* opera.

This "trick" adds much to its charm.

The leather-silhouette show is a unique dramatic form. Actors, while manipulating leather- or papercut-silhouettes of human figures, with shadows cast on a white curtain, sing to accompanying music. With a history of more than 1,000 years, it is widespread in China. Many celebrities often write in their memoirs about the joys of watching leather-silhouette shows in their childhood. But with the development and expansion of television, cinema and the Internet, this form of entertainment is gradually fading, though recollections linger of the simple and deep pleasure it has imparted.

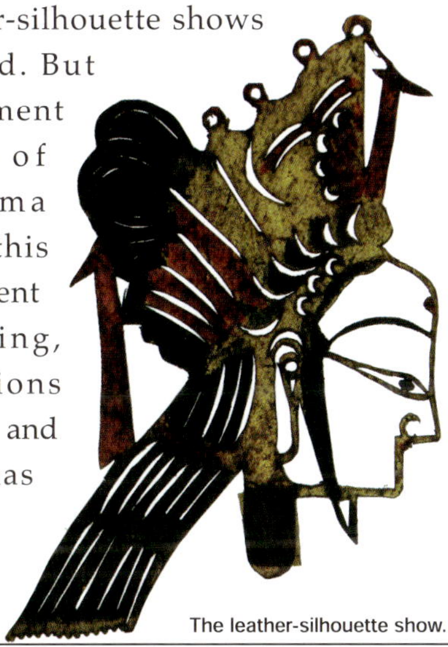

The leather-silhouette show.

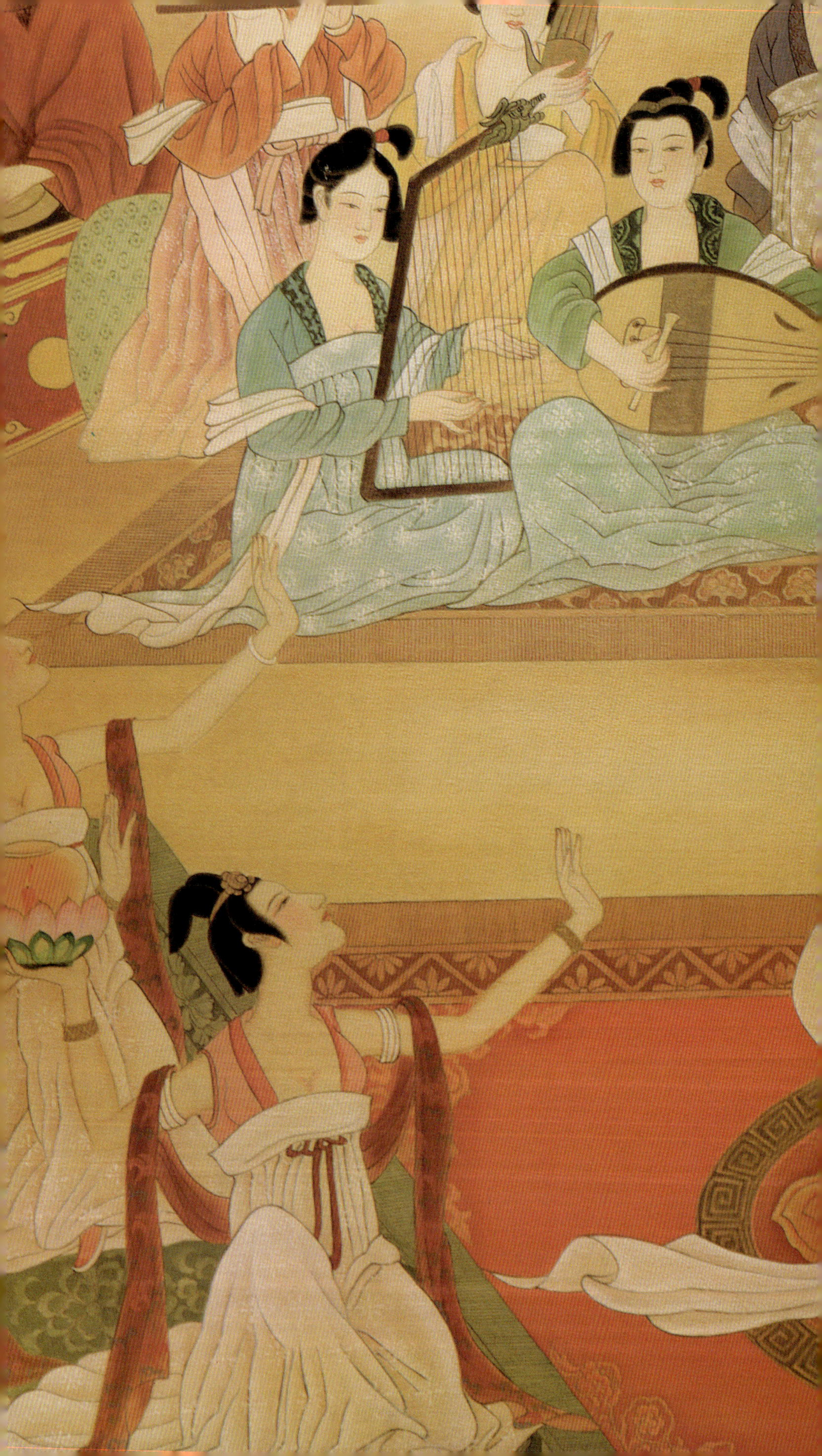

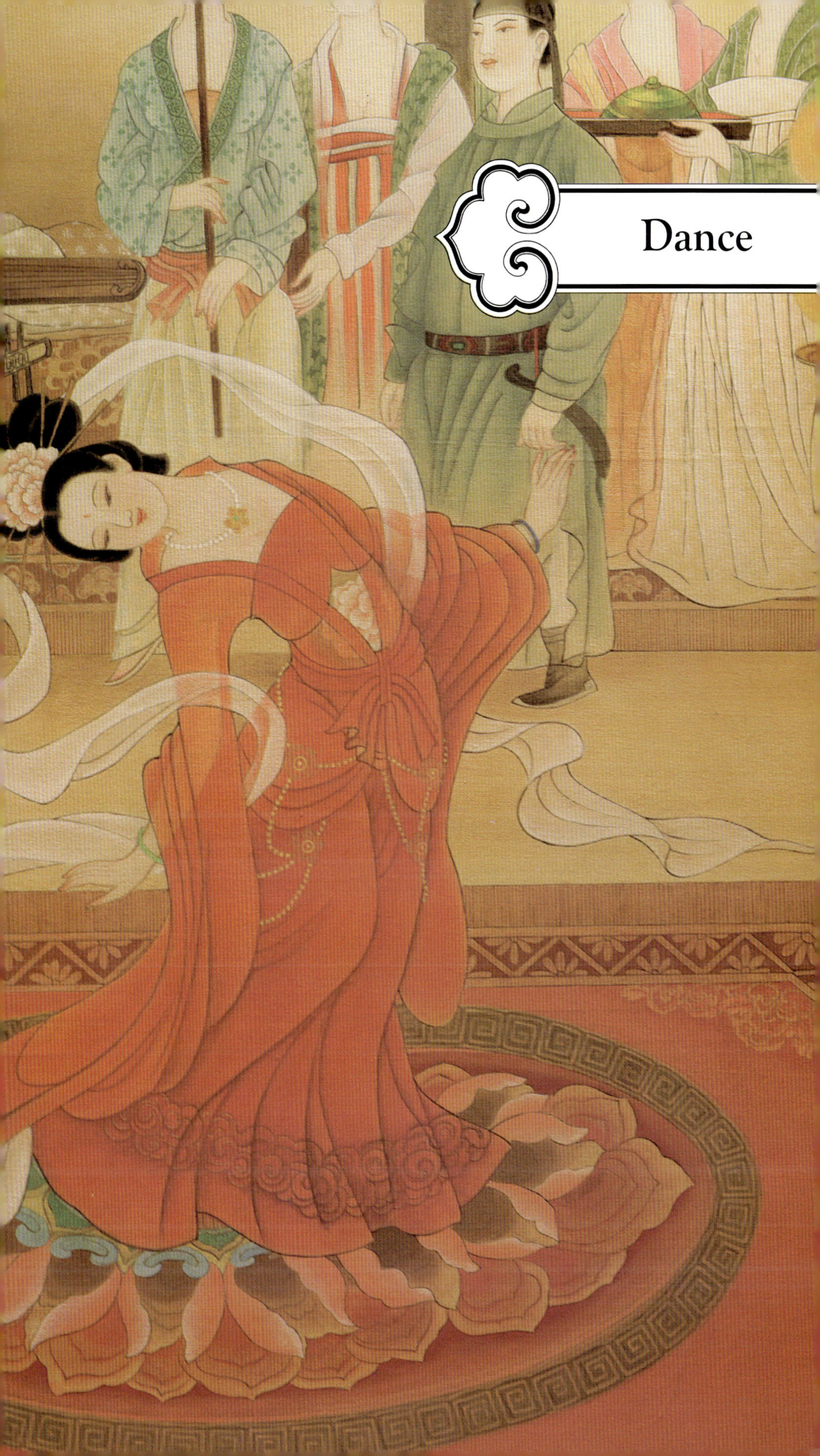

Dance

Chinese Dance: Close Ties with Music and Opera

It is widely known that dance is a companion art of music and opera, and this is especially true of Chinese dance, for dance was an important part of the "music dance" in ancient China. According to a Confucian canon, poems express our feelings, songs express our aspirations and dances move us by images. In ancient Chinese rituals and music, poetry, music and dance could all perform educational, exemplary and aesthetic functions.

Because of this special feature, the development of Chinese dance has been influenced not only by productive labor and lifestyle, but also by cultural environments, religious beliefs and even political ethics. The long history of Chinese civilization has provided the art of dance with sufficient room for germination, development and flourishing. China's vast size and her eco-environmental diversity also lend color to the art of dance. The harmonious unity of various nationalities contributes greatly to the development of dance in China as well.

The art of dance in China originated in ancient society and gradually became refined in the Bronze Age; it developed further in the feudal society, and, with the assimilation of a number of foreign elements, moved on to its peak in the Sui and Tang dynasties. After the Song Dynasty, with the overall transformation of Chinese culture and art, dance gradually became eclipsed by other art forms. Since the beginning of modern times, influenced by Western dance, traditional Chinese dance, in an effort to merge with Western dance, has taken on new styles.

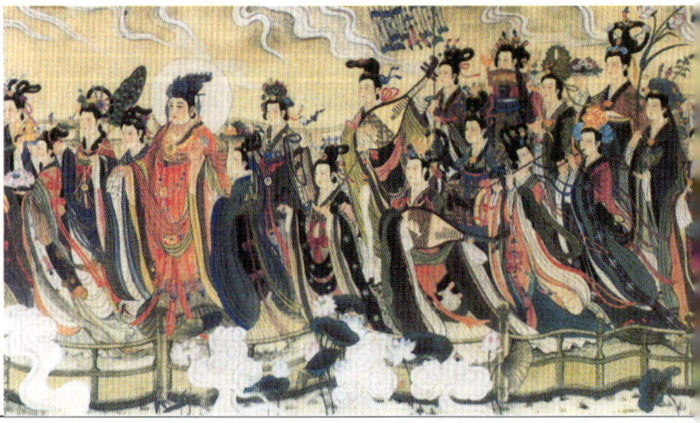

A painting from the Tang Dynasty, which illustrates the close unification of music and dance.

Primitive Dance: The Dancing Shadows of the Primitive People

In the remote past, dance occurred in close association with labor, sacrifice rituals and witchcraft. Many Chinese characters, in the ancient style, seem to relate to dance. For example, "舞(*wu*)," the very word meaning "dancing," and "巫(*wu*)," meaning "witchcraft," contain both a description of a dancing scene. The ancient people took witchcraft very seriously and depended heavily on it; the primeval dance occurred amid this powerful, mystical environment.

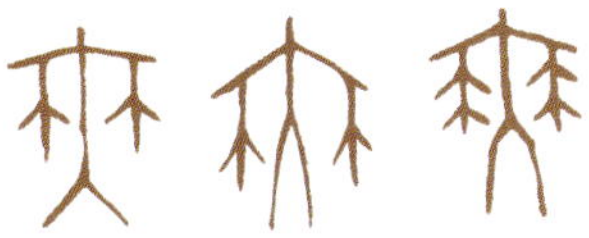

the Chinese character, 舞 (*wu*), in bone inscriptions

The colored pottery basin with dancing patterns, found in 1973 in Sunjiazhai, Datong County, Qinghai Province, is the oldest relic of Chinese dance available today, and provides a striking image of Chinese primeval dancing about 5,000 years ago. The patterns are painted on the inner and upper sides of the basin, with 15 dancers divided into three groups. The dancers join hands and form neat lines; they are dressed similarly; and judging by their hairstyles and suggested movement of the swaying clothes, they seem to be in synchronization. Therefore, it is easy to imagine the solemnity and enthusiasm with which they are dancing.

The dancing shadows of Chinese ancestors can also be found on the many rock paintings that have been discovered in abundance in such regions as Xinjiang, the Inner Mongolia, Yunnan, etc. The rock paintings in the Yinshan Mountains, Inner Mongolia, display a collective dancing scene, and those in the Helan Mountains, Ningxia, depict a dual-dance scene. These pictures express in simple, light strokes the pleasure that the primeval people received from the straightforward, unpretentious dance.

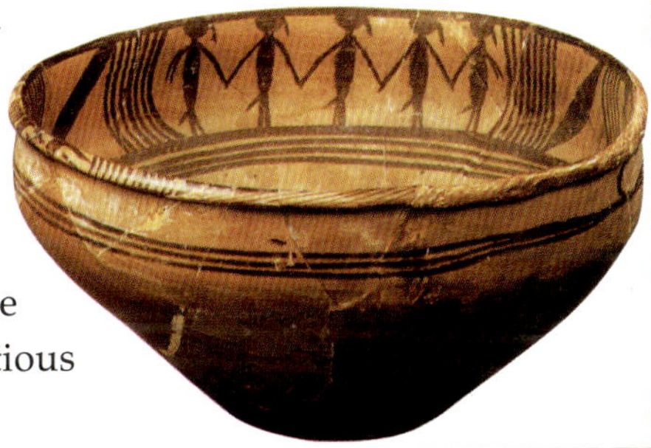

Colored pottery basin with dancing patterns, unearthed in Sunjiazhai, Datong County, Qinghai Province,

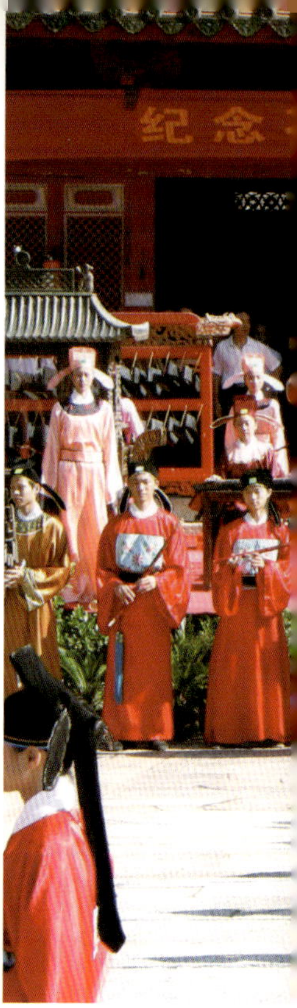

Ceremonial and Music Dance: Dancing for Ceremony and Propriety

Chinese dance became sophisticated in the Western Zhou Dynasty and the system of ceremonial and music dance designed in this period was a landmark in symbolizing the maturation of dance with accompaniment.

Since its very foundation, the Western Zhou Dynasty established a strict system of ceremony and music, which was actually a political strategy for strengthening the social estate system through ceremonial and music regulation. A special term, "*Jiaohua* (to enlighten by education)" was reserved for this practice. As a means of enlightening by education, the status and function of dance with accompaniment were raised to unprecedented heights and received strong approval from the ruling class; therefore, the culture of dance with accompaniment flourished. Because dance with accompaniment as advocated by the ruling class aimed at being ceremonially correct, the accompanying music was called ceremonial music, and the dance was called ceremonial dance. Being an important part of Chinese culture of dance with accompaniment and reflecting the aesthetic taste and dignity of the ruling classes, it retained its dominant status throughout the feudal society which lasted for thousands of years.

Throughout Chinese feudal culture, a tendency occurred of trying to restore the ancient ways in the belief that a good and just society existed only in the past, especially the remote past ruled by Yao, Shun, Yu and other august and wise sovereigns, whom Confucius admired most. It is no wonder that dances extolling their feats with vivid images became classics of the ceremonial music dances. There are six masterpieces of the ceremonial dances, responding to the feats of the six august and wise sovereigns, the best known of which is *Shao*, extolling the feat of Shun. According to literature,

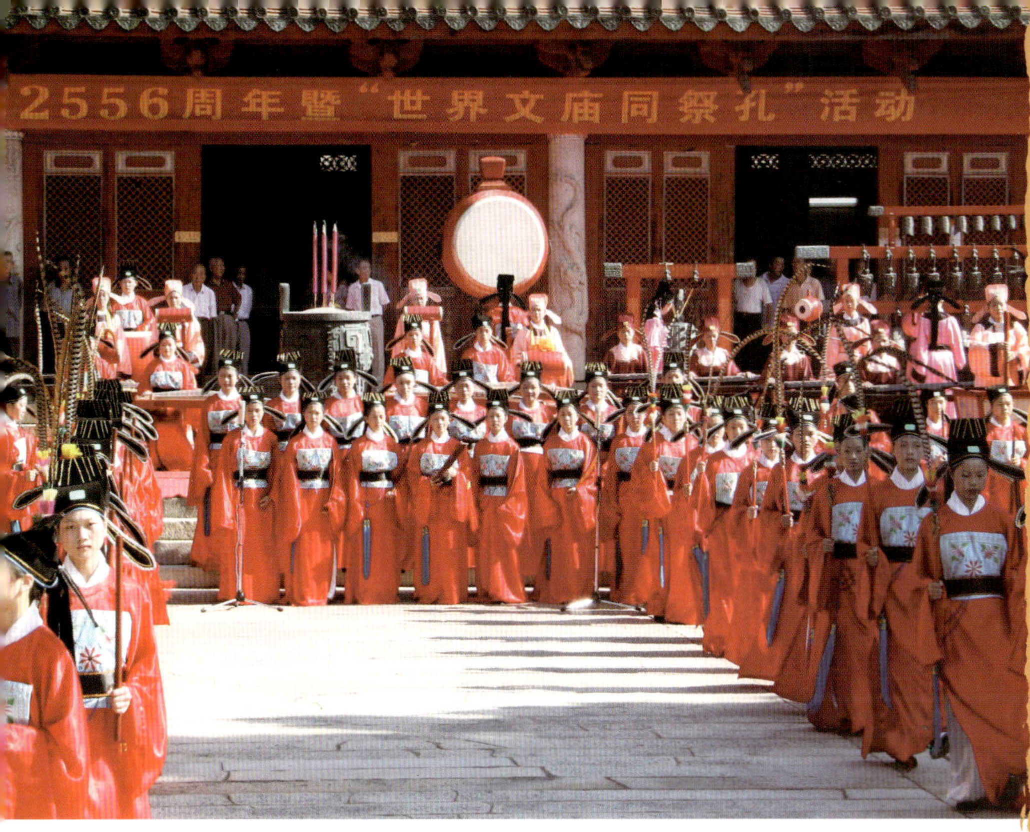

Contemporary music and dance memorial ceremony for Confucius

this dance was so appealing that even the magic bird phoenix and the various animals were attracted and they all joined in the dancing. As mentioned in our previous discussion about music, Confucius, in his appreciation of this dance, was so immersed in the music that he forgot the taste of deliciously cooked meat for months.

So, it is easy to see that ceremonial music and dance brought about more enlightenment and was strongly utilitarian. Learning music and dance was once compulsory for the noble juniors in their education. Such dances emphasized order, regulation and restraint, and made the learners envious of their ancestors' glorious deeds and thus stimulated their ambition to achieve similar feats and to be august and wise, but such dances also undermined their recreational value and left the audiences listless. The decrease in these goals led to the decline of ceremonial music and dance. Despite this inevitable decline, ceremonial music and dance retain its traditional status in Chinese history.

Professional Female Dance: Carefree Soft Music and Graceful Dance

Since ceremonial music and dance undertook the educational function, the recreational function had to be left to the professional female dance, which served as a symmetrical contrast with ceremonial music and dance. While ceremonial music and dance tended to be serious and solemn, professional music and dance tended to be vivid and graceful.

The professional female dance, performed by professional musicians and dancing girls, aimed at being recreational and attracted a greater audience than ceremonial music and dance, thereby occupying the actual mainstream status during a very long period of history. This type of music and dance was highly developed in the Spring and Autumn and the Warring States periods. For example, a dancing girl was carved on a copper kettle handed down from the Warring States; with long, coiled hair and flowing sleeves, she dances gracefully. On another copper kettle was carved a female musician, who, with her elegant carriage, strikes an

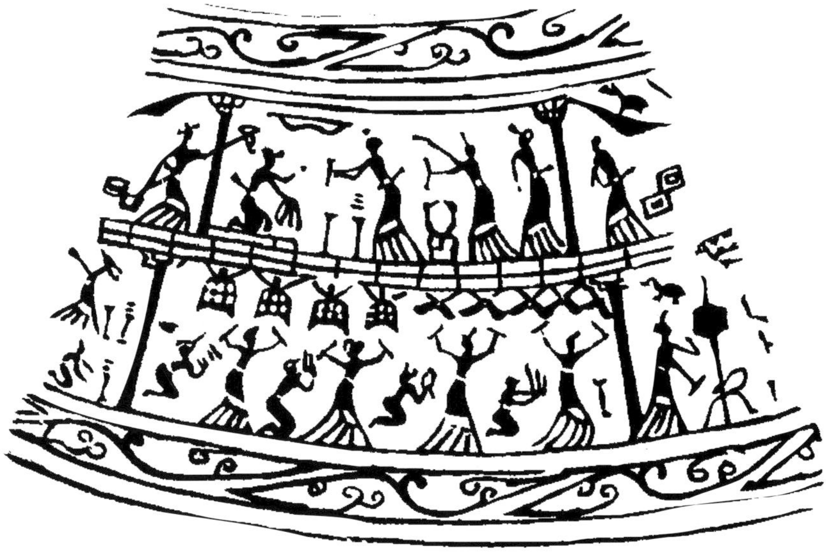

Female dancers on a bronze pot of the Warring States Period.

The dancers are striking the chime stones while dancing.

inverted bell gracefully. These two relics of music and dance reflect the taste of the periods.

Professional female music and dance flourished during the Han Dynasty. Of the many famous dancers, the most famous was Zhao Feiyan, who was once the empress. We can gather some of the reasons for her fame from her name, Feiyan, which means literally a flying swallow, and serves as a fitting metaphor in describing her graceful dancing. Actually, the emperor appreciated her superb dancing before she became the empress. It is said that she was so light that she could dance trippingly on a man's palm. On a brick relief unearthed in Zhengzhou, Henan, a dancing girl had been carved who, with one foot on the floor and the other raised and with long, fluttering sleeves, appears to dance high in the air. Her dance appears so light and elegant and forms an interesting contrast with the nearby flying swallows.

It is said in our previous discussion of Chinese music that the music played at the court feasts in the Sui and Tang dynasties symbolized the peak of the music and dance culture of these periods. Because of the booming Silk Road, Western music and dance were imported into central China and exerted great influence upon traditional Chinese music and dance. As with music, dance developed greatly because of the preferences of the emperors, and the sitting dancers, the standing dancers and the grand dance music represented the highest level of the professional female dance. *Watching Madam Gongsun Performing a Sword-Dance*, a famous poem by the great poet, Du Fu, and *Dancing in a Feather Robe*, an equally famous poem by another great poet, Bai Juyi, describe vividly the superb skills of great dancers in the Tang Dynasty. Today, from the handed-down female dancing figurines, their moving grace can be imagined easily.

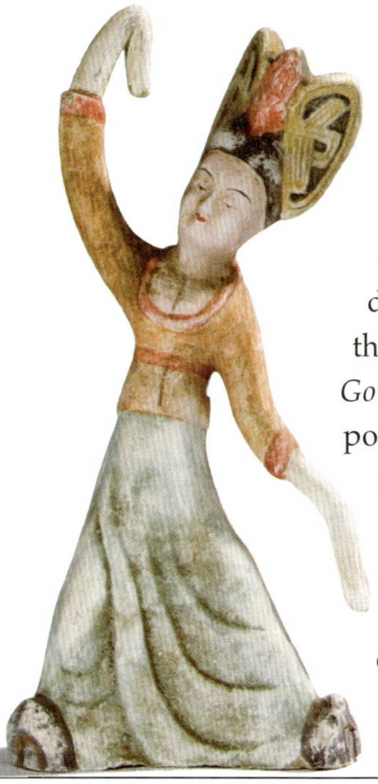

A dancer figurine of the Tang Dynasty.

Religious Dance: Dancing upon the Encounter between Gods and Humans

The origin of dance is related to witchcraft. When performing sacrifices for their ancestors and gods, the ancient people used to dance to please the gods. The witches, who were mediators between gods and humans, needed to dance in a special manner to convey the will of the gods and express the aspirations of the men. With the development of religion and the decline of witchcraft, religious dance became an important part of Chinese dance and continued at a very high level.

Among the religious dances, the most sophisticated is the Buddhist dance. In order to attract followers and to

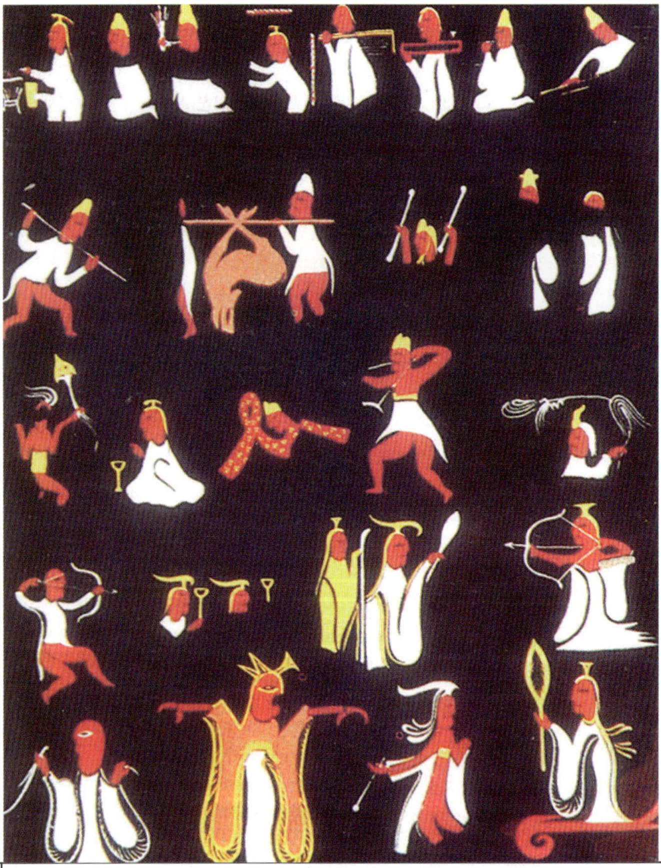

Colored painting of dancing witches, Warring States, unearthed in Henan Province.

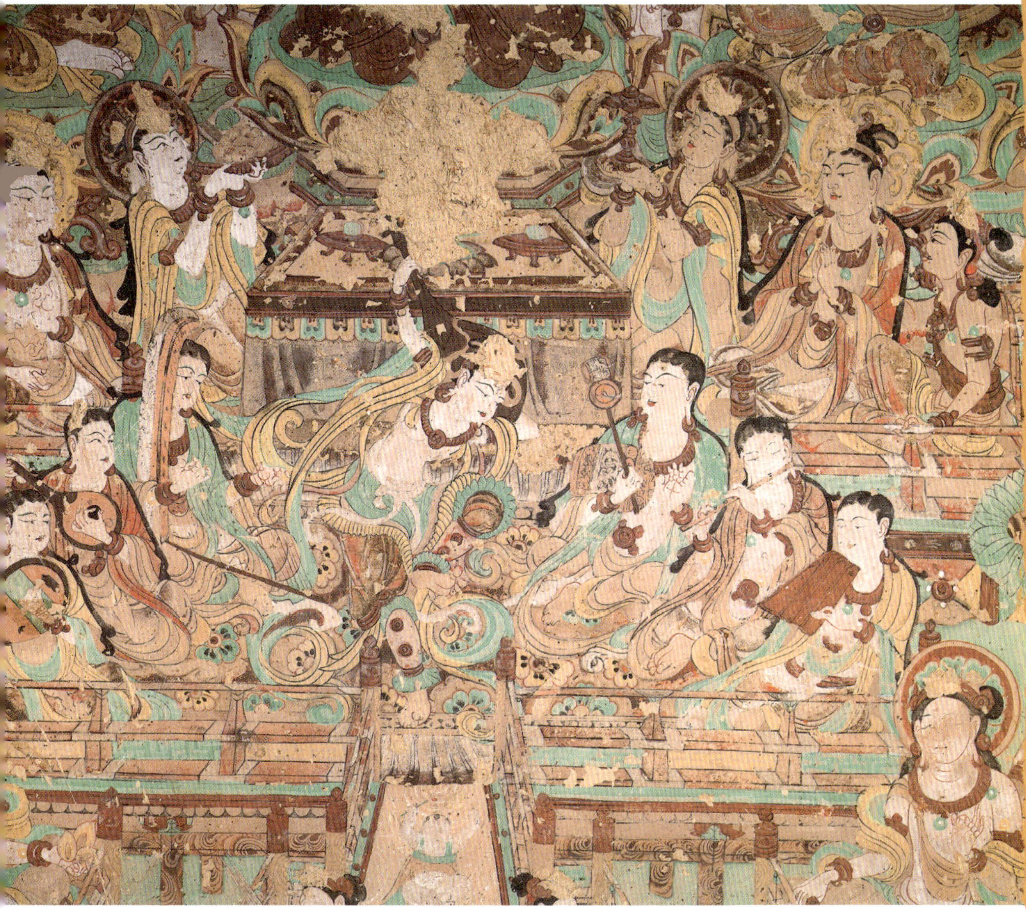

A Tang Dynasty female dancer in the Mogao Grottos, Dunhuang, Gansu.

teach doctrine, Buddhist dances were characteristically organized upon important Buddhist occasions. By assimilating the best of native ethnic dances and by drawing on the exotic flavor of the Indian Buddhist dance, the Chinese Buddhist dance constituted a new element in Chinese dance. According to written documents, the Buddhist dance approached its peak during the Northern and Southern Dynasties, and when magnificent Buddhist dances were performed in the temples the audiences often seemed to forget where they were, even thinking that they had been transported to the heavenly kingdom as described in Buddhist doctrine. From these writings the grandeur and attraction of the Buddhist dances can be appreciated.

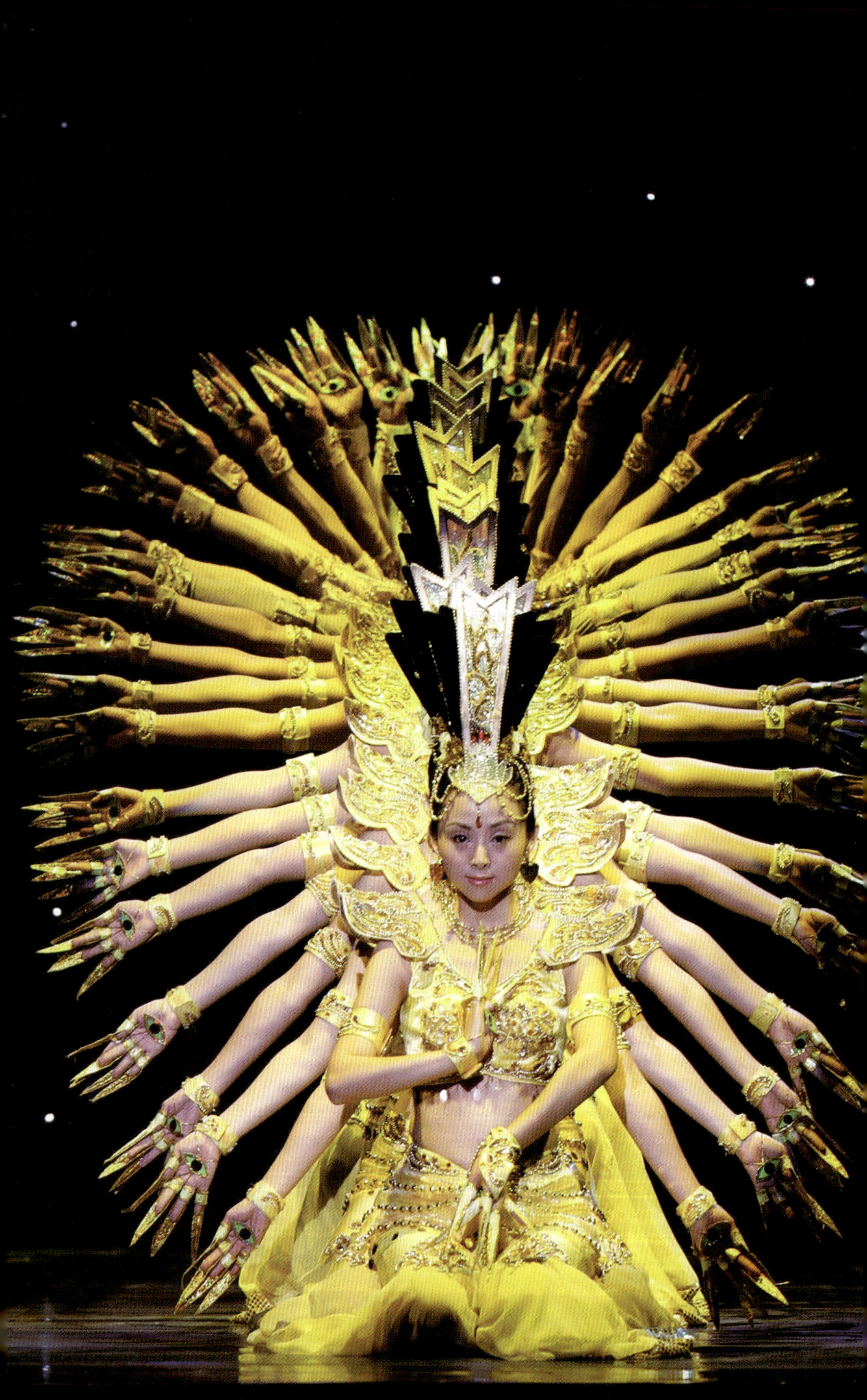

Contemporary dance, *The 1,000-handed Buddhist Guanyin*

Despite its decline, the many Buddhist dancing images that were left in grottoes offer a glimpse of the charming beauty of the Buddhist dance. Many Buddhist dance artifacts produced during the 3rd to 9th century are kept in the Kizil Grottoes. The nimble posture and romantic charm of the immortal dancers are strong reminders of exotic customs. One female musician-dancer in No.175 grotto deserves our special attention. Well-developed, strong and in a light gauzy dress, she is falling from a great height; the moment her feet touch the floor, with her left arm slightly raised and the right naturally down, she casts a glowing look around her. This artifact, certainly influenced by Western tastes, is representative of the communication of Oriental and Western dancing cultures. If you have an opportunity to be in the Mogao Grottoes in Dunhuang, Gansu, do not miss the superb collections of dancing images on the murals; they represent the highest level of Chinese dance of the period. For example, from the female musicians in the No.148 grotto the aesthetic taste of the Buddhist dance and the secular dance in the Tang Dynasty can be discerned.

Religious dance, especially the Buddhist dance, has played a major role in promoting the development and flourishing of the art of Chinese dance. The religious dance can still inspire audiences, such as the 2005 CCTV Spring Festival party, where *The 1,000-handed Buddhist Guanyin,* a dance program, was performed jointly by 21 deaf and mute dancers. This dance, inspired by Buddhist art, not only ranked among the most favorite programs of the year, but was also performed many times abroad upon invitation. That is, its charm has not only moved Chinese audiences but also won the love of the world.

Ethnic Dances: Flowing Customs

As a large family of ethnic unity and harmony, 56 ethnic groups live in China, each of which has its own special art of dance. The satisfaction of work, the pleasure of good harvest, the chastity of love, and the piety and reverence towards ancestors all find sustenance in dance. The reed-pipe wind instrument dance of the Miao, the bronze drum dance of the Zhuang , the *saman* dance of the Man, *kuiyi* dance of the Kazak and the *sainaim* dance of the Uygur are all typical ethnic dances. Therefore, it is easy to see people of all ethnic groups expressing their pleasures and sorrows in their favorite dance.

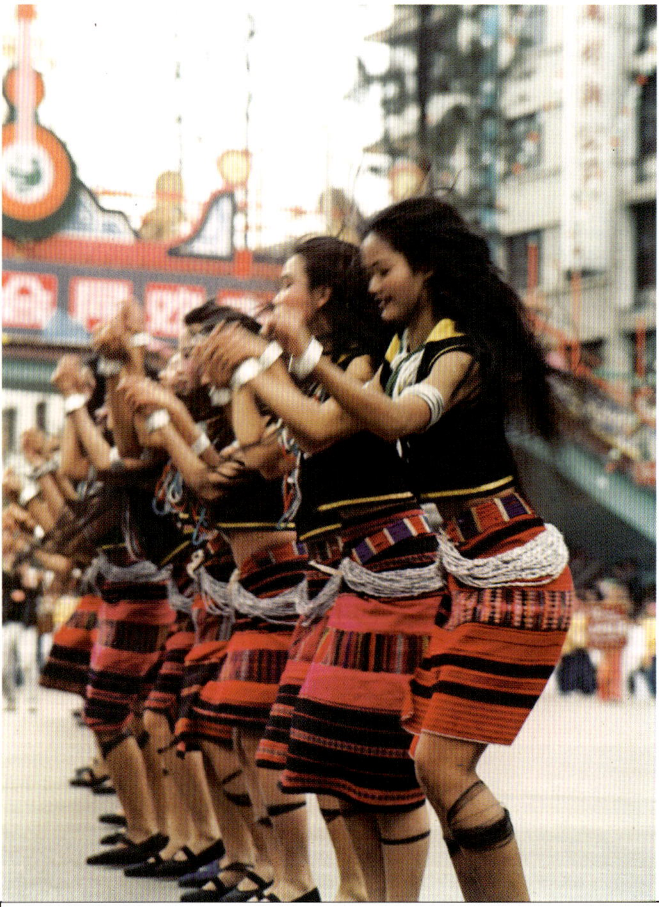

Girls of the Wa ethnic group greeting their guests.

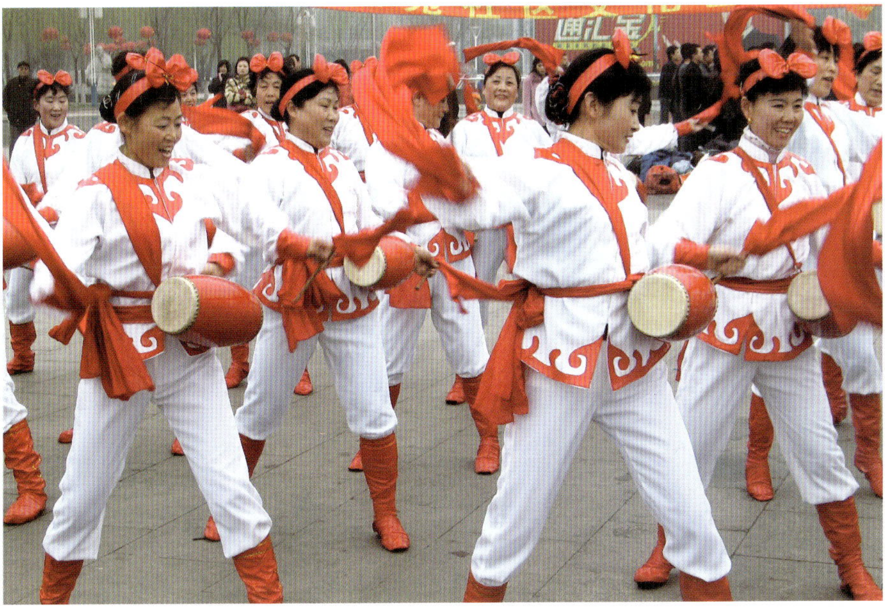

Yangge

Two kinds of dance, *yangge* and stilts, which you might have seen on previous trips to China, are prevalent in most of the country. Since they both originated in the praise of agricultural productive labor and the celebration of bumper harvests, these two simple, animated dances are performed on New Year's Day and other festivals. The style of dance might vary but the joyous atmosphere is the same. Children, without much special training, can join in the enormous dancing line and get caught up in the strong, rhythmic accompaniment of gongs and drums. You may even find foreign friends in the *yangge* parade in Beijing or other large cities.

These simple, natural dances provide contemporary dance artists with great inspiration. Yang Liping, a female dancer of Bai ethnic group, born into a family located at the foot of Mountain Cangshan and along the shore of Erhai, in Dali Bai Ethnic Autonomous Prefecture, Yunnan, is internationally famous for her peacock dance. In order to strengthen the ethnic, artistic and primeval quality of her dancing, she visits the areas near her hometown that are populated by Dai, Bai, Yi and other ethnic groups and observes and learns from real life. Meanwhile, she spends

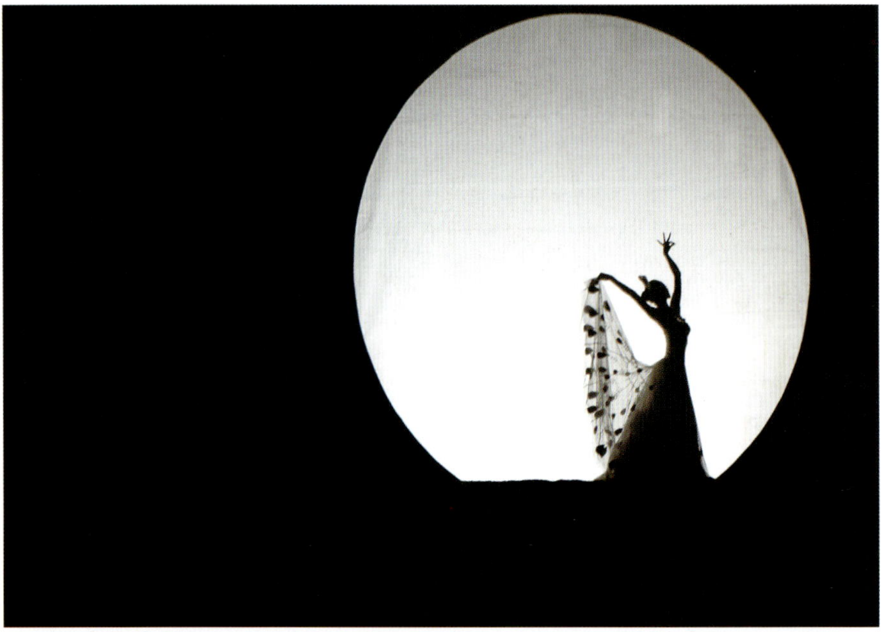

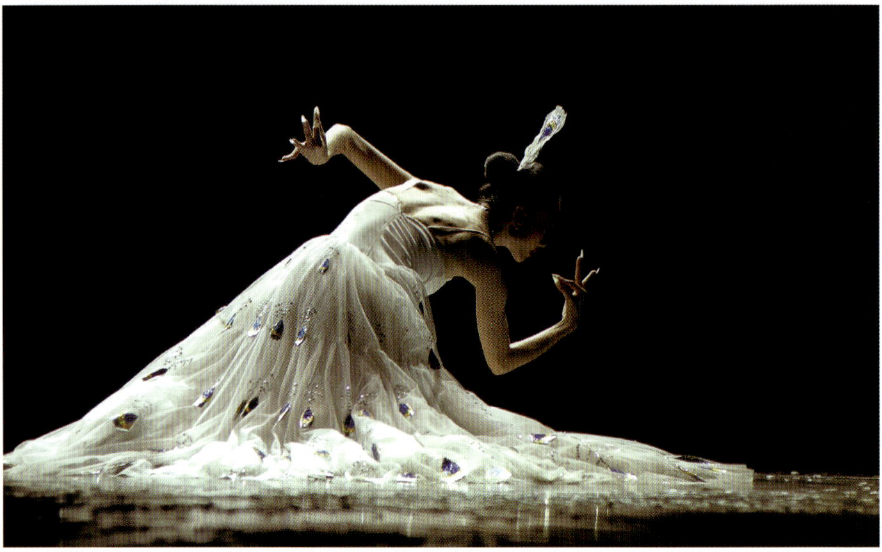

Yang Liping performing *The Spirit of the Peacock.*

a lot of time studying the habits of peacocks and other wild birds. Yang Liping's unique dancing, which deploys all her physical energy in conveying her understanding of life, has been praised as a flower of art, because she combines so wonderfully local color with stage classics.

Modern Dance: Confluence of Oriental and Western Dance

Chinese dance, an open and dynamic art, has never rejected the nourishing influence of the positive elements of foreign dances. Since the beginning of the 20th century, Western dance has exerted enormous influence upon traditional Chinese dance, causing great changes in its substance and appearance. Ballet and music dancing epic are two cases in point.

In 1964, the full-length song-and-dance epic, *Dongfanghong*, which describes the course of the Chinese people from plight to victory in the trinity of song, dance and poetry, was performed on stage. With its imposing momentum, rigorous structure and ingenious design, this epic gives a passionate representation of the history of the Chinese revolution. In its inaugural performance, almost all of the contemporary renowned musicians and dancers in China had gathered, and the performers totaled 3,000. Without doubt, it was a huge success. This is perhaps the grandest scene in the history of Chinese dance. If so inclined, you can appreciate the grandeur of this epic by watching a documentary film of the same name.

In 1965, a ballet, named *A White-*

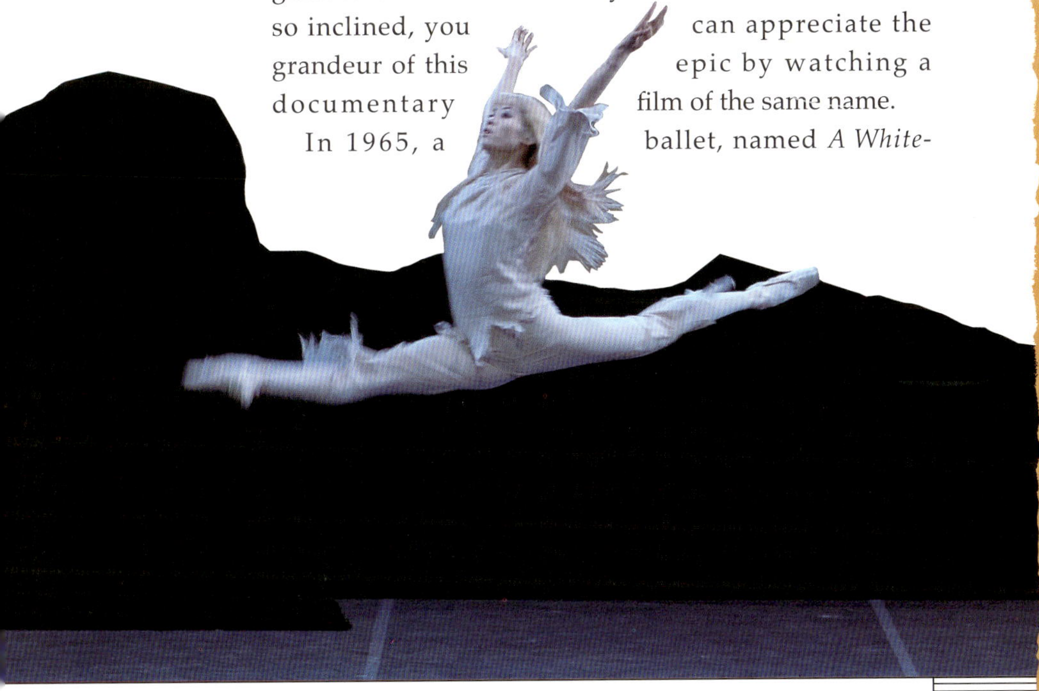

A White-haired Girl, a milestone in the development of ballet in China.

haired Girl, which tells about the miserable life of the daughter of a poor family in the old society, with the theme that the old society makes a ghost of a man while the new society makes a man of a ghost, was put on stage for the first time. It draws ingeniously on the classic and folk source materials, and represents the plots in the unification of realism and romanticism. Having moved millions upon millions of Chinese common people, it has become a milestone in the development of ballet in China. The effort at assimilating foreign artistic nutrients produced a classic.

Epilogue

Chinese arts are like a vast ocean and our travel covers only a small part of this spacious territory. The several kinds of Chinese arts just introduced are like a few beautiful shells scattered along the shore. If you take an interest in the mysterious, vast sea during or after the trip, then the effort certainly has been worthwhile.

The Chinese nation is now undergoing a historic moment of rejuvenation. The cultural development in accordance with shaping a harmonious society, which China aims for, is conducive to thriving artistic creation. China respects and appreciates the creations of other nations just as she cherishes the glories created by her ancestors. An open China opens her heart to the world. If you come to Beijing to watch the 2008 Olympic Games, you will surely have a better chance to listen to the heartbeat of this nation.

Close this humble book and our journey of the arts will come to a stop. It is our sincere hope that it can serve as the starting point of your journey to China, which certainly would be wonderful and unforgettable. Once in Beijing, the capital of China, you would not only have a chance to experience the charm of Chinese culture, but also witness her great historic rejuvenation, which has long been anticipated by the world.

Appendix: Chinese Dynasties

The Paleolithic Age	c. 1.7 million years ago – 10,000 years ago
The Neolithic Age	c. 10,000 years ago – 4,000 years ago
Xia Dynasty	2070 BC – 1600 BC
Shang Dynasty	1600 BC – 1046 BC
Western Zhou Dynasty	1046 BC– 771 BC
Spring and Autumn Period	770 BC– 476 BC
Warring States Period	475 BC – 221 BC
Qin Dynasty	221 BC– 206 BC
Western Han Dynasty	206 BC – AD 25
Eastern Han Dynasty	AD 25 – AD 220
Three Kingdoms Period	AD 220 – AD 280
Western Jin Dynasty	AD 265 – AD 316
Eastern Jin Dynasty	AD 317 – AD 420
Southern and Northern Dynasties Period	AD 420 – AD 589
Sui Dynasty	AD 581 – AD 618
Tang Dynasty	AD 618 – AD 907
Five Dynasties Period	AD 907 – AD 960
Northern Song Dynasty	AD 960 – AD 1127
Southern Song Dynasty	AD 1127 – AD 1279
Yuan Dynasty	AD 1271 – AD 1368
Ming Dynasty	AD 1368 – AD 1644
Qing Dynasty	AD 1644 – AD 1911